FREEDOM OF ASSOCIATION

OTHER BOOKS IN AMERICA'S FREEDOMS

Donald Grier Stephenson, Jr., Series Editor

Cruel and Unusual Punishment,
Joseph A. Melusky and Keith A. Pesto

Equal Protection, Francis Graham Lee

Freedom of Speech, Ken I. Kersch

Property Rights, Polly J. Price

Religious Freedom, Melvin I. Urofsky

The Right to Bear Arms, Robert J. Spitzer

*The Right to Counsel and
Privilege against Self-Incrimination,* John B. Taylor

The Right to Privacy, Richard A. Glenn

FREEDOM OF
ASSOCIATION

Rights and Liberties
under the Law

ROBERT J. BRESLER

A B C 🮥 C L I O

Santa Barbara, California • Denver, Colorado • Oxford, England

Library of Congress Cataloging-in-Publication Data
Bresler, Robert J., 1937 –
    Freedom of association : rights and liberties under the law / Robert J. Bresler.
        p. cm. — (America's freedoms)
    Includes bibliographical references and index.
    ISBN 1-57607-772-1 (hardcover : alk. paper)   ISBN 1-57607-773-X (e-book)
1. Freedom of association—United States.
I. Title. II. Series.
    KF4778.B74 2004
    342.7308'54—dc22   2004003209

07 06 05 04   10 9 8 7 6 5 4 3 2 1

This book is also available on the World Wide Web as an e-book. Visit abc-clio.com for details.

ABC-CLIO, Inc.
130 Cremona Drive, P.O. Box 1911
Santa Barbara, California 93116-1911

This book is printed on acid-free paper.
Manufactured in the United States of America

To Linda

CONTENTS

SERIES FOREWORD

America's Freedoms promises a series of books that address the origin, development, meaning, and future of the nation's fundamental liberties, as well as the individuals, circumstances, and events that have shaped them. These freedoms are chiefly enshrined explicitly or implicitly in the Bill of Rights and other amendments to the Constitution of the United States and have much to do with the quality of life Americans enjoy. Without them, America would be a far different place in which to live. Oddly enough, however, the Constitution was drafted and signed in Philadelphia in 1787 without a bill of rights. That was an afterthought, emerging only after a debate among the foremost political minds of the day.

At the time, Thomas Jefferson was in France on a diplomatic mission. Upon receiving a copy of the proposed Constitution from his friend James Madison, who had helped write the document, Jefferson let him know as fast as the slow sailing-ship mails of the day allowed that the new plan of government suffered one major defect—it lacked a bill of rights. This, Jefferson argued, "is what the people are entitled to against every government on earth." Madison should not have been surprised at Jefferson's reaction. The Declaration of Independence of 1776 had largely been Jefferson's handiwork, including its core statement of principle:

> We hold these truths to be self-evident, that all men are created equal,
> that they are endowed by their Creator with certain unalienable
> Rights, that among these are Life, Liberty, and the pursuit of Happi-
> ness. That to secure these rights, Governments are instituted among
> Men, deriving their just powers from the consent of the governed.

Jefferson rejected the conclusion of many of the framers that
the Constitution's design—a system of both separation of powers
among the legislative, executive, and judicial branches, and a
federal division of powers between national and state
governments—would safeguard liberty. Even when combined
with elections, he believed strongly that such structural checks
would fall short.

Jefferson and other critics of the proposed Constitution
ultimately had their way. In one of the first items of business in
the First Congress in 1789, Madison, as a member of the House of
Representatives from Virginia, introduced amendments to protect
liberty. Ten were ratified by 1791 and have become known as the
Bill of Rights.

America's Bill of Rights reflects the founding generation's
understanding of the necessary link between personal freedom
and representative government, as well as their experience with
threats to liberty. The First Amendment protects expression—in
speech, press, assembly, petition, and religion—and guards against
a union of church and state. The Second Amendment secures
liberty against national tyranny by affirming the self-defense of
the states. Members of state-authorized local militia—citizens
primarily, soldiers occasionally—retained a right to bear arms.
The ban in the Third Amendment on forcibly quartering troops in
houses reflects the emphasis the framers placed on the integrity
and sanctity of the home.

Other provisions in the Fourth, Fifth, Sixth, Seventh, and
Eighth Amendments safeguard freedom by setting forth standards
that government must follow in administering the law, especially

regarding persons accused of crimes. The framers knew firsthand the dangers that government-as-prosecutor could pose to liberty. Even today, authoritarian regimes in other lands routinely use the tools of law enforcement—arrests, searches, detentions, as well as trials—to squelch peaceful political opposition. Limits in the Bill of Rights on crime-fighting powers thus help maintain democracy by demanding a high level of legal scrutiny of the government's practices.

In addition, one clause in the Fifth Amendment forbids the taking of private property for public use without paying the owner just compensation and thereby limits the power of eminent domain, the authority to seize a person's property. Along with taxation and conscription, eminent domain is one of the most awesome powers any government can possess.

The Ninth Amendment makes sure that the listing of some rights does not imply that others necessarily have been abandoned. If the Ninth Amendment offered reassurances to the people, the Tenth Amendment was designed to reassure the states that they or the people retained those powers not delegated to the national government. Today, the Tenth Amendment is a reminder of the integral role states play in the federal plan of union that the Constitution ordained.

Despite this legacy of freedom, however, we Americans today sometimes wonder about the origin, development, meaning, and future of our liberties. This concern is entirely understandable, because liberty is central to the idea of what it means *to be American.* In this way, the United States stands apart from virtually every other nation on earth. Other countries typically define their national identities through a common ethnicity, origin, ancestral bond, religion, or history. But none of these accounts for the American identity. In terms of ethnicity, ancestry, and religion, the United States is the most diverse place on earth. From the beginning, America has been a land of immigrants. Neither is there a single historical experience to which all current citizens can directly relate: someone who arrived a decade ago from, say, Southeast Asia and was naturalized as a citizen only last year is just as much an American as someone whose forebears served in General George Washington's army at Valley Forge during the American War of Independence (1776–1783). In religious as in political affairs, the United States has been a beacon to those suffering oppression abroad: "the last, best hope of earth," Abraham Lincoln said. So, the American identity is ideological. It consists of faith in the value and importance of liberty for each individual.

Nonetheless, a longstanding consensus among Americans on the *principle* that individual liberty is essential, highly prized, and widely shared hardly ensures agreement about liberty *in practice.* This is because the concept of liberty, as it has developed in the United States, has several dimensions.

First, there is an unavoidable tension between liberty and restraint. Liberty means freedom: we say that a person has a "right" to do this or that. But that *right* is meaningless unless there is a corresponding *duty* on the part of others (such as police officers and elected officials) not to interfere. Thus, protection of the liberty of one person necessarily involves restraints imposed on someone else. This is why we speak of a *civil* right or a *civil* liberty: it is a claim on the behavior of another that is enforceable through the legal process. Moreover, some degree of order (restrictions on the behavior of all) is necessary if everyone's liberties are to be protected. Just as too much order crushes freedom, too little invites social chaos, which also threatens freedom. Determining the proper balance between freedom and order, however, is more easily sought than found. "To make a government requires no great prudence," declared English statesman and political philosopher Edmund Burke in 1790. "Settle the seat of power; teach obedience; and the work is done. To give freedom is still more easy. It is not necessary to guide; it only requires to let go the rein. But to form a *free government;*

that is, to temper together these opposite elements of liberty and restraint in one consistent work, requires much thought; deep reflection; a sagacious, powerful, and combining mind."

Second, the Constitution does not define the freedoms that it protects. Chief Justice John Marshall once acknowledged that the Constitution was a document "of enumeration, and not of definition." There are, for example, lists of the powers of Congress in Article I, or the rights of individuals in the Bill of Rights, but those powers and limitations are not explained. What is the "freedom of speech" that the First Amendment guarantees? What are "unreasonable searches and seizures" that are proscribed by the Fourth Amendment? What is the "due process of law" secured by both the Fifth and Fourteenth Amendments? Reasonable people, all of whom favor individual liberty, can arrive at very different answers to these questions.

A third dimension—breadth—is closely related to the second. How widely shared is a particular freedom? Consider voting, for example. One could write a political history of the United States by cataloging the efforts to extend the vote or franchise to groups such as women and nonwhites that had been previously excluded. Or consider the First Amendment's freedom of speech. Does it include the expression of *all* points of view or merely *some?* Does the same amendment's protection of the "free exercise of religion" include all faiths, even obscure ones that may seem weird or even irritating? At different times questions like these have yielded different answers.

Similarly, the historical record contains notorious lapses. Despite all the safeguards that are supposed to shore up freedom's foundations, constitutional protections have sometimes been worth the least when they have been desperately needed. In our history the most frequent and often the most serious threats to freedom have come not from people intent on throwing the Bill of Rights away outright but from well-meaning people who find the Bill of Rights a temporary bother, standing in the way of some objective they want to reach.

There is also a question that dates to the very beginning of American government under the Constitution. Does the Constitution protect rights not spelled out in, or fairly implied by, the words of the document? The answer to that question largely depends on what a person concludes about the source of rights. One tradition, reflected in the Declaration of Independence, asserts that rights predate government and that government's chief duty is to protect the rights that everyone naturally possesses. Thus, if the Constitution is read as a document designed, among other things, to protect liberty, then protected liberties are not limited to those in the text of the Constitution but may also be derived from experience, for example, or from one's assessment of the requirements of a free society. This tradition places a lot of discretion in the hands of judges, because in the American political system, it is largely the judiciary that decides what the Constitution means. Partly due to this dynamic, a competing tradition looks to the text of the Constitution, as well as to statutes passed consistent with the Constitution, as a *complete* code of law containing *all* the liberties that Americans possess. Judges, therefore, are not free to go outside the text to "discover" rights that the people, through the process of lawmaking and constitutional amendment, have not declared. Doing so is undemocratic because it bypasses "rule by the people." The tension between these two ways of thinking explains the ongoing debate about a right to privacy, itself nowhere mentioned in the words of the Constitution. "I like my privacy as well as the next one," once admitted Justice Hugo Black, "but I am nevertheless compelled to admit that government has a right to invade it unless prohibited by some specific constitutional provision." Otherwise, he said, judges are forced "to determine what is or is not constitutional on the basis of their own appraisal of what laws are unwise or unnecessary." Black thought that was the job of elected legislators who would answer to the people.

Fifth, it is often forgotten that at the outset, and for many years afterward, the Bill of Rights applied only to the national government, not to the states. Except for a very few restrictions, such as those in section 10 of Article I in the main body of the Constitution, which expressly limited state power, states were restrained only by their individual constitutions and state laws, not by the U.S. Bill of Rights. So, Pennsylvania or any other state, for example, could shut down a newspaper or barricade the doors of a church without violating the First Amendment. For many in the founding generation, the new central government loomed as a colossus that might threaten liberty. Few at that time thought that individual freedom needed *national* protection against *state* invasions of the rights of the people.

The first step in removing this double standard came with ratification of the Fourteenth Amendment after the Civil War in 1868. Section 1 contained majestic, but undefined, checks on states: "*No State* shall make or enforce any law which shall abridge the privileges or immunities of citizens of the United States; nor shall any *State* deprive any person of life, liberty, or property, without due process of law; nor deny to any person within its jurisdiction the equal protections of the laws" (emphasis added). Such vague language begged for interpretation. In a series of cases mainly between 1920 and 1968, the Supreme Court construed the Fourteenth Amendment to include within its meaning almost every provision of the Bill of Rights. This process of "incorporation" (applying the Bill of Rights to the states by way of the Fourteenth Amendment) was the second step in eliminating the double standard of 1791. State and local governments became bound by the same restrictions that had applied all along to the national government. The consequences of this development scarcely can be exaggerated because most governmental action in the United States is the work of state and local governments. For instance, ordinary citizens are far more likely to encounter a local police officer than an agent of the Federal Bureau of Investigation or the Secret Service.

A sixth dimension reflects an irony. A society premised on individual freedom assumes not only the worth of each person but citizens capable of rational thought, considered judgment, and measured actions. Otherwise democratic government would be futile. Yet, we lodge the most important freedoms in the Constitution precisely because we want to give those freedoms extra protection. "The very purpose of a Bill of Rights was to . . . place [certain subjects] beyond the reach of majorities and officials and to establish them as legal principles to be applied by the courts," explained Justice Robert H. Jackson. "One's right to life, liberty, and property, to free speech, a free press, freedom of worship and assembly, and other fundamental rights may not be submitted to vote; they depend on the outcome of no elections." Jackson referred to a hard lesson learned from experience: basic rights require extra protection because they are fragile. On occasion, people have been willing to violate the freedoms of others. That reality demanded a written constitution.

This irony reflects the changing nature of a bill of rights in history. Americans did not invent the idea of a bill of rights in 1791. Instead it drew from and was inspired by colonial documents such as the Pennsylvania colony's Charter of Liberties (1701) and the English Bill of Rights (1689), Petition of Right (1628), and Magna Carta (1215). However, these early and often unsuccessful attempts to limit government power were devices to protect the many (the people) from the few (the English Crown). With the emergence of democratic political systems in the eighteenth century, however, political power shifted from the few to the many. The right to rule belonged to the person who received the most votes in an election, not necessarily to the firstborn, the wealthiest, or the most physically powerful. So the focus of a bill of rights had to shift too. No longer was it designed to shelter the majority from the minority, but to shelter the minority from the majority. "Wherever the real power in a Government lies, there is the danger of oppression," commented Madison in his exchange of letters with Jefferson in 1788. "In our Government, the real power lies in the majority of the Community, and the invasion of private rights is *chiefly* to be apprehended, not from acts of government contrary to the sense of its constituents, but from acts in which the Government is the mere instrument of the major number of the Constituents."

Americans, however, do deserve credit for having discovered a way to enforce a bill of rights. Without an enforcement mechanism, a bill of rights is no more than a list of aspirations: standards to aim for, but with no redress other than violent protest or revolution. Indeed this had been the experience in England with which the framers were thoroughly familiar. Thanks to judicial review—the authority courts in the United States possess to invalidate actions taken by the other branches of government that, in the judges' view, conflict with the Constitution—the provisions in the Bill of Rights and other constitutionally protected liberties became judicially enforceable.

Judicial review was a tradition that was beginning to emerge in the states on a small scale in the 1780s and 1790s and that would blossom in the U.S. Supreme Court in the nineteenth and twentieth centuries. "In the arguments in favor of a declaration of rights," Jefferson presciently told Madison in the late winter of 1789 after the Constitution had been ratified, "you omit one which has great weight with me, the legal check which it puts into the hands of the judiciary." This is the reason why each of the volumes in this series focuses extensively on judicial decisions. Liberties have largely been defined by judges in the context of deciding cases in situations where individuals thought the power of government extended too far.

Designed to help democracy protect itself, the Constitution ultimately needs the support of those—the majority—who endure its restraints. Without sufficient support among the people, its freedoms rest on a weak foundation. The earnest hope of *America's Freedoms* is that this series will offer Americans a renewed appreciation and understanding of their heritage of liberty.

Yet there would be no series on America's freedoms without the interest and support of Alicia Merritt at ABC-CLIO. The series was her idea. She approached me originally about the series and was very adept at overcoming my initial hesitations as series editor. She not only helped me shape the particular topics that the series would include but also guided me toward prospective authors. As a result, the topic of each book has been matched with the most appropriate person as author. The goal in each instance as been to pair topics with authors who are recognized teachers and scholars in their field. The results have been gratifying. A series editor could hardly wish for authors who have been more cooperative, helpful, and accommodating.

Donald Grier Stephenson, Jr.

Preface and Acknowledgments

Unlike such rights as freedom of speech, assistance of counsel, trial by jury, and protection against the infliction of cruel and unusual punishment, freedom of association is never mentioned in the Constitution and was not given explicit recognition by the Supreme Court until the 1950s. Freedom of association is thus marked by the issues of that era, when civil rights and domestic communism were center stage. Recently, in the late decades of the twentieth century and the early years of the twenty-first century, associational freedom has been given a fuller definition. Now it is involved with the questions of gender equality and gay rights.

The study of constitutional law requires a degree of detachment from the immediate passions of an era. Few issues have garnered more emotional baggage than those with which freedom of association cases have been entangled—civil rights, McCarthyism and domestic communism, gender equality, and gay rights. The charged atmosphere from which they emerge is intensified by the other values with which freedom of association inevitably clashes. It is the purpose of this book to disentangle readers from the hotly contested issues in one particular case or series of cases in order to allow them to appreciate the full complexity of the law.

In the 1950s it was hard to find a middle ground between those who were concerned about the internal threat from domestic communism and those who felt that an obsession with the issue was endangering our civil liberties. In the 1960s passions on that question cooled a bit, allowing the Supreme Court to take a more measured view of associational rights and the government's interest in internal security. In the 1980s women's rights were in the foreground, as many exclusive male bastions were battered down. The Supreme Court, as we shall see, stepped into that controversy in one of most important cases discussed in this book, *Roberts v. United States Jaycees.* Since then few issues have provoked more emotion than gay rights, the issue at the center of perhaps the Supreme Court's most significant freedom of association case to date, *Boy Scouts of America v. Dale.* It is likely that new freedom of association issues and court decisions will come of the recent laws intended to prevent domestic terrorism and limit the activities of those associated with such groups.

It is because freedom of association is embroiled in such highly charged political issues that its story is compelling. The evolution of this right is deeply embedded in the history of America during the past half-century and was frequently in conflict with other values: domestic security and equality of opportunity. Consequently, Americans often have ambivalent feelings toward freedom of association. Many want the liberty to join whatever groups they choose and to allow those groups their autonomy. At the same time, many are suspicious of certain groups and practices that may be outside the American mainstream. The Communist Party in the 1950s was certainly one such group, and its associational rights were for a time severely restricted. The political establishment of the White South considered the National Association for the Advancement of Colored People (NAACP) a threat to the segregated order over which they presided and used their power to suppress that organization's associational rights. The Boy Scouts of America, in general a well-regarded organization, found itself in the middle of a political maelstrom when its policy of excluding gays clashed with state antidiscrimination laws. Many communities sympathetic to gay rights engaged in retaliatory policies directed at the Boy Scouts.

Freedom of association also raises difficult questions about what is within the sphere of purely private activity and what should be subject to public regulation. In many regards freedom of association is designed to protect that private sphere against unwanted governmental intrusion. But where do we draw the line? What are the kinds of associational activities that states can legitimately restrict?

This book gives no definite answers to these questions, if there are any. It does explain how the courts and the Congress have grappled with them. In addition to the historical and analytical narrative, the book includes a list of key events, cases, and people and excerpts from selected court decisions, important public pronouncements, and landmark congressional laws. For those who wish to explore these questions further, there is a list of suggested readings at the end of each chapter and an annotated bibliography.

I would not have undertaken the journey to write this book without the encouragement and wisdom of my dear colleague Donald Grier Stephenson, Jr., the general editor of this series, and without the patience and guidance of my editors at ABC-CLIO, Alicia S. Merritt and Melanie Stafford. I particularly want to thank Peggy Waddle, who patiently helped this neophyte overcome his persistent vexations with the world of computers. I also wish to thank my wife, Linda, to whom this book is dedicated, for her frequent good humor, love, and patience throughout its writing. There are still a few leaves waiting to be picked up.

Robert J. Bresler
Franklin and Marshall College

1

INTRODUCTION

Writing in the late eighteenth century, both Jeremy Bentham and Thomas Paine argued that liberty of public association was essential to the prevention of tyranny. People need to exercise their rights in concert and to develop their lives in a vast variety of associations. Yet as we know from recent history, not all associations are benign and not all serve the cause of human liberty or happiness.

ASSOCIATIONAL RIGHTS AND THE WAR ON TERROR

In the aftermath of two terrorist bomb attacks, one at the World Trade Center in 1993 and another at the Oklahoma City federal building in 1995, the Congress, alarmed at the threat of domestic terrorist groups, passed and President Bill Clinton signed the Anti-Terrorism and Effective Death Penalty Act of 1996. The law made it a crime and a deportable offense to "knowingly provide material support or resources to a foreign terrorist organization." Material support was defined as any "physical asset," "personnel," "training," or "expert advice or assistance." At the time, the law elicited little public debate. After the horrific terrorist attacks of September 11, 2001, concern about terrorist organizations operating in the United States became a central political issue. Consequently, Congress strengthened the penalties of the law in the Patriot Act of 2001, and the administration of George W. Bush issued numerous indictments under it, including those of six men from Lackawanna, New York, who allegedly trained at a camp run by the terrorist Al Qaeda group in Afghanistan. The law prohibits material support to those groups the secretary of state designates as terrorist organizations. This provision, section 215 of the Patriot Act, which has drawn sharp criticism from civil libertarians, allows counterterrorism agents of the Federal Bureau of Investigation (FBI) to obtain secret court orders requiring any private business—including libraries and hospitals—to produce business records for foreign intelligence and international terrorism investigations. The law can require businesses to hand over to authorities "any tangible things," including books, records, and documents.

Supporters of these laws argue that they are an essential law enforcement tool for choking off funds to foreign terrorist groups and in pursuing Al Qaeda "sleeper cells." Given the disasters of September 11th and the possibility of yet worse attacks, law enforcement cannot wait until the crime has been committed to take action. In the war against terrorism, law enforcement, working closely with intelligence agencies here and abroad, must concentrate on prevention, not just prosecution.

Critics of the law claim that its material support section is a classic case of guilt by association and infringes on individuals' right of freedom of association. They argue that the law could be used to punish a host of innocent associations and activities defined as "material support," such as filing lawsuits or writing newspaper columns on behalf of organizations. The law could also punish donors to charitable aims of so-called terrorist groups. Civil libertarians warn that the law could be used to violate a series of Supreme Court decisions that ensure freedom of association and protect against guilt by association such as those guaranteeing one a right to be a member of a subversive group so long as one does not specifically intend to further violence or cause any other illegal actions. The government counters that material support does not constitute guilt by association since it does not criminalize membership. Critics contend that if one can join an organization but not support it, freedom of association is an empty vessel. They cite Supreme Court decisions that link soliciting donations and making contributions as acts of association. The Court has said in regard to political contributions, "The right to join together for the advancement of beliefs and ideas ... is diluted if it does not include the right to pool money through contributions, for funds are often essential if advocacy is to be truly or optimally effective" (*Buckley v. Valeo*, 424 U.S. 65–66; 1976).

In its efforts to starve terrorist groups, the government claims that money is fungible so that any funds, no matter what their specific purpose, would have the indirect effect of aiding and abetting terrorism. As Congress saw it, "Foreign organizations that engage in terrorist activity are so tainted by their criminal conduct that any contribution to such an organization facilitates that conduct" (Public Law 104-132, 104th Cong., 2nd sess., April 24, 1996). Money given to such organizations and intended for humanitarian purposes, in other words, could end up paying for a truck bomb or some dastardly radiological weapon.

The Antiterrorism Act and the Patriot Act place a much heavier burden on those charged with association with any terrorist organizations. Defenders of the young American-born Muslim men charged in Lackawanna say that they are misguided zealots who were on a religious quest, happened to stumble into an Al Qaeda training camp, and never intended to engage in terrorist action; their association was innocent and without criminal intent. Their defense lawyers claim that it would be an infringement on their constitutional freedom of association for the government to prosecute these men unless it can be proven that they specifically intended to commit terrorist crimes. The 1996 law, however, requires no such proof. By showing that these men traveled to Afghanistan, went to an Al Qaeda camp, heard a speech by terrorist mastermind Osama bin Laden, and trained in the use of weapons and explosives, the government believes the law makes their association criminal. In the war against terrorism, the government argues that it must be able to prosecute those with such connections without shouldering the burden of proving criminal intent.

In its responsibility to enforce both the Antiterrorism Act and the Patriot Act, the Justice Department has asserted that it will protect the freedom of association. But what is freedom of association, and exactly what does it protect? The Constitution of the United States does not grant such an explicit right. It emanates from the First Amendment guarantees of freedom of speech and assembly and the Fourteenth Amendment protection that one cannot be denied life, liberty, or property without due process of the law. The concept of associational freedom is rooted in the notion that liberty cannot be defined merely as an individual guarantee. In a vast and complex society of almost 300 million people such as the United States, individuals, standing alone, have great difficulty in making their voices heard loud enough to make an impact. If people can band together in a variety of causes, however, freedom of speech can be amplified and made meaningful.

Also, most people do not want to live their lives in isolation. They find meaning in connecting with others in everything from neighborhood associations to civic clubs to religious groups or even Internet chat groups. Such connection flows voluntarily and naturally from the choices that people make. They are not coerced; people can enter and leave at their own discretion; they make these connections because they find meaning, benefit, and satisfaction from them. Totalitarianism, a hideous twentieth-century phenomenon in Nazi Germany and the Soviet Union, attempted to order every aspect of common life—religious, economic, and educational. Beyond the ghastly crimes committed by those regimes was the deprivation of the cultural richness and economic innovation that comes from allowing people to make their own associations.

The choice is not between a highly regimented totalitarian society, where everything is state controlled, and a completely libertarian society, where everyone is allowed to associate without any state interference. The question of where freedom of association ends and the society's interests begin is a more complex one in the American experience. Not all associations are valuable; not all their policies enhance individual welfare or the common good; and some, as in the case of terrorist organizations, are downright criminal. Residential community associations can design zoning rules to make their neighborhoods economically, ethnically, and racially homogeneous; the Augusta National Golf Club, which hosts the prestigious Masters Tournament, is an all-male organization; many religious associations preach nontolerance, if not downright hatred of other religions. Freedom of association can foster a bewildering variety of groups—racist, sexist, authoritarian—that hardly contribute to the common good. Such organizations can deepen the divisions in society, making it less stable and governable. A democratic society, such as Weimar Germany in the 1920s and 1930s, can allow a totalitarian party, such as the Nazi Party, to spring up and then strangle the very democracy that allowed it to exist.

Even those organizations with more benign intentions—special interest groups, such as the National Rifle Association (NRA), the American Association of Retired People (AARP), labor unions, trade association, and trial lawyers—can exercise disproportionate influence on the political arena, making change and innovation difficult. This is what Jonathan Rauch has called the hardening of the democratic arteries, or demosclerosis.

As with any right, freedom of association does not guarantee a good outcome. Without it, however, life would be much worse, if not intolerable. Like all other rights, it is not absolute. In one case involving a state regulation restricting admission to certain dance halls to those between the ages of fourteen and eighteen so they would not be subject to the potentially detrimental influences of older teenagers and young adults, the Supreme Court declared that there was no "generalized right of social association that would include chance encounters in the dance halls" (*Dallas v. Stanglin,* 490 U.S. 19; 1989).

At some point the rights of association may conflict with the needs of society. Where is the line drawn between social interests and associational freedom? The question requires a complex balancing test. A government restriction on associational freedom has to be measured by weighing the legitimacy and necessity of the social need against the degree of infringement on the right. This is the job of the courts. Since freedom of association is not found in the text of the Constitution, it lacks the history inherent in textually based rights—congressional and state ratification hearings and debate. The courts have much greater leeway in delineating the contours of the right and balancing it against state interests.

Courts are also confronted with determining what is legitimate association. For example, when does a political party become a conspiracy against liberty—the issue concerning the Nazi Party or the Communist Party? The courts have given such organizations as the National Association for the Advancement of Colored People (NAACP) greater protection from state interference than it has the Ku Klux Klan or the Communist Party. As with terrorist groups, does mere membership in a suspected organization make one legally vulnerable?

Equally vexing is the question of what belongs legitimately within the public sector and what belongs to the private sector. What is the appropriate reach of the state? What makes an association private, and when does it take on the attributes of a public accommodation? What is the status of large, influential organizations such as the Boy Scouts and Jaycees? Are they purely private organizations, or are they so entwined with the public schools and other public agencies so as to be covered by a public accommodation law? How far should the government go in defining what is in the public sector before it drains associational life of its spontaneity and its participants of their liberty?

Disputes can also arise between an association and its members. This creates the problem of whose rights are at stake: the member or the organization? And when, if at all, should the courts step in? When a member can voluntarily leave an organization without losing a job or any such benefit, the courts are reluctant to intervene. However, they have protected the right of public employees who objected to having their union dues go to political causes they did not support (*Abood v. Detroit Board of Education,* 431 U.S. 209; 1977).

PLAN OF THE BOOK

The burdens of defining and sifting through these complex questions have fallen to the courts, and to the Supreme Court for its final judgment. Its decisions have inevitably emerged from the political environment and the issues that dominated in any particular era. In the 1950s and early 1960s, civil rights and domestic communism were at center stage. In the later decades of the twentieth century and the early years of the twenty-first century, the question of discrimination in regard to gender and sexual preferences become central political concerns. It should not be surprising, therefore, that many of the Supreme Court's landmark decisions on freedom of association come out of disputes related to those issues. It is impossible to trace the development of any constitutional right outside of its historical context. Freedom of association has grown out of the political struggles of the past and is defined by them. Thus, the story of what freedom of association involves must be told historically, as this book intends to do.

Chapter 2 traces the historical origins of associational freedom from the early years of the Republic to the present. Since the Bill of Rights, prior to the passage of the Fourteenth Amendment, applied only to the federal government, not the states, there was relatively scant litigation in regard to the First Amendment. The Court in the first half of the nineteenth century gave very little guidance as to the contours of free speech and assembly and said nothing about freedom of association. In Chapter 2 we look at the writings of the most astute observer of young America, the French aristocrat Alexis de Tocqueville. In his classic study *Democracy in America*, we find the first explanation of why habits of voluntary association were so essential for democratic culture to take root in a fledgling republic. Despite Tocqueville's admiration of American volunteerism, two of our most important founding fathers, George Washington and James Madison, had deep suspicions about associations, particularly about political associations, and feared conspiracies. John Adams, our second president, shared their concerns and so signed the Sedition Act of 1798. Yet, we shall see that this view was in a minority.

We will therefore examine how Tocqueville's thinking has influenced a current generation of political philosophers—Robert Putnam, Amy Guttman, William Galston, Nancy Rosenblum, and George Kateb—who have written on the importance of civic engagement to democracy. Their argument is based not on a constitutional interpretation but rather on an empirical and moral basis. To wit, freedom of association in the American experience has proven to be related to economic development, individual self-sufficiency, charitable generosity, and political stability. Many of them, especially Robert Putnam, fret that the values of a liberal democracy may be threatened by the decline of voluntary civic engagement.

Chapter 2 also looks at the first glimmers of freedom of association as a constitutional doctrine in the years following the Civil War with the ratification of the Fourteenth Amendment. I focus particular attention on the first Supreme Court case to give even a hint of recognition to freedom of association, *United States v. Cruikshank* (92 U.S. 542; 1875).

In Chapter 3 freedom of association emerges as a judicially determined yet fully recognized constitutional right. In the last two-thirds of the twentieth century, civil rights and civil liberties became a central concern of the Supreme Court, particularly when it interpreted the due process clause of the Fourteenth Amendment as applying most of the Bill of Rights to the states. We will see in Chapter 3 how the Court finds the properties of associational freedom in the First and Fourteenth Amendments, making freedom of association applicable to federal, state, and municipal laws. Nonetheless, the Supreme Court decisions defining freedom of association come out of some of the most important political struggles of the twentieth century: the battles over civil rights and discrimination, domestic communism, and the expansion of the voting franchise. In the Court decisions of the 1950s, the conflicts over civil rights and domestic communism allowed the Supreme Court to define both the limits and the breadth of freedom of association.

In Chapter 4 we explore two major Supreme Court cases decided in the first year of the twenty-first century, *Boy Scouts of America v. Dale* (530 U.S. 640; 2000) and *California Democratic Party v. Jones* (530 U.S. 567; 2000). Both go a long way in sharpening the contours of freedom of association. The debate in *Dale* revolves around the emotionally charged issue of gay rights and associational rights. In the effort of James Dale, a gay man, to prevent the Boy Scouts from removing him from his position, we see a clash of values and a clash of rights. How far can society go in attempting to remove the vestiges of discrimination before it controls heretofore private groups? What guidance can the courts give in refereeing disputes between state antidiscrimination laws and rights of association? The *Dale* case, decided 5–4, shows how complex the problem is and how deep the divisions on the issue can be. The *Jones* case is equally complex but less emotionally charged. It examines where the states' authority to regulate primary elections ends and the rights of political parties to control their membership and message begins.

Chapter 5 provides a list of important Supreme Court cases and congressional laws, key personalities, terms, and concepts. Chapter 6 offers excerpts of seminal Supreme Court cases, key provisions of important legislation, and public statements. The book also includes a chronology of events in the evolution of freedom of association and an annotated bibliography.

References and Further Reading

Burns, J. H., and H. L. A. Hart. 1977. *The Collected Works of Jeremy Bentham.* London: Athlone Press.

Cole, David. 2003. "The New McCarthyism: Repeating History in the War on Terrorism." *Harvard Civil Rights—Civil Liberties Law Review* 38 (Winter): 1–29.

Cole, David, and James X. Dempsey. 2002. *Terrorism and the Constitution: Sacrificing Civil Liberties in the Name of National Security.* 2nd ed. New York: New Press.

Gunther, Gerald, and Kathleen M. Sullivan. 2003. *Constitutional Law.* 14th ed. Westbury, NY: Foundation Press.

Harris, George. 2003. "Terrorism and the Constitution: Sacrificing Civil Liberties in the Name of National Security." *Cornell International Law Review* 36 (Spring): 135–150.

Macedo, Stephen. 2000. *Diversity and Distrust: Civic Education in a Multicultural Democracy.* Cambridge: Harvard University Press.

Paine, Thomas. 1995. *Rights of Man, Common Sense, and Other Political Writings.* Edited by Mark Philp. Oxford: Oxford University Press.

Rauch, Jonathan. 1994. *Demosclerosis: The Silent Killer of American Democracy.* New York: New York Times Books.

Soifer, Aviam. 1995. *Law and the Company We Keep.* Cambridge: Harvard University Press.

Taylor, Stuart, Jr. 2002. "Making Plans with Al Qaeda: The War on Terrorism Justifies Some Limits on American Freedom to Associate." *Legal Times,* October 28: 86.

2

ORIGINS

America is often described as a nation of joiners. It has been that way since the beginning of the republic. As early as the 1830s, Alexis de Tocqueville, in his classic study *Democracy in America,* observed that "Americans of all ages, all conditions, all minds constantly united. Not only do they have commercial and industrial associations in which all take part, but they also have a thousand other kinds: religious, moral, grave, futile, very general, and very particular, immense and very small" (2000, 489). Associations have been defined as:

- "any group of persons pursuing a common purpose or system or aggregation of purposes by a course of cooperative action extending beyond a single act, and, for this purpose, agreeing together upon certain methods of procedure, and laying down in however rudimentary a form, rules for common action" (Cole 1950, 37);
- "any kind of formalized, non-governmental, human interaction" (Tamir 1998, 216);
- "those kinds of attachments we choose for specific purposes—to further a cause, form a family, play a sport, work through a problem of identity or meaning, get

ahead in a career, or resolve a neighborhood problem"
(Warren 2001, 39).

There are voluntary associations that individuals enter by
choice. Within these voluntary associations, there are different
types with important distinctions. Primary intimate associations
are those such as family and friends; other personal associations,
such as religious groups, reading clubs, and hobby groups, involve
face-to-face contact. In the Internet age there are more remote
personal associations such as chat rooms. Secondary associations
are large membership organizations of people who may never see
each other—political parties, special interest groups such as the
American Association of Retired People (AARP) or the National
Rifle Association (NRA). The *Encyclopedia of Associations* lists
23,000 nonprofit membership organizations of national scope.
The Nonprofit Almanac found 576,133 tax-exempt organizations
of 645 types as of 1995. One survey estimates that there are about
3 million small, informal groups such as support groups, book
clubs, and neighborhood associations (Mazzone 2002, 691). In
fact, it is impossible to achieve even an approximate count of all
the associations in the United States, since many are small and do
not bother to publicize their existence.

Political theorists, sociologists, and other social commentators
have long considered associations to be an essential part of democratic political culture, making up what is often called civic society. For most contemporary observers, the right to associate is so
vital to a free society that it must be given constitutional protection. However, the precise contribution associations make to a
democratic society is subject to differing interpretations. Some
observers have argued that associational freedom is simply an extension of freedom of speech and must be yoked to the First
Amendment. Others believe that associational freedom has its
own intrinsic value and should be given constitutional standing
independent of the First Amendment. Before one can begin the

constitutional discussion, it is important to review the various arguments about what associational freedom contributes to a free society.

Associations as a Counterweight to the Power of the State

Tocqueville believed that "freedom of association has become a necessary guarantee against the tyranny of the majority" (2000, 182). Associative freedom, according to Tocqueville, had an intrinsic value. He believed that civil associations were essential to the success of a self-governing people. The innovation and the vitality of this young nation fascinated Tocqueville, and he credited it to the formation of voluntary associations, which were not only business associations but touched virtually every aspect of life. "In America," Tocqueville observed, "I encountered sorts of associations of which, I confess, I had no idea, and I often admired the infinite art with which the inhabitants of the United States managed to fix a common goal to the efforts of many men and to get them to advance to it freely" (2000, 489).

Tocqueville was one of the first social commentators to see the importance of social mores to a stable democracy. Tocqueville believed that formal governmental arrangements and a constitutional design were not enough. The voluntary secondary associations that stood between the state and the primary associations of family and other intimates were essential to developing democratic habits among ordinary citizens.

Tocqueville understood democracy as a culture, not simply as a set of governmental arrangements. A stable and successful democracy requires the qualities of self-reliance and responsibility in its people, which must be cultivated and developed. Otherwise people will, in their thirst for equality, grant greater and greater powers to a centralized state. Tocqueville feared a democratic despotism that would be subtle and mild, caring for its people's needs and regulating their affairs. "It does not tyrannize," Tocqueville wrote; "it hinders, compromises, enervates, extinguishes, dazes, and finally reduces each nation to being nothing more than a herd of timid and industrious animals of which the government is the shepherd"(quoted in Wood 2001, 49). Thus, voluntary associations, along with a free press, local self-government, and independent judges and juries, can teach the habits of self-reliance and social responsibility.

Voluntary associations become an essential element in the formation of a liberal democracy. They create a sphere of activity, independent from state regulation, that allows people to sharpen their personal identities, find a sympathetic community, and amplify their own ideas. Associations give each citizen a megaphone to influence the direction of state politics.

According to Tocqueville, voluntary associations promote the norms of reciprocity and the materials that bind a society together through interlocking networks. These associations allow America to be both experimental and self-governing. Tocqueville believed that associations amplified the influence of the individual citizen who could easily become lost and isolated in a country as vast as the young American republic. Associations also drew the individuals out of their narrow primary group into a wider network of social relations. As he described it, "All citizens are independent and weak: they can do almost nothing by themselves, and none of them can oblige those like themselves to lend them their cooperation. They therefore all fall into impotence if they do not learn to aid each other freely" (2000, 496). Freedom of association provides two essential ingredients for a stable democracy: social reciprocity and citizen efficacy. Both ingredients, if insinuated into the fabric of culture, could become an important buffer against unwarranted state intrusion, a kind of moat between the citizen and the state.

The formation of so many voluntary associations in America was, from Tocqueville's perspective, an important explanation of how democratic culture was taking root in this new country. Tocqueville was struck by the contrast between the voluntary associations among equals found in America and the top-down aristocratic associations of Europe. He compared the American openness to voluntary associations to the European experience: "Among all the peoples of Europe, there are certain associations that can only be formed after the state has examined their statutes and authorized their existence. Among several, efforts are being made to extend this rule to all associations. One readily sees where the success of such an undertaking would lead" (2000, 658). Tocqueville feared that once the state could authorize associations, it would regulate them, impose its own rules, and enforce a general orthodoxy. Truly voluntary associations were, in Tocqueville's view, a buffer between individuals and the state, filling functions that government could eventually dictate. Democracy was as much an expression of culture as it was a reflection of constitutional forms. The vibrancy and innovation that Tocqueville observed in America came not from the governmental leadership but from the local communities. Both the secular associations and the religious communities provided the foundation of a self-regulating order (McGinnis 2002).

In contemporary American politics, interest groups, an important form of association, are designed to make the state responsive to various private groups, a condition far more beneficial to liberty than the reverse. Americans have placed far more trust in those associations they freely join than the government itself. The historian Arthur Schlesinger Sr. observed, "Traditionally, Americans have distrusted collective organization as embodied in government while insisting upon their own untrammeled right to form voluntary associations"(Schlesinger 1949, 23).

Freedom of association, rooted in the protection of a constitution and protected from the whims of a temporary majority, could be an essential guarantee in creating an authentically private sector where beliefs and cultural expressions could be embraced without the approval and clearance of the state. "A government," claimed Tocqueville, "can no more suffice on its own to maintain and renew the circulations of sentiments and ideas in a great people than to conduct all its industrial undertakings. As it tries to leave the political sphere to project itself on this new track, it will exercise an insupportable tyranny even without wishing to; for a government knows only how to dictate precise rules; it imposes the sentiments and the ideas that it favors, and it is always hard to distinguish its counsels from its orders" (2000, 492).

ASSOCIATIONS AS A SOURCE OF SOCIAL CAPITAL

Contemporary scholar Robert D. Putnam considers voluntary associations as important to the more mature American democracy of the late twentieth and early twenty-first centuries as Tocqueville did to the America of the early nineteenth century. In *Bowling Alone: The Collapse and Revival of American Community* (2000), Putnam builds his argument around the concept of social capital. He cites the progressive reformer L. J. Hanifan, who first defined the social capital as "those tangible substances [that] count for most in the daily lives of people: namely good will, fellowship, sympathy, and social intercourse. . . . The community as a whole will benefit by the cooperation of all its parts, while the individual will find in his associations the advantages of the help, the sympathy, and the fellowship of his neighbors" (quoted in Putnam 2000, 19). Social capital can increase the efficiency of society by facilitating cooperative action. Citizens who are a part of strong social networks are more likely to assist each other in the mundane but important everyday aspects of life by lending money, finding a job, carpooling to work, and generally sharing resources. Empirical studies have shown that the social capital produced from various associations results in a great deal of individual and social benefits. For example, when children grow up in neighborhoods and families that produce the reciprocal norms characterized by high levels of social capital, they suffer from less risk of abuse, have fewer behavioral problems, perform better in school, and have improved prospects for the future (Mazzone 2002, 710). A society with a high level of social capital will reap the benefits of mutual trust and cooperation in the form of increased productivity. Without the social capital that associations can provide, a society may be rife with suspicion and self-dealing.

According to Putnam, voluntary associations produce social capital by the development and bonding of exclusive groups such as ethnic and fraternal organizations. They also promote what Putnam calls bridging, the bringing together of different ethnic, religious, and racial groups in civic societies and ecumenical religious groups. In particular, voluntary civic associations produce both the private good that Hanifan refers to as well as a public good. For example, service clubs such as the Rotary Clubs and the Lions fund scholarships and raise money to fight disease. Thus, such associations generate a beneficial set of social norms, and their autonomy keeps alive a peaceful, productive, and spontaneous social order. As John McGinnis puts it, "Preserving the autonomy of these civil associations helps sustain the subtleties and complexities of this spontaneous order, which in turn improves the behavior and character of individuals without the intervention of the centralized state" (2002, 530).

The vital civic engagement that Tocqueville witnessed in the early nineteenth century has diminished dramatically. Putnam fears a loss of social capital as participation of all kinds waned at the end of the twentieth century, even in bowling leagues (thus the title of his book). He calls the generation born between 1910 and 1940 a "long civic generation" and those born between 1925 and 1930 in particular "exceptionally civic—voting more, joining more, giving more."

Sadly, he sees in the succeeding generations, namely, the baby boomers and the generation X-ers, a precipitous decline in civic engagement. In echoing Putnam's claim, Paul Starr writes, "Our public experience has changed dramatically since the Depression and World War II. Politics and civic life once seemed to make imperative claims on Americans, to offer avenues for participation, and to reinforce the sense that government could be made to work. The public world has since become less urgent, more remote, and more tainted" (2000, 36). Putnam and Starr may be overly pessimistic. There is evidence that Americans are still a nation of joiners. A recent national survey on citizen participation in associations found that 79 percent of the respondents were affiliated with one or more associations through financial contributions. Of those who were affiliated with at least one association, 65 percent had attended a meeting within the past year, 42 percent were active members, and 28 percent had served as board members or officers (Verba et al. 1995, 74–79).

Implicit in both Tocqueville's and Putnam's appreciation of associational life is the recognition that liberty is more than an individualistic concept, that its social and communal dimension are equally important. Associational freedom is an ingredient of pluralism, the concept that a democratic society requires multiple and competing centers of power separate from those that are politically organized. As Laurence Tribe put it, "Believers in the richness and diversity of a pluralist society, where a variety of voluntary private associations and groups operate simultaneously to maximize opportunities for self-realization and minimize the strength of centralized power, may begin to find comfort in the freedom of association" (1998, 35).

ASSOCIATIONS AS A SOURCE OF PERSONAL ENRICHMENT

Building on Tocqueville's observations, political philosopher George Kateb has argued that freedom of association has an independent and intrinsic value apart from protecting liberty and enhancing civil society. Voluntary nongovernmental associations can teach mutual assistance, cultivate habits of civic engagement, perform valuable public work, build community, and reduce the danger of anomie. They can become the mechanism through which raw self-interest is transformed into what Tocqueville called "self-interest rightly understood"—a willingness to sacrifice some self-interest for the greater good. When individuals cooperate in voluntary association, they learn the values of moderation, self-command, and the need to compromise. Thus, such associations foster the habits of a democratic, self-governing people (Galston 2000, 64–70). Kateb voices his disquiet when "association is intrinsically yoked to speech and is protected only because speech is protected" (1998, 35). Voluntary associations are not, he says, merely instrumental purposes of free speech.

Kateb does not reduce the inherent value of freedom of association to intimate associations, such as marriage, family relationships, and child rearing. He would also include businesses, economic corporations, labor unions, professional guilds, lobbying groups, political parties, private social clubs, fraternities, sororities, charities, universities, and other nonprofit entities. Kateb (1998) believes freedom of association should not only be broadly defined but should receive its own judicial protection. "In a constitutional democracy," he argues, "people should have the right, recognized by government, to associate in these ways for any appropriate purpose that does not harm the vital claims of others" (36–37). He asserts, "There is a basic truth about almost all associative life and activity, a truth not confined to love and friendship. People find in association a value in itself. The point is obvious, but it has not received enough judicial attention or protection. In pursuing their ends, and needing to associate in order to do so, people discover numerous sources of pleasure apart from the pleasure of success in their specific pursuits" (36–37). Kateb would look to the due process clauses of the Fifth and Fourteenth Amendments and follow the concept of substantive due process that he defines as "the idea that the widest possible scope of general liberty is mandated by the Constitution" (38). Procedural due process, the rights embodied in the Fourth through Eighth Amendments, protects defendants or suspected or convicted persons. They stem from a "refined conception of personhood and a sense that the law should treat all people with a respect for their dignity" (62). Kateb holds that the same respect for personhood should "set limits as well to government's encroachments on the liberty of individuals who are not subject to criminal procedure" (62).

Kateb thinks that freedom of association has an inherent value for ordinary human experience in that "the desire to rid society of oppression so that a life of decent adventure would become more available for a larger number of people" (39). The importance of an association and its value to society are not issues for governments to decide. Kateb admits, "Much of protected freedom is misspent or misused, is wasted, from one dignified perspective or another. Government, however, is not supposed to look skeptically or censoriously at how freedom is used (except when vital claims are involved) if people are to live free in a free society. One's life is one's own" (40).

Arguing along the same lines, Amy Guttman sees freedom of association as essential "to create and maintain intimate relationships of love and friendship, which are valuable for their own sake, as well as the pleasure that they offer. Freedom of association is increasingly essential as a means of engaging in charity, commerce, industry, education, health care, residential life, religious practice, professional life, music and art, recreation and sports. . . . By associating with one another we engage in camaraderie, cooperation, dialogue, deliberation, negotiation, competition, creativity, and the kinds of self-expression that are possible only in association with others" (1998, 3). Freedom of association from this perspective is considered an intrinsic right and not simply an instrumental right, serving as a function of free speech. According to this justification, freedom of association has a value apart from self-government. It is also rooted in a notion of *self-realization*, a term perhaps foreign to Tocqueville's nineteenth-century sensibility. At this point one can argue that the right to association and the right to privacy are conflated. Guttman and Kateb's view of association is similar to the position of Justice Anthony Kennedy in *Lawrence v. Texas* (2003), the case in which the Court overturned the Texas law prohibiting homosexual sodomy. As Justice Kennedy explained it, "Freedom extends beyond spatial bounds. Liberty presumes an autonomy of self that includes freedom of thought, belief, expressions, and certain intimate conduct. The instant case involves liberty of the person both in its spatial and more transcendent dimensions." Is this "certain intimate conduct" not association?

ASSOCIATIONS AS AN ELEMENT IN STRENGTHENING SELF-GOVERNMENT

In a recent study of associations, Mark E. Warren identifies three ways in which associations might produce potentially democratic effects: (1) They contribute to the capacities of citizens to participate in collective judgment and to develop autonomous judgments that reflect their wants and beliefs; (2) they contribute to the formation of public opinion by developing agendas, testing ideas, and providing a voice for various interests; (3) they transform autonomous judgments into collective decisions, enabling individuals to have some leverage on the political system (Warren 2001, 61). Nancy Rosenblum argues that associations build habits among those who participate in them by tempering individual self-interest and integrating otherwise disconnected individuals into society (1994).

All these observers see freedom of association as part of the right of self-government and associations as a function of popular sovereignty. Associations are a form of political participation. If the ideal of democracy is a process whereby enlightened citizens reason together in the formation of public policy, the more participation the better. Participation creates more informed citizens, promotes mutual discourse, and may allow for a deeper understanding of the country's common purposes.

First Constitutional Origins

As does any right, freedom of association needs restraints. There is a concept of the common good that the state must defend. Civil associations cannot use their freedom to violate the law, such as religious groups that engage in human sacrifice or withhold medical treatment from children. But where is the line between protecting the general welfare and preserving the rights of individuals to enter into free associations with their fellow citizens?

Popular sovereignty, the notion that people can govern themselves, is at the heart of the American experiment. The phrase "freedom of association" appears nowhere in the Constitution, yet it grows out of the concept of popular sovereignty. The Preamble to the Constitution, which begins, "We, the People of the United States, in Order to form a more perfect Union," is emblematic of this fundamental idea. It was first articulated by Thomas Jefferson in the Declaration of Independence: "Governments are instituted among men, deriving their just powers from the consent of the governed." The First Amendment is also part of this fabric. It protects freedom of speech but also the right of assembly and the right to petition for the redress of grievances. The notion of assembly implies that self-government allows groups to meet to protest or to influence the direction of the state. Despite the concern of James Madison and others that factions could tear at the fabric of a well-ordered, self-governing society, the First Amendment protects their existence.

In a sense the popular rebellion that became the American Revolution was itself a demonstration of the importance of collective action and voluntary association. Collective action sprang from the soil of the Revolution when Americans, as Tocqueville observed, began to form political parties and an extensive network of civic associations. Associations became deeply embedded in the events that preceded and followed the Civil War: the abolitionist movement and the vast number of associations that emerged after that war to link Northern and Southern citizens into groups with shared purposes. During the progressive era, Americans formed an unprecedented number of associations in order to cure the social injustices of industrialization.

Despite the growing importance of associations, many feared that associations would disrupt the political order. James Madison, in his famous *Federalist* No. 10, warned about the "mischiefs of faction." President Washington was fearful of the new Democratic-Republican societies that formed in the years 1793–1794 and felt they may have had a role in the Whiskey Rebellion. In his farewell address, published in 1796, Washington made it clear that association could be a threat to representative government:

> All combinations and associations, under whatever plausible character, with the real design to direct, control, counteract, or awe the regular deliberation and action of the constituted authorities, are . . . of fatal tendency. They serve to organize faction, to give it an artificial and extraordinary force; to put, in the place of the delegated will of the nation, the will of a party, often a small but artful and enterprising minority of the community; and, according to the alternate triumphs of different parties, to make the public administration the mirror of the ill-concerted and incongruous projects of faction, rather than the organ of consistent and wholesome plans digested by common councils, and modified by mutual interests (Washington 1931, 34).

Washington's suspicion of associations was confined to his public and private statements. Soon after he left office, however, these suspicions became manifest in congressional legislation. Two years after Washington published his farewell address, the Congress passed the Sedition Act of 1798. This law made it a crime for any person to "unlawfully combine or conspire together, with intent to oppose any measure or measures of the government of the United States." The Sedition Act was one of the first examples of how government, fearful of certain associations, has used its power to curb and limit their freedoms. The act reflected a concern that societies that supported the French Revolution would bring its instability to American shores and a fear of political societies that could upset a fragile young republic.

Washington's view on associations was far from unanimously held. The Sedition Act was allowed to lapse in 1801, and President Thomas Jefferson pardoned all those who had been convicted under it. Many essayists of the day saw associations as mediating institutions that could facilitate the dialogue between citizens and their elected leaders. Even those who shared Washington's suspicion of the Democratic-Republican societies took a more generous view of other associations such as the Masons. Many prominent early Americans such as Benjamin Franklin and Washington himself were Masons. The Masons were held in such high esteem that President Washington dedicated the United States Capitol dressed in Masonic garb, and when he placed a silver plate on the corner, he identified the date as "the thirteenth-year of American independence and . . . the year of Masonery" (quoted in Mazzone 2002, 733).

The contrasting attitudes toward the Masons and the Democratic-Republican societies were an early sign that government leaders, even those as admirable as our founders, could not resist the temptation to favor some associations over others. It was certainly within the power of the state to coerce those associations it suspected and reward those it favored. The possibilities could include preventing citizens from forming certain associations, denying them the use of public facilities, excluding their members from public employment, or publicizing the names of those who belonged to unpopular groups. In the twentieth century, federal and state governments have used their power to limit such organizations as the NAACP, the Communist Party, and the Ku Klux Klan and in the twenty-first century those with known ties to terrorist groups. The question is, Where does the government's interest in public order begin and the right of association end? This issue eventually found its way into the debates over U.S. constitutional law. The results reflect the complexity of the issue and the uncertain contours of the right.

It is possible to argue that freedom of association, although not specifically mentioned in the Constitution, can find some textual support in the First Amendment guarantee of freedom of assembly. The Constitution and the Bill of Rights were written in the era prior to modern communication. With mail delivery in its primitive form and before the telephone, it was difficult to associate without physically assembling. Today this is no longer necessary. As David Cole has noted, "If one asks why the Framers protected the right of assembly, the reasons would have little to do with the physical act of gathering together in a single place, and everything to do with the significance of coordinated action to a republican political process. Today we are connected by telephones, faxes, modems, and the Internet, and association can more often than not take place without any physical assembly" (Cole 1999, 227).

The constitutional concept has emerged slowly. Its first traces are found the Reconstruction-era case *United States v. Cruikshank* (92 U.S. 542; 1875). This case involved the Enforcement Act, a Reconstruction law that made it a crime to "band or conspire together to oppress any citizen or hinder his free exercise . . . of any right . . . secured to him by the Constitution" or federal law. A group of white defendants had conspired to deprive a number of black citizens their right to assemble for peaceful and lawful purposes. Although the Supreme Court declared the indictment too broad (the black group was not meeting to petition the federal government), the Court did declare that "the very idea of a government, republican in form, implies a right on the part of its citizens to meet peaceably for consultation in respect to public affairs and to petition for a redress of grievances" (*Cruikshank,* 548). In his interpretation of *Cruikshank,* Cole has argued, "If the right of assembly is implicit in a republican government, so too is the right of association, since the very reason assembly was considered implicit was that it made association possible" (Cole 1999, 228). Thus, the constitutional doctrine of freedom of association in its embryonic form begins with *Cruikshank.*

REFERENCES AND FURTHER READING

Cole, David. 1999. "Hanging with the Wrong Crowd: Of Gangs, Terrorists, and the Right of Association." *Supreme Court Review* 199: 203–252.

Cole, G. D. H. 1950. *Essays in Social Theory.* New York: Macmillan.

Galston, William A. 2000. "Civil Society and the Art of Association." *Journal of Democracy* 11, 1: 64–70.

Guttman, Amy. 1998. "Freedom of Association: An Introductory Essay." In *Freedom of Association,* edited by Amy Guttman. Princeton, NJ: Princeton University Press.

Hunt, Kimberly N., ed. 2002. *Encyclopedia of Associations.* 38th ed. New York: Gale Research.

Kateb, George. 1998. "The Value of Association." In *Freedom of Association,* edited by Amy Guttman. Princeton, NJ: Princeton University Press.

Mazzone, Jason. 2002. "Freedom's Associations." *Washington Law Review* 77 (July): 639–767.

McGinnis, John O. 2002. "Reviving Tocqueville's America: The Rehnquist Court's Jurisprudence of Social Discovery." *California Law Review* 90 (March): 530–571.

Putnam, Robert D. 2000. *Bowling Alone: The Collapse and Revival of American Community.* New York: Simon and Schuster.

Rosenblum, Nancy L. 1994. "Civil Societies: Liberalism and the Moral Uses of Pluralism." *Social Research* 61, 3: 539–562.

Schlesinger, Arthur. 1949. *Paths to the Present.* New York: Macmillan.

Skocpol, Theda. 1999. *Civic Engagement in American Democracy.* Washington, DC: Brookings Institution.

Starr, Paul. 2000. "The Public Vanishes." *New Republic,* August 14: 35–37.

Tamir, Yael. 1998. "Revisiting the Civic Sphere." In *Freedom of Association,* edited by Amy Guttman. Princeton, NJ: Princeton University Press.

Tocqueville, Alexis de. 2000. *Democracy in America.* Edited by Harvey C. Mansfield and Delba Winthrop. Chicago: University of Chicago Press.

Tribe, Laurence H. 1998. *American Constitutional Law.* 2d ed. Mineola, NY: Foundation Press.

Verba, Sidney, Kay Lehman Schlozman, and Henry E. Brady. 1995. *Voice and Equality: Civic Voluntarism in American Politics.* Cambridge: Harvard University Press.

Warren, Mark E. 2001. *Democracy and Association.* Princeton, NJ: Princeton University Press.

Washington, George. 1931. Sixth annual address to Congress (November 19, 1794). In *The Writings of George Washington.* Vol. 35. Edited by John C. Fitzpatrick. Washington, DC: Government Printing Office, pp. 214–238.

Wood, Gordon. 2001. "Tocqueville's Lesson." *New York Review of Books,* May 17: 46–49.

3

TWENTIETH-CENTURY
ISSUES

In order for freedom of association to take root in the Constitution, the Supreme Court had to expand both the protection and the meaning of the First and Fourteenth Amendments. In *Gitlow v. New York* (268 U.S. 652; 1925), the Supreme Court incorporated both the free speech and press clauses of the First Amendment into the due process clause of the Fourteenth Amendment, thus applying them to state and municipal law. As the Court put it, "Freedom of speech and of the press are among the fundamental personal rights and 'liberties' protected by the due process clause of the Fourteenth Amendment from impairment by the states."

In *De Jonge v. State of Oregon* (299 U.S. 353; 1937), the Supreme Court incorporated the right of peaceable assembly into the Fourteenth Amendment. Overturning the conviction of a political organizer who had simply attended a Communist Party rally, Chief Justice Charles Evans Hughes wrote:

> The right of peaceable assembly is a right cognate to those of free speech and free press and is equally fundamental. The First Amendment of the

Federal Constitution expressly guarantees that right against abridgment by Congress. But explicit mention there does not argue exclusion elsewhere. For the right is one that cannot be denied without violating those fundamental principles of liberty and justice which lie at the base of all civil and political institutions—principles which the Fourteenth Amendment embodies in the general terms of its due process clause. These rights may be abused by using speech or press or assembly in order to incite to violence and crime. The people through their legislatures may protect themselves against that abuse. But the legislative intervention can find constitutional justification only by dealing with the abuse. The rights themselves must not be curtailed. The greater the importance of safeguarding the community from incitements to the overthrow of our institutions by force and violence, the more imperative is the need to preserve inviolate the constitutional rights of free speech, free press and free assembly in order to maintain the opportunity for free political discussion, to the end that government may be responsive to the will of the people and that changes, if desired, may be obtained by peaceful means. Therein lies the security of the Republic, the very foundation of constitutional government.

In giving a peaceful Communist Party rally the protection of the Constitution, the Court in *De Jonge* was acknowledging that freedom of association could serve as an important safety valve in a free society. When individuals can associate without fear of government interference, conspiracies are less likely to occur. As Tocqueville observed, "In the country where associations are free secret societies are unknown. In America there are factious persons, but no conspirators" (2000, 184). As we shall see, in the 1940s and 1950s many Americans in fact saw the Communist Party as a conspiracy.

Eight years after *De Jonge*, in *Thomas v. Collins* (323 U.S. 516; 1945), the Court expanded on the right of free assembly. In this case a union leader had been cited for contempt for ignoring a court order that he obtain a license for union organizers. Writing for the Court, Justice Wiley Rutledge saw this as a prior restraint on Thomas's right to speak as well as upon his audience's right to hold a public meeting. These rights were in Rutledge's view "necessarily correlative." It was, according to Rutledge,

> the right of the union, its members and officials, whether residents or nonresidents of Texas and, if the latter, whether there for a single occasion or sojourning longer, to discuss with and inform the employees concerning matters involved in their choice. The First Amendment protects these rights of assembly and discussion. Whatever would restrict them, without sufficient occasion, would infringe its safeguards. The occasion was clearly protected. The speech was an essential part of the occasion, unless all meaning and purpose were to be taken from it. And the invitations, both general and particular, were parts of the speech, inseparable incidents of the occasion and of all that was said or done.

By acknowledging that the rights of both the speaker and the audience were reciprocally related, or "necessarily correlative," Rutledge was implying that the right of association was instrumental to the First Amendment. The right of free speech minus the right of an audience to hear the speaker is vacuous. At the same time the right to speak is amplified by collective action. In neither case was the actual phrase "freedom of association" invoked. Nonetheless, the seeds of a constitutional doctrine had been planted. The Court had understood that freedom of speech, apart from a social context, could not be reduced to the right of a solitary figure shouting in an empty hall.

Freedom of Association and the Civil Rights Movement: The Court Defines a Doctrine

Free speech, as Alexander Meiklejohn argued in his classic study (1948), is an essential component of self-government. As society became more complex, political action required collective support; and as government undertook more social and economic functions, the need to protect civil society became more urgent. A statist society, Tocqueville warned, would inevitably promote social and political orthodoxies. In the white South during the 1950s, the doctrine of racial integration and racial equality was a political heresy. Those civil rights leaders and organizations who fought for such issues did so at their own peril. An individual black man or woman speaking alone stood little chance of breaking down the walls of racial separation and discrimination. Collective action was an imperative.

It was against this background that the Supreme Court understood the need to expand the protection of the First Amendment and to articulate freedom of association as a constitutional right, as it did in *NAACP v. Alabama ex rel. Patterson* (357 U.S. 449; 1958). In 1956 Alabama had sought an injunction against the NAACP to prevent it from "doing business" in the state. Alabama claimed that the NAACP had not complied with a legal requirement that out-of-state corporations doing business in the state must file their corporate charters with the state, designating a place of business and an agent. The NAACP, a New York membership corporation, operated in Alabama through local affiliates that were unincorporated associations, and it considered itself exempt from the state requirement. During the course of the proceedings, the state moved for a large number of the NAACP's records. The organization produced most of this material with the exception of its membership list. The trial court then judged the NAACP to be in contempt and fined it $100,000. Having failed to get the judgment reversed in the Alabama Supreme Court, the NAACP appealed to the United States Supreme Court.

In a unanimous opinion written by Justice John M. Harlan, the Court reversed the judgment of contempt and, for the first time, recognized an independent "right of association." Citing *De Jonge* and *Thomas,* Justice Harlan wrote, "Effective advocacy of both public and private points of view, particularly controversial ones, is undeniably enhanced by group association, as this Court has more than once recognized by remarking upon the close nexus between freedoms of speech and assembly. It is beyond debate that freedom to engage in association for the advancement of beliefs and ideas is an inseparable aspect of the 'liberty' assured by the Due Process Clause of the Fourteenth Amendment, which embraces freedom of speech."

Although he defined freedom of association as an element of free speech, Harlan did not restrict the right to core political speech. "It is beyond immaterial," Harlan wrote, "whether the beliefs sought to be advanced by association pertain to political, economic, religious or cultural matters; state action which may have the effect of curtailing the freedom to associate is subject to the closest scrutiny" (*NAACP v. Alabama,* 460). Harlan considered Alabama's desire to compel disclosure of the NAACP's membership list an "effective restraint on freedom of association." He saw a vital connection between freedom to associate and privacy. In a less than oblique reference to the Nazi era, Harlan compared Alabama's demand to "a requirement that adherents of particular religious faiths or political parties wear identifying arm-bands." Given the general hostility to the civil rights movement by Alabama's white political establishment, disclosure of the NAACP membership list could very well subject members to serious economic and even physical retaliation.

Harlan made what he thought was a clear distinction between this case and a much earlier case, *Bryant v. Zimmerman* (278 U.S. 63; 1928), which involved the state of New York's demand for forced disclosure of the membership rolls of the Ku Klux Klan (KKK). New York law called for the disclosure of membership lists of any organization requiring an oath as a condition of membership. In that case the Court had upheld the disclosure requirement because of the "particular character of the Klan's activities, involving acts of unlawful intimidation and violence." In addition, the KKK had refused to turn over any information, whereas the

NAACP had agreed to divulge names of those members whom it employed and those who held official position.

Although *NAACP v. Alabama* was a major step in the development of freedom of association, the Court did not mark it as an unqualified right. Membership lists were not immune from state scrutiny. But Alabama had not shown a "controlling justification" for obtaining such lists. In *Bryant* New York had, in contrast, made its case. As Harlan noted in his opinion, the NAACP had "made an uncontroverted showing that on past occasions revelation of the identity of its rank-and-file members has exposed these members to economic reprisal, loss of employment, threat of physical coercion, and other manifestations of public hostility." Forced disclosure, Harlan concluded, "is likely to affect adversely the ability of petitioner and its members to pursue their collective effort to foster beliefs which they admittedly have the right to advocate. . . . It may induce members to withdraw from the Association and dissuade others from joining it because of fear of exposure of their beliefs shown through their associations and of the consequences of this exposure." Harlan cited precedents that involved "witnesses demurring before legislative investigating committees, lobbyists resisting registration and reporting requirements, and media executives protesting governmental regulations or taxes"(O'Neill 2001, 58).

As one scholar has noted, "The direct and unequivocal recognition of freedom of association in *NAACP v. Alabama* represented something quite novel, a highly significant expansion of First Amendment freedoms at a time that was especially crucial to the civil rights movement, but in time would prove invaluable to a host of other organizations, even eventually to the Ku Klux Klan"(O'Neill 2001, 61). It was not clear from Harlan's formulation whether he was creating an independent constitutional right or making freedom of association a subsidiary right of free speech and assembly. Nor was it clear where the rest of the Court stood, since Harlan's was the only opinion in the case.

A Doctrine Reaffirmed

Yet two years later, in *Bates v. City of Little Rock* (361 U.S. 516; 1960), the Court showed its uncertainly as to exactly what Harlan had meant. The Court ruled that a local NAACP branch did not have to disclose its membership list as a requirement of its licensing tax in two Arkansas cities. Writing for the majority, Justice Potter Stewart indicated that freedom of association derived its standing from free speech and assembly. Stewart declared, "Like freedom of speech and a free press, the right of peaceable assembly was considered by the Framers of our Constitution to lie at the foundation of a government based upon the consent of an informed citizenry. . . . It is now beyond dispute that freedom of association for the purpose of advancing ideas and airing grievances is protected by the Due Process Clause of the Fourteenth Amendment from invasion by the States. Freedoms such as these are protected not only against heavy-handed frontal attack, but also from being stifled by more subtle governmental interference."

Stewart also indicated that freedom of association could be treated as an independent right and reaffirmed Harlan's view in *NAACP v. Alabama:* "Inviolability of privacy in group association may in many circumstances be indispensable to the preservation of freedom of association, particularly where a group espouses dissent beliefs." As was the case in *NAACP v. Alabama,* states had to show a compelling interest before they could require the disclosure of membership lists. Stewart asserted, "Where there is a significant encroachment upon personal liberty, the State may prevail only upon showing a subordinating interest which is compelling"(*Bates,* 524). The two cities had shown "no relevant correlation" between the power to impose a licensing tax and the compulsory disclosure of membership.

In their brief concurring opinion, Justices Hugo Black and William O. Douglas made it clear that freedom of association was simply one of the rights included in the First Amendment, implying it was not an independent right. Justice Black supported a literal reading of the Constitution and did not believe in creating rights not in the original text. He therefore took great pains to declare, "First Amendment rights are beyond abridgment either by legislation that directly restrains their exercise or by suppression or impairment through harassment, humiliation, or exposure by government. One of these rights, freedom of assembly, includes of course freedom of association; and it is entitled to no less protection than any other First Amendment right."

As with any First Amendment right, the Court could not define freedom of association as a limitless right. In many ways the Court was defining a right without an explicit textual base in the Constitution. Although it was yoked to freedom of speech and particularly assembly, the Court did not consider the rights coterminous. Association can encompass almost all of human activity, more so than even speech or assembly. One can easily go through life without uttering a public opinion or participating in a political assembly. By contrast, few live in isolation from each other. Most of us associate in one way or another. If all associations were free of government regulations, the society could verge on anarchy; some regulations are essential for an orderly society. Parents cannot deprive their children of health care and education; all organizations must obey public health, safety, and environmental laws; schools (even private schools) must meet certain educational standards. All associations must obey the laws intended for the general population, and no association can engage in a criminal conspiracy.

Thus, the Court did not look upon all organizations with the same benign eye. For example, the Communist Party and the Ku Klux Klan were not granted the same deference that was given to the NAACP. In *Bryant v. Zimmerman* the Court upheld New York's demand that the Ku Klux Klan disclose its membership list. The justification was based on the theory that the requirement would deter any illegal activities the organization was tempted to undertake. Years later the Court upheld a federal law that required the Communist Party to reveal its membership. The law was justified, the Court said, on the basis that the government rationally concluded that the Communist Party was part of "a world-wide integrated movement which employs every combination of possible means, peaceful and violent, domestic and foreign, overt and clandestine, to destroy the government itself" (*Communist Party of the United States v. Subversive Activities Control Board*, 367 U.S. 1; 1961). However, in *Gibson v. Florida Legislative Investigation Committee* (372 U.S. 539; 1963), the Court held that the Miami branch of the NAACP could not be forced to disclose names of its members and contributors simply because a legislative committee was investigating alleged Communist infiltration of the organization. The Court found no link between the Communists or any subversive activity and the NAACP.

The Court continued to conflate free speech and freedom of association in *NAACP v. Button* (371 U.S. 415; 1963). This case involved a Virginia law that prohibited the NAACP from urging its members to institute litigation through the association's legal staff. Justice William Brennan, writing for the majority, began by declaring that litigation can be a form of speech. "In the context of NAACP objectives," Brennan contended, "litigation is not a technique of resolving private differences; it is a means for achieving the lawful objectives of equality of treatment by all government, federal, state and local, for the members of the Negro community in this country. It is thus a form of political expression." Brennan found protection for this activity not "under a narrow, literal conception of freedom of speech, petition or assembly. For there is no longer any doubt that the First and Fourteenth Amendments protect certain forms of orderly group activity. Thus we have affirmed the right 'to engage in association for the advancement of beliefs and ideas'" (*Button*, 429–430). Just as in the membership disclosure cases, Virginia did not have a compelling interest in regulating this kind of litigation.

The political effect of the NAACP cases was clear. They prevented hostile, segregationist state governments from using neu-
tral business regulations to destroy an important civil rights organization. The NAACP had to struggle in a threatening
atmosphere in the South of the 1950s. Public disclosure of its
membership list would put the organization and its supporters in
grave risk. As Laurence Tribe has commented, "Anonymity has
long been recognized as absolutely essential for the survival of
dissident movements; the glare of public disclosure, so healthy in
other settings, may operate in the context of protected but unpopular groups or beliefs as a clarion call to ostracism or worse"
(1998, 1019). By expanding free speech to include expressive associations, the Court extended the protection of the Constitution to
unpopular groups that resisted the pressure of the state to con-
form to the dominant ideology—in these cases, the principle of
racial separation.

FREEDOM OF ASSOCIATION AND
THE COMMUNIST PARTY:
THE QUESTION OF GUILT BY ASSOCIATION

During World War II the Soviet Union was an ally in the fight
against Nazi Germany. Consequently, the Communist Party of
the United States of America adopted a full-throated patriotic
stance in favor of the war. Anticommunism was a muted cause,
and many Americans admired the Soviet resistance to Germany in
the battle of Stalingrad and beyond. The American Communist
Party tried to ingratiate itself into the mainstream of American
politics, denouncing any interference with the war effort, endorsing Franklin D. Roosevelt's reelection in 1944, helping to build
the powerful Congress of Industrial Organizations, and supporting parts of the New Deal program. It may be going too far to say
that the Communist Party was an accepted part of American life

during World War II, but it was not the pariah it was to become. The Communist Party's move to the fringes of American politics began soon after the war, when, taking its lead from Moscow, it adopted an adversarial position against the U.S. policy of containing the Soviet Union. The strains of the Cold War tested the limits of associational freedom. The permissive attitude toward radical dissent and the Communist Party that was reflected in *De Jonge* and *Thomas v. Collins* was not to be found in later Supreme Court decisions. The prevailing opinion was that the Communist Party had lost many of the rights that other associations, even unpopular ones, could claim.

The so-called Communist issue reached its greatest intensity as the result of two jolting events in 1949: the explosion of the first Soviet atomic bomb and the Communist takeover of China. Those events, combined with the North Korean invasion of South Korea and a number of sensational spy cases involving alleged Communist Party members, convinced the overwhelming majority of Americans that the party was a menace to national security. The two most notorious cases involved Alger Hiss, a onetime senior State Department official who was convicted of perjury for denying his espionage activities and Communist Party affiliation, and Julius and Ethel Rosenberg, who were convicted and later executed for their part in a Soviet spy ring that had penetrated the super secret Manhattan Project responsible for building the atomic bomb. These cases lent public credence to the charges of Senator Joseph R. McCarthy (R–WI) in February 1950 that the State Department was rife with known Communists.

Against this background there was a strong consensus that members of the party needed to be subject to sanctions, exposure, and even criminal prosecution. At the height of Cold War tensions in the 1950s, the phrase "guilt by association" acquired an ominous meaning. Many who were linked to the Communist Party or to other left-wing organizations risked the loss of employment, denial of a U.S. passport, disbarment, blacklisting, and social ostracism. During those years the Congress and the executive branch took measures that the courts mostly ratified, designed to limit the rights of members of the Communist Party.

The first major prosecution of the Communist Party came in 1948, when the Justice Department brought charges against the party's eleven top members under the Smith Act of 1940, which outlawed membership in "any society, group, or assembly of persons who teach, advocate, or encourage the overthrow or destruction of any government in the United States by force or violence" (Public Law 670, 76th Cong., 1st sess., June 28, 1940). They were convicted in federal court, and in *Dennis v. United States* (341 U.S. 494; 1951) the Supreme Court upheld the conviction. Even though the party posed no immediate threat of violence, the Court argued that a political party organized around the doctrines of Marxism-Leninism and aligned with a hostile foreign power such as the Soviet Union constituted a gravity of evil that must not be discounted by the improbability of its success.

The Communist Party of the United States of America: Heretics or Conspirators?

In 1950 the Congress, not satisfied that the Smith Act was adequate, took a further step and passed over President Harry Truman's veto the Internal Security Act. This law required Communists and members of other so-called subversive groups to register with the attorney general, and it established the Subversive Activities Control Board (SACB) with broad authority to hold hearings and identify such groups. Membership in such organizations would prohibit one from holding a passport, a government job, or a defense job. All literature published by such an organization would have to be stamped "Disseminated by _____, a Communist organization." Two years later, in 1952, Congress passed, again over President Truman's veto, the McCarran-Walter Immigration Act, which gave the attorney general authority to deport aliens who were thought to be subversive.

What was the justification for making association with the Communist Party and organizations affiliated with it subject to such draconian governmental sanctions? The issue sparked a serious debate over what constituted a legitimate association and what actions the government could rightly take against an organization that was perceived to be a threat to the democratic order. Sidney Hook, a Social Democrat and staunch anticommunist, felt the legal restrictions placed on the associational freedom of the party were thoroughly justified. In an essay written in 1953 (which later appeared as the book *Heresy, Yes, Conspiracy, No*), Hook argued that the Communist Party did not play by the rules of the democratic system. Its aim is to overthrow the democratic state and to use all means necessary toward that end, including secrecy and deceit. "A conspiracy, as distinct from a heresy, is a secret or underground movement which seeks to attain its ends not by normal political or educational processes but by playing outside the rules of the game. . . . The signs of a conspiracy are secrecy, anonymity, the use of false names and labels and the calculated lie" (1953, 22). Hook argued that Communist ideas were heresies that were afforded constitutional protections but that the Communist movement was a conspiratorial organization directed by Moscow. Joining the party was a conscious decision to work outside the democratic process while pretending otherwise. Hook disparaged the phrase "guilt by association" and argued that it clouded the issue. "All members of the Communist Party must 'associate' with its purposes or be expelled," he wrote (84). Hook felt that membership in Communist front organizations (those clandestinely controlled by the party) was a more difficult question. It would depend, according to Hook, upon the number of such organizations an individual has joined, the time that he joined, and his function and activities upon joining (93). All of

these questions would determine whether an individual constituted a security risk and could be denied certain privileges and opportunities.

Was the American Communist Party a legitimate party or a
conspiracy? Its defenders believe that it often disguised its purposes but that such tactics were justified. Ellen Schrecker has written, "The CP's attempts at secrecy—its underground organizations, secret conclaves, forged passports, and false names—were
self-defeating. They fooled no one and just reinforced the party's
image as a conspiracy. Though most of the CP's clandestine practices had been adopted as defensive measures, the party's opponents put a far more malevolent spin on them" (1998, 140). Those
who considered the party a clandestine conspiracy argued that
public exposure would be one justified remedy.

So-called friendly witnesses were expected not only to reveal
their own past or present affiliations but also to name others who
had been party members in order to be given a chance to resume
their careers. Refusal categorized one as a hostile witness with all
the risks that entailed. Exposure was the rationale for the registration provisions of the Internal Security Act of 1950 as well as the
rationale for the hearings of the House Un-American Activities
Committee (HUAC), in which witnesses were asked the prover-
bial question, "Are you now or have you ever been a member of
the Communist Party?"

Private organizations, unions, the entertainment industry, defense
contractors, and the universities took far-reaching measures to exclude Communists. Failure to cooperate with government investigating committees and to disclose any political affiliation with the
party could lead to dismissal. The academic community was a major
target of legislative committees' attempts to expose Communists,
and most of its leaders were willing to cooperate. In 1953 thirty-
seven presidents of leading public and private organizations published a position paper justifying their right to fire faculty members
who refused to answer questions about possible Communist Party

members. The statement read, "As in all acts of association, the professor accepts conventions which become morally binding. . . . If he is called upon to answer for his convictions it is his duty as a citizen to speak out." The university presidents insisted that the invocation of the Fifth Amendment right against self-incrimination "places upon a professor a heavy burden of proof of his fitness to hold a teaching position and lays upon the university an obligation to re-examine his qualifications for membership in its society." The statement made it quite clear that membership in the Communist Party constituted a legitimate ground for dismissal. "Appointment to a university position and retention after appointment require . . . the affirmative obligation of being diligent and loyal in citizenship. This renders impossible adherence to such a regime as that of Russia and its satellites. No person who accepts or advocates such principles and methods has any place in the university. Since present membership in the Communist Party requires the acceptance of these principles and methods, such membership extinguishes the right to a university position" (quoted in Fried 1997, 141).

During the late 1940s and 1950s, more than 100 college and university professors were dismissed for refusing to cooperate with various investigating committees. Most colleges and universities required faculty members to sign a loyalty oath forswearing membership in the party as a condition of employment. The issue of whether Communist Party membership automatically disqualified someone for a faculty position haunted the academic community throughout this period. Some argued that party membership alone was not sufficient grounds for dismissal and that deciding it was would lead to witch-hunts, limiting academic freedom. Membership in the party did not mean that one would slavishly follow the party line in all one's academic endeavors. The philosopher Victor Lowe argued that not all Communists were perfect Communists, committed to indoctrinating students, and that "we should judge an individual first of all (though not exclusively) by his record than by that of any group, whenever and

wherever special circumstances do not make that too dangerous."
A. O. Lovejoy, Lowe's colleague in the Johns Hopkins Philosophy Department, argued that membership in the Communist
Party should lead to dismissal, since it contributed to the triumph
of totalitarianism and was the equivalent of allegiance to the Nazi
Party and the Ku Klux Klan. Sidney Hook claimed that membership in the Communist Party was ample evidence that a faculty
member would be unfit to pursue the ideals of democratic education. According to Hook, the party was a conspiracy contrary to
"the ethics of free inquiry essential to a liberal education" and was
"functioning as a fifth column in every sector of democratic life."
Thus, membership was proof of guilt without the need to show
any actual harm (*Journal of Philosophy,* February 14, 1952: 110,
121). Others said these academic purges affected many who were
not even current members of the Communist Party. According to
Ellen Schrecker, "Most of these people were former party members who had refused to name names or cooperate with anticommunist investigators" (Schrecker 1998, 404).

Was the Communist Party engaged in political conspiracy and
a tool of the Soviet Union, as Hook claimed over fifty years ago?
Or was it "a political movement that was both subservient to the
Kremlin and genuinely dedicated to a wide range of social reforms, a movement whose adherents sometimes toed the party
line and sometimes did not even receive it," as Schrecker claims
(Schrecker 1998, xv)? The answer may lie somewhere in the middle, but recent disclosures may put it closer to Hook's assertion
than to Schrecker's.

The end of the Cold War has resulted in the declassification of
the Venona Project tapes (the super secret deciphering of Soviet
cables to and from Moscow), the opening of some KGB files, and
the published accounts of former KGB agents. These new sources
revealed a far closer relationship between the American Communist Party and Soviet espionage than the general public realized at
the time. The conviction of party leaders in the *Dennis* case was

based upon their violation of the sedition laws, not for any overt act of espionage or sabotage. Although the famous spy trials of Hiss and the Rosenbergs during the 1940s and 1950s involved people who were identified as Communists, the top leadership of the party was never implicated in such activities. The recently revealed documents indicate that they should have been. According to two leading scholars of the subject, "The American Communist Party as an organization covertly cooperated with Soviet espionage. The CPUSA made party members available to Soviet intelligence when they were needed." Senior American Communists, these documents suggest, had important relationships with Soviet intelligence (Haynes and Klehr 2000, 46–47, 233).

Since these materials were highly classified, they could not be revealed at the time without compromising the Venona decryptions. Law enforcement officials had no knowledge of such information and could not have used it in court even if they had. The gap between the intelligence community—the Central Intelligence Agency (CIA) on the one side and the FBI on the other—was wide and made the sharing of such sensitive data difficult. Intelligence agencies by their nature fear compromising their sources and do not want them exposed to the scrutiny of the judicial process. Without this information on the public record, indictments and convictions of Communist Party members had to be based on the Sedition Laws. After the *Dennis* case the federal government brought charges against 120 Communists who were in the party's lower echelons. The constitutional challenge involved in these Cold War cases was balancing the government's right to monitor an association with close ties to a hostile foreign power against individuals right to some privacy in their associations.

THE COURT ASSERTS ASSOCIATIONAL RIGHTS

By the late 1950s and the early 1960s, the intensity of the Communist issue had faded. The Korean War ended in 1953, the same year that Soviet dictator Joseph Stalin died; Senator McCarthy was censured by the Senate in 1954; and President Dwight Eisenhower met with the new Soviet leaders in 1955 and talked about the importance of preventing another nuclear war. The Supreme Court began to take a more critical look at the laws aimed at Communist Party membership and moved hesitantly and at times erratically toward a more tolerant view. In the process it focused more on the rights of association. One of the first cases to indicate a new attitude was *Watkins v. United States* (354 U.S. 178; 1957). In this decision the Court challenged the right of congressional committees to examine an individual's political beliefs and associations. Chief Justice Earl Warren declared that there was no power to "expose for the sake of exposure." Witnesses had to be informed of the pertinence of any questions put to them about such associations. Two years later, in *Barenblatt v. United States* (360 U.S. 109; 1959), the Court stepped back from *Watkins* and upheld the right of the House Un-American Activities Committee to ask a witness about past and present membership in the Communist Party. Lloyd Barenblatt, a former college professor, had refused on First Amendment grounds to answer any questions about his past affiliation with the party. Writing for the Court, Justice John Marshall Harlan claimed that Congress, as a part of its interest in Communist infiltration into the field of education, had "the right to identify a witness as a member of the Communist Party." This was not the exposure for exposure's sake that the Court had warned against in *Watkins*.

In *Yates v. United States* (354 U.S. 298; 1957), the Court set aside the conviction of fourteen defendants, contrasting "the advocacy of abstract doctrine and advocacy directed at promoting unlawful action." The result was that membership in the party was not by itself considered sufficient evidence for a conviction. This was made clearer in *Scales v. United States* (367 U.S. 205; 1961). Junius Scales had been a member of the Communist Party and was arrested in 1954 on charges of violating the Smith Act.

The Court did uphold his conviction under the Smith Act's membership clause, but it made an important distinction. The majority opinion in the case, written by Justice Harlan (who had written the Court opinions in both *Yates* and *Barenblatt*), distinguished between active and nominal membership. The party member, according to Harlan, had to have specific intent "to accomplish [the goals of the organization] by resort to violence." If a member of the party joined in order to advance "legitimate aims and policies . . . he lacked the requisite specific intent" (*Scales*, 205). Scales was considered to be an active member of the party, and thus his conviction was upheld. He was, however, the last defendant convicted under the Smith Act. In *Noto v. United States* (367 U.S. 290; 1961), the Court reversed a conviction for membership in the Communist Party because the evidence did not suffice to establish that the party had engaged in unlawful behavior.

That same year the Court did uphold a Subversive Activities Control Board order that the Communist Party register with the attorney general as a "Communist-action organization." Writing for the Court in *Communist Party v. SACB* (367 U.S. 1; 1961), Justice Felix Frankfurter asserted that freedom of speech and association did not prevent the Congress "from requiring the registration and filing of membership lists, by organizations substantially dominated or controlled by the foreign powers controlling the world Communist movement." This order was eventually challenged and overturned in *Albertson v. SACB* (382 U.S. 70; 1965), the Court recognizing that such registration would violate the self-incrimination clause of the Fifth Amendment, as it could be used as evidence for prosecution under the Smith Act. In *Aptheker v. Secretary of State* (378 U.S. 500; 1964), the Court also struck down as a restriction on the right to travel the provision of the Internal Security Act denying passports to members of the Communist Party. With *United States v. Robel* (389 U.S. 258; 1967), the Court invalidated a provision denying Communist Party members employment in any defense facility, calling this a violation of freedom of association. Thus, the SACB was reduced to holding hearings and reverted to the backwaters of the federal government. In 1973 the Congress abolished the SACB with little notice or opposition from the public.

These cases expanded associational rights. They made it difficult for the government to force disclosure of membership lists and punish mere passive membership in the Communist Party even if its leaders had been convicted of sedition.

The Question of Loyalty Oaths

The other question was whether party membership, passive or not, could disqualify someone from a particular government benefit. Could a government agency or one funded by the government require someone to take a loyalty oath or disavow membership in a disfavored group such as the Communist Party as a condition for a job or a license?

In the 1950s and early 1960s, loyalty oaths were a common requisite of employment in public institutions. The Supreme Court, reflecting the strong anticommunist public consensus, initially upheld most loyalty oaths and accepted in *Adler v. Board of Education* (342 U.S. 485; 1952) the argument that membership in the Communist Party could make one unfit for a teaching position or a government job. The Court also upheld the right of a state to dismiss employees or deny licenses to those who refused to answer questions about Communist Party membership. In *Konigsberg v. State Bar of California* (366 U.S. 36; 1961), the Court ruled in favor of the California Bar Association, which had denied admission to Konigsberg. He had refused to answer questions about his political associations and beliefs on First Amendment grounds, claiming that questions about his Communist Party membership infringed on his rights of free speech and association. The Court, speaking again through Justice Harlan, asserted that "the State's interest in having lawyers who are devoted to the law in its broader sense [including] its procedures for orderly change, is clearly sufficient to outweigh the minimal effect upon free association occasioned by the compulsory disclosure in the circumstance presented here." In dissent Justice Hugo Black wrote, "The inevitable effect of the majority's decision is to condone a practice that will have a substantial deterrent effect upon the associations entered into by anyone who may want to become a lawyer in California" (*Konigsberg*, 36).

As the 1960s wore on, fear of domestic communism subsided and the Court, reflecting a different attitude in a completely different political climate, took a more critical view of loyalty oaths and a more sympathetic view of the rights of associations. In *Baggett v. Bullitt* (377 U.S. 360; 1964), the Court struck down a loyalty oath requirement that obligated state employees to swear that they were not members of a "subversive organization." The Court found this oath "unduly vague, uncertain and broad." In *Elfbrandt v. Russell, et al.* (384 U.S. 11; 1966), the Court struck down an Arizona oath that did not distinguish between active and nonactive members of the Communist Party. Finally, the Court overturned *Adler* by a 5–4 vote in the landmark case *Keyishian v. Board of Regents* (385 U.S. 589; 1967). In this case the Court ruled that a New York State loyalty oath requiring state employees to disclaim that they were members of the Communist Party was unconstitutional. Justice William Brennan, speaking for the majority, claimed, "Legislation which sanctions membership unaccompanied by specific intent to further the unlawful goals of the organization or which is not active membership violates constitutional limitations." By punishing both active and passive membership in the Communist Party, the oath was considered to "sweep over broadly into association which may not be proscribed." In dissent, Justice Tom Clark, voicing the fears of the previous decades, saw danger in overturning *Adler*. Clark and the other dissenters refused to consider simple membership in the Communist Party as an act to which government should be indifferent. He warned in unusually strong language, "The majority by its broadside swept away one of our most precious rights, namely, the right of self-preservation" (*Keyishian*, 589).

Keyishian did not mean that all loyalty oaths concerning membership in the Communist Party were unconstitutional. The Court upheld loyalty oath requirements for bar membership that specifically asked about an applicant's knowing membership in the party or any other organization with the specific intent to advance its illegal goal of overthrowing the government by force or violence (*Law Students Civil Rights Research Council v. Wadmond*, 401 U.S. 154; 1971).

The Issue of Blacklisting

The issue of blacklisting—identifying people with alleged Communist associations or sympathies with the purpose of denying them private employment—raises other and perhaps even more complex questions of freedom of association. The most notorious instance was the Hollywood blacklist of the late 1940s and early 1950s. The punishments were largely economic and were enforced by private organizations—movie studios and radio and television networks. The blacklist, as it evolved, was not without the encouragement and support of certain parts of the federal government, namely, the House Un-American Activities Committee and the FBI. In 1947 HUAC began its investigation into Communist influence in Hollywood. The committee subpoenaed major Hollywood figures such as Jack L. Warner, Louis B. Mayer, Ayn Rand, and Ronald Reagan, who were known for their public opposition to the Communist Party's activities in Hollywood. These so-called friendly witnesses identified over 100 members of the Hollywood branch of the Communist Party. Soon after this testimony the committee subpoenaed John Howard Lawson, a prominent screenwriter, president of the Screen Writers Guild, and head of the Hollywood branch of the Communist Party, along with other prominent writers and directors. These witnesses, known as the Hollywood Ten, were asked the famous question, "Are you now or have you ever been a member of the Communist Party of the United States?" After a raucous committee hearing, all refused to answer on First Amendment grounds. They were cited for contempt of Congress and eventually imprisoned. At first there was a burst of sympathy for the Hollywood Ten from such prominent film figures as Humphrey Bogart, Lauren Bacall, and William Wyler, who formed a group known as the Committee for the First Amendment. When it was revealed that most of the Hollywood Ten were in fact Communists, sympathy evaporated, as did the Committee for the First Amendment.

The public reaction against the Hollywood Ten and the fear of boycotts led the studios to begin a purge of known Communists and their supporters. The heads of the major studios signed the famous Waldorf Statement, in which they pledged not to hire any known member of the Communist Party or of any group advocating the forceful overthrow of the government. This was the beginning of the blacklist. There was no formal or official list in Hollywood, but it was widely known that people suspected of membership in certain organizations would be denied employment. Blacklisting soon spread to radio and television and became more systematic. It was eventually made public with the publication of "Red Channels," a list of 151 actors, writers, musicians, and other entertainers who had alleged Communist affiliations. No network or sponsor would hire anyone listed in "Red Channels." CBS had a loyalty oath, and most networks had full-time investigators (Schrecker 1994).

Getting your name removed from the blacklist required coming forward to HUAC or the FBI and purging yourself. Those blacklisted would have to recant their membership in the party as a mistake and name names of those they knew in the party. Some willingly came forward to save their careers. Others refused to testify against their friends or associates and suffered the consequences. Some directors sought work in Europe, and some writers found fronts to pass off scripts as their own. Actors had a more difficult time. As the years passed, the blacklist lost its hold on the entertainment industry. In 1959 producer-director Otto Preminger announced that he had hired blacklisted writer Dalton Trumbo to write the screenplay for the film *Exodus.* Kirk Douglas also hired Trumbo to do the script for the big-budget film *Spartacus.* Both movies were box-office successes and suffered no observable damage from Trumbo's association with them. By the mid-1960s, when the political climate had changed, the blacklist was tossed out, and many others besides Trumbo resumed their careers. There was clearly an economic motive behind blacklisting. In an intensely anticommunist climate, movie studios and television networks feared the public reaction if they hired anyone with the slightest association with communism, whether it was just or not. When the public fears of domestic communism dissipated, there was no box-office recrimination. The success of *Exodus* and *Spartacus* had shown that.

Decades after the practice ended, blacklisting still brings up strong feelings. Film director Elia Kazan, who openly cooperated with HUAC and named names, found himself the subject of great controversy when Hollywood gave him an Academy Award for lifetime achievement in 1999. Blacklisting ruined the lives and careers of many innocent people, deprived the public of the talents of many gifted artists, and contributed to Hollywood's reluctance to make films with serious social themes. It also forced many to make the agonizing choice between losing their careers or harming their friends.

Was there any justification in punishing such political associations? Blacklisting by the entertainment industry, a private enterprise, raises somewhat different constitutional issues than do certain government sanctions against political associations, such as loyalty oaths and membership disclosure requirements. The First Amendment, which begins, "Congress shall make no law," places restrictions on how government can limit expression and association. If the film studios did not wish to associate with people whose political views they found odious, were they not asserting their own associational rights? Would blacklisting have raised the same objections if the targets had been members of the Nazi Party or the Ku Klux Klan? Many considered communism the moral equivalent of Nazism and fascism, and the Soviet Union as evil as Nazi Germany. Two of the most prominent liberal groups, the Americans for Democratic Action (ADA) and the American Civil Liberties Union (ACLU), denied membership to Communists during that same era, as did many of the labor unions. The Court in its famous flag-salute case, *West Virginia State Board of Education v. Barnette* (319 U.S. 624; 1943), made it clear that forced speech was as much a violation of the First Amendment as was forced silence. Could the same be said of forced association? Did the film studios and the networks have the right to decide who should be associated with them? If those organizations found Communists to be politically offensive or economically harmful to their business, did they have a right to keep these people off their payrolls? And did they have a right to find out who was or was not a Communist—the alleged function of the blacklist (Redish and McFadden 2001, 1669)? Screenwriter John Howard Lawson, the leader of the Hollywood Communist Party, had made it clear that party members had an obligation to push the party line. He had publicly written before he was hauled before the HUAC, "I do not hesitate to say that it is my aim to present the Communist position and to do so in the most specific manner." A witness before the Committee testified that Lawson urged fellow Communists to get five minutes of party doctrine into the most expensive scenes of every film so they would not be cut (Goodman 1964, 215). Although Lawson and others had little success in getting pro-Soviet or Communist propaganda into their films, supporters of the blacklist felt that they had reason to be leery of hiring people with such strong loyalties to the party line. Did studio heads have a right to find out whether or not they were hiring a Communist?

Most party members kept their affiliation secret. Such secrecy was a commonplace tactic in order to penetrate various institutions. Did the public have the right to know the political affiliations of those who were making films?

In the late 1930s Hollywood was a prime source for raising funds for party activities (Klehr, Haynes, and Firsov 1995, 9). Supporters of the blacklist argued that if the public went to films made with and by Communists, they could be indirectly putting money into party coffers. In the early 1950s, films made by those thought to be Communists were picketed with messages such as "This picture written by a Communist. Do not patronize" (Redish and McFadden 2001, fn. 64). Numerous radio and television corporate sponsors had an explicit policy against providing support of any kind to those with Communist sympathies. A statement from Procter and Gamble in the mid-1950s was quite clear: "We would never knowingly engage a Communist for any of our radio or television programs. Also we would never knowingly engage anyone who aids either directly or indirectly the Communist cause. We carry out this policy in the employment of literally thousands of people in connection with our radio and television programs" (Cogley 1971, 192).

Although many consider the blacklisting period a shameful era in American life, its practice was not limited to anti-Communists. Some ex-Communists who had broken with the party said that they, too, were blacklisted. *New York Times* art critic Hilton Kramer described "the 'other blacklist'—the black list drawn up by Communists in Hollywood, Broadway, book publishing, and journalism—that prohibited certain anticommunists, many of them former Party members who had broken with the Party, from working in their industries. Everyone who worked in those fields was well aware of this phenomenon" (Kramer 1999, 73).

Efforts to shun individuals for their ideas have not ceased. In recent years liberals discouraged sponsors and affiliate stations in an attempt to drive conservative talk show host Laura Schlessinger off the air because of her critical views on homosexuality. In 2003 some urged people to boycott the works of actors and performers who had opposed the war in Iraq. The Screen Actors Guild that had barred Communists from membership in the late 1940s issued a statement in March 2003 declaring, "We deplore the idea that those in the public eye should suffer professionally for having the courage to give voice to their own views. Even a hint of the blacklist must never again be tolerated in this nation"(Associated Press, March 4, 2003). In those cases nothing as pervasive as the 1950s blacklist resulted. But there were efforts to develop one, at least implicitly.

Was the blacklist a purely private action, untainted by governmental participation and therefore not a weapon of government coercion? The Supreme Court did recognize the right of a legislative committee to ask questions about an individual's Communist Party activities in the name of national security. Government exposure of an individual's political associations did raise constitutional issues. Chief Justice Warren in *Watkins* did warn the House Un-American Activities Committee, "There is no congressional power to expose for the sake of exposure" (*Watkins*, 198). The argument was that such exposure could chill free speech and dissent. Much of the material to support the blacklist came from the HUAC and the FBI. There was another way of looking at the issue. Were the House Un-American Activities Committee and the FBI merely assisting employers and sponsors in their right of nonassociation?

Many liberals such as the playwright Arthur Miller consider the practice of naming names to be an ultimate crime. In his 1953 play *The Crucible,* about the Salem witch trials, Miller equated the informers to those who named names before congressional committees. Many did not consider informing to be inherently bad. In a criticism of Miller's attitude, the journalist Richard Rovere wrote, "If any agency of the community is authorized to undertake a serious investigation of any of our common problems, then the identities of others—names—are of great importance" (Rovere 1957, 18).

The issue of the Hollywood blacklist will not go away easily, and it does not lend itself to a simple, pious response. Forced exposure of an individual's political associations can chill constitutional rights. At the same time, do private individuals or businesses, particularly those involved in expressive activity, have a right to know about what they perceive to be the odious political associations of those they may hire? Does a civil rights group need to know if one of its employees is a member of the Ku Klux Klan? Does a Jewish organization have a right to know whether or not it is hiring a neo-Nazi?

In *Barenblatt,* the case involving congressional investigations into Communist Party activity, the Court had argued that because of the threat the party posed, the Congress had "wide power" to inquire into individual associations. In the NAACP cases, the Court was concerned that the forced disclosure of member lists by state action would subject members of a legitimate organization to public scorn and ostracism in the white South. In the Communist Party cases, the Court saw a legitimate reason for exposing a group considered likely to present possible dangers to the republic. The participation of Communist Party members in state employment could raise security issues about which the government has a valid concern. Did the government have a legitimate right to inform private companies such as the film studios and the networks about the political associations of potential employees? That is a different matter than the right of private employers to screen employees because of unwanted associations. Antidiscrimination laws have not traditionally protected people because of their political associations. The blacklist controversy raises issues both of chilling dissent and assisting the right of nonassociation.

THE LEGACY OF THE NAACP AND COMMUNIST PARTY CASES

The long-term constitutional effect of the NAACP and Communist Party cases was also ambiguous. Even though the Court had linked freedom of association to the First Amendment, these early cases left important questions unanswered. Was freedom of association an independent constitutional right with different rules for its protection? Or was it simply another form of free speech and assembly? Writing in 1970, free speech theorist and constitutional scholar Thomas I. Emerson expressed serious doubts about association as an independent constitutional right. He thought the concept too vague: "There can be no doubt that freedom of association, as a basic element in the democratic process, must receive constitutional protection. But the freedom to be safeguarded is so inclusive, appears in so many different forms, and is subject to such varied restrictions, that the rules for its protection cannot be capsuled in a single doctrine called the right to association." Emerson thought the term could be "stretched to cover so many things, and be limited by so many qualifications, as to be meaningless." The right should be clearly enveloped in the First Amendment, as "associational expression is simply an extension of the individual right of expression and, for the same reasons and to the same extent, should be free of governmental abridgement" (Emerson 1970, 431, 528, 432).

Emerson's comment was closer to the Supreme Court's thinking in the 1950s and 1960s than George Kateb's sweeping definition of freedom of association. In the 1980s and later, the issue of antidiscrimination and private clubs would provide occasions for the Court to define the concept somewhat more clearly.

ASSOCIATIONAL RIGHTS VERSUS CIVIL RIGHTS

One of the great tasks of American democracy is balancing the imperatives of liberty and equality. They are rights with different properties, often at odds with each other. Traditionally, liberty has been defined as freedom from unwarranted interference by the states in the lives of individuals. This notion of liberty is embodied in the original Bill of Rights, which contains explicit restrictions on the power of government to infringe upon the individual. Equality, defined as protection from discrimination, has required the active intervention of the state. The conflict between these two concepts produces a constant, elastic tension.

The framers of the Constitution were more enamored of liberty than of equality. Some, such as Madison, felt that liberty was essential to protect the efforts of the productive and industrious few, whereas equality was the justification of the unproductive to confiscate the property of those who toiled for it. An excessive demand for equality could turn the states into a weapon for such confiscation. The political enemy of liberty was the combination of rampant democracy and state power. Suspicious of simple majoritarianism that may feed an appetite for greater economic equality at the expense of property holders, the framers designed a government of limited powers, a system of checks and balances, and an independent judiciary. These institutional arrangements, they hoped, would provide protection from the tyranny of the majority, manifest in an intrusive national government. Tocqueville saw the clash between the impulses for equality and liberty as an inevitable result of the contradictory impulses of a democratic society. He observed that the passion for equality is a natural instinct in the democratic society and follows from a hatred of privilege. Nonetheless he felt such a passion constituted a threat to liberty. "Every central power," wrote Tocqueville, "that follows these natural instincts loves equality and favors it; for equality singularly facilitates the action of such a power, extends it, and secures it" (Tocqueville 2000, 645). What would prevent this fledging democracy from becoming a centralized bureaucratic society if majoritarianism would inflame a desire for equality? Equality, be it racial or social, was simply not the business of government, at any level. Hence, Americans tolerated until the Civil War the persistence of slavery in the South and after the Civil War racial discrimination and segregation well into the twentieth century.

The experience of black people in the South made it clear that the intervention of the federal government would be necessary to protect discrete and insular minorities from the tyranny of the majority. Much of the opposition to such new laws was racist at the core. However, the idea of such intervention also brought opposition from those who believed that the hallmarks of liberty—property rights and limited government—would the first victims of any egalitarian legal regime. Thus, the obstacles to insinuating the imperatives of equality into the Constitution were considerable. Even after the Thirteenth Amendment abolished slavery and the Fourteenth Amendment guaranteed all persons the equal protection of the law, Americans were reluctant to grant the government the full powers to enforce these amendments. Many still harbored the sentiment of the eccentric Virginian John Randolph, an early champion of states' rights and limited government, who declared without apology, "I love liberty. I hate equality" (Kirk 1964, 28). The constitutional guarantees of liberty, certainly as Randolph must have understood them, did not preclude the majority's relegating certain groups to the status of outsiders.

By the middle of the twentieth century, the rising tide of social egalitarianism overcame the impulses of eighteenth- and nineteenth-century libertarianism. In endless court battles and later through nonviolent direct action, the civil rights leadership insisted that the concept of equality of opportunity become an important element of the American legal system. Although unrecognized at the time (for good reason), one of the first signs of this eventual victory came in the most unlikely of Supreme Court cases, *Korematsu v. United States* (323 U.S. 214; 1944), where the Supreme Court upheld the internment of Japanese Americans during World War II. In this otherwise discredited decision, Justice Hugo Black stated, "All legal standards which curtail the civil rights of a single racial group are immediately suspect. That is not to say that all such restrictions are unconstitutional. It is to say that courts must subject them to the most rigid scrutiny." Although Justice Black ignored his own admonition in this case by upholding a racially based internment, his statement was a harbinger of future court decisions. Ten years later, in *Brown v. Board of Education* (347 U.S. 483; 1954*)*, the Supreme Court declared racial segregation in public schools to be unconstitutional and overturned *Plessy v. Ferguson* (163 U.S. 537; 1896), an almost sixty-year-old precedent. In the years that followed, the Court, citing *Brown,* held all forms of state-sponsored segregation to be unconstitutional. Responding to the demands of the civil rights movement, Congress, with the prodding of Presidents John F. Kennedy and Lyndon B. Johnson, eventually passed the Civil Rights Law of 1964.

The 1964 law granted the federal government broad enforcement powers to end discrimination in public accommodation, education, employment, and federal contracts. The liberty of employers and the owners of restaurants, hotels, theaters, and other public places to discriminate were now subordinated to imperatives of racial and gender equality (discrimination on the basis of sex was originally included in Title VII, the employment section of the law). This landmark bill was the central part of a movement in American law and politics in which the agencies of government as well as corporations, unions, and universities committed themselves to the principle of equality of opportunity. Consequently, antidiscrimination laws now exist in practically every state and in countless municipalities, and no longer do they focus on race as the only protected class. In the past several decades, the definition of protected classes has been broadened to include gender, disability, and sexual orientation.

As the categories of protected classes have been extended, so has the reach of enforcement. Although the Civil Rights Act of 1964 had exempted from its public accommodation section all clubs and institutions "not in fact open to the public," many states have adopted a broader definition of what constitutes a public accommodation. In recent decades many state and municipal antidiscrimination statutes have been interpreted to include groups heretofore considered private associations, such as the Boy Scouts of America. This expansion of state authority has brought about a classic constitutional confrontation between liberty and equality, raising complex questions: antidiscrimination laws in particular call for the expansion of government authority; freedom of association requires protection against unwarranted state intrusion into people's private affairs. Where is the line between freedom of association and equality of opportunity? What constitutes a private association? When does a private association become so open and accessible to the public that it loses its private character? What limits can the state place upon an association's membership policies? When does the right to associate include the right to discriminate or, put another way, the right not to associate?

Ironically, both antidiscrimination laws and the freedom of association can be justified as a guarantee against the tyranny of the majority. Antidiscrimination laws protect vulnerable minorities from social and economic exclusion by the dominant majority; conversely, freedom of association provides constitutional protection against governmental attempts to interfere with groups that defy conventional orthodoxy. Protection against discrimination and protection of associational freedom alike are designed to make society more open to new ideas and new groups. Yet libertarians fear that antidiscrimination laws will extend the authority of the state and weaken the vitality and the diversity of associations—families, churches, social clubs, service organizations, political parties—that give free society its vitality. And for their part, egalitarians fear that freedom of association will become a cover to preserve the habits and traditions of discrimination. Such a complex debate cannot be understood as an either-or choice. It is a question of balancing two competing values essential to a free society.

In 1976 the Court dealt with this problem in *Runyon v. McCrary* (427 U.S. 160; 1976). Several southern states, in order to avoid desegregation decrees, had dramatically reduced funds for their public schools and had in turn provided funding for white-only private academies. Michael McCrary and several other black students were denied admission to these schools, and their parents brought suit against the schools under a Reconstruction-era federal law prohibiting racial discrimination in the making and enforcement of private contracts. The Court ruled in the favor of the black students, concluding that the schools were "more public than private" and did not fall under any exceptions in the statute.

The Court also dismissed the school's claim of freedom of association on relatively narrow grounds. It did not deny a school's right to promote the belief that segregation was desirable but said that ending its discriminatory practices would not inhibit its teaching "of any ideas or dogma." The Court emphasized that the case did not challenge "the right of a private social organization to limit its membership on racial or any other grounds [or] the right of a private school to limit its student body to boys, to girls, or to adherents of a particular religious faith [or] the application of [the federal statute] to private sectarian schools that practice racial exclusion on religious grounds." As one scholar put it, "The lesson of *Runyon v. McCrary* might simply be that race is different, and racial discrimination in education is a unique evil" (Brody 2002, 844).

THE *ROBERTS* DECISION AND
THE RIGHT NOT TO ASSOCIATE

In the mid-1980s the Supreme Court dealt with the issues of associational freedom and antidiscrimination in three cases, *Roberts v. United States Jaycees* (468 U.S. 609; 1984), *Rotary International v. Rotary Club of Duarte, California* (481 U.S. 537; 1987), and *New York State Club Association v. City of New York* (487 U.S. 1; 1988), often referred to as the *Roberts* trilogy. It was in these cases that the Supreme Court developed a framework for analyzing freedom of association claims against those of antidiscrimination laws.

In *Roberts* the United States Jaycees had challenged an order of the Minnesota Department of Human Rights alleging that the exclusion of women from full membership in the Jaycees violated the Minnesota Human Rights Act. The Jaycees argued that such an order violated their rights of free speech and free association. In a unanimous opinion the Court denied the Jaycees' claim and ordered the admission of women to its membership. Justice William Brennan's opinion for the Court was its first important statement on the question of associational freedom and antidiscrimination and the fullest explanation of what the Court considered the parameters of this inchoate constitutional right. To the chagrin of commentators like George Kateb and John O. McGinnis, Brennan gave a limited definition of the right and did not include, as McGinnis put it, "the Tocquevillian paradigm of mediating institutions" (McGinnis 2002, 531).

Brennan recognized only two dimensions of freedom of association: freedom of intimate association and freedom of expressive association. The former was derived from the general concept of liberty found in the Fourteenth Amendment. As Brennan explained it, "The Court has long recognized that, because the Bill of Rights is designed to secure individual liberty, it must afford the formation and preservation of certain kinds of highly personal relationships a substantial measure of sanctuary from unjustified interference by the State" (*Roberts,* 619). Examples of such relationships were marriage, childbirth, raising and educating children, and cohabitation with one's relatives. Brennan did not restrict these associations only to family relationships. Other characteristics, according to Brennan, were "relative smallness, a high degree of selectivity in decisions to begin and maintain the affiliation, and seclusion from others in critical aspects of the relationship. . . . Only [these] relationships are likely to reflect the considerations that have led to an understanding of freedom of association as an intrinsic element of personal liberty." In determining what constitutes an intimate association, Brennan claimed it "entails a careful assessment of where that relationship's objective characteristics locate it on a spectrum from the most intimate to the most attenuate of personal attachments" (*Roberts*, 620).

Brennan noted that the Jaycees were large and basically unselective and with the exception of age and sex (membership was limited to males between the ages of eighteen and thirty-five), the Jaycees recruited new members with no inquiry into their backgrounds. Brennan dismissed the Jaycees' claim of intimate association. Brennan did not recognize, as did Kateb, that distant or mediated relationships could also contribute to the process of self-discovery or self-expression and were thus worthy of constitutional protection.

Brennan then considered the second dimension of freedom of association, freedom of expressive association. It was on this dimension of the right that Brennan devoted most of his opinion and where future courts were to focus as well. Unlike the freedom of intimate association that was intrinsic to the concept of liberty and protected by the due process clause of the Fourteenth Amendment, Brennan considered expressive association as instrumental to the First Amendment and an essential corollary to that amendment. In Brennan's words expressive association was "a corresponding right to associate with others in pursuits of a wide variety of political, social, economic, educational, religious, and cultural ends"(*Roberts*, 623). Given the facts of the case, Brennan gave greater consideration to the Jaycees' claim of expressive association. He also recognized that it included the right to disassociate or the right of groups to exclude others under certain circumstances. As Brennan put it, "There can be no clearer example of an intrusion into the internal structure of affairs of an association than a regulation that forces the group to accept members it does not desire. Such a regulation may impair the ability of the original members to express only those views that brought them together.

Freedom of association therefore plainly presupposes a freedom not to associate" (*Roberts*, 623).

Brennan was expanding on the groundwork the Court had laid for the doctrine of disassociation in *Abood v. Detroit Board of Education* (431 U.S. 209; 1977). The Court in that case ruled that an agency shop agreement between the school board and the union could not require nonunion employees to support ideological causes with which they disagreed. Writing for the majority, Justice Potter Stewart conceded that the union could support ideological causes, but it had to finance such expenditures with dues from employees "who do not object to advancing those ideas and who are not coerced into doing so against their will." In a concurring opinion Justice Lewis Powell argued that "compelling a government employee to give financial support to a union in the public sector—regardless of the uses to which the union puts the contribution—impinges seriously upon the interests in free speech and association protected by the First Amendment." Powell felt the burden for justifying such expenditures should fall on the union and state. He disagreed with the part of the majority opinion that required the dissenting employee to identify the causes to which he objected in order to obtain a rebate from the union. The decision in *Abood* was also applied to the use of state bar dues for supporting gun control and a nuclear freeze initiative (*Keller v. State Bar of California*, 496 U.S. 1; 1990). However, the Court upheld in *Board of Regents of the University of Wisconsin v. Southworth* (529 U.S. 217; 2000) a public university's charge of a compulsory fee that was used in part to support student political and ideological organizations. The Court in this case did not find *Abood* and *Keller* controlling because of the need to protect the academic freedom of the university. Justice Anthony Kennedy, writing for a unanimous Court in *Southworth*, stated, "The speech the University seeks to encourage in the program before us is distinguished not by discernable limits, but by its vast unexplored bounds. To insist upon asking what speech is germane would be contrary to the very goal the University seeks to pursue. It is not for the Court to say what is or is not germane to the ideas pursued in an institution of higher learning" (*Southworth*, 232).

Freedom not to associate was the other side of the freedom of association coin and was an essential element of that right. It involved the right of groups to determine their own membership, and membership was connected to the nature of a group's voice and message. The question at the heart of *Roberts* was, How far did the right of a group to control its message go in allowing it to also control its membership? Did the admittance of women into the Jaycees dilute their message and alter their voice?

Brennan acknowledged that the right to associate for expressive purposes, like other freedoms, was not absolute. The right could be limited by a state regulation "adopted to serve compelling state interests, unrelated to the suppression of ideas, that cannot be achieved through means significantly less restrictive of associational freedom." Brennan concluded that Minnesota's interest in eliminating discrimination against its female citizens was compelling and justified any burden on the Jaycees' associational freedoms. The burden for justifying such discrimination fell upon the Jaycees. Brennan found that "the Jaycees . . . failed to demonstrate that the [Minnesota] Act imposes any serious burden on the male members' freedom of expressive association." Brennan argued that the admission of females as full voting members would not "impede the organization's ability to engage in these protected activities or to disseminate its preferred views [and would] impose no restrictions on the organization's ability to exclude individuals with ideologies or philosophies different from those of its existing members." The Jaycees' position on public issues, according to Brennan, had nothing to do with gender. He considered it sexual stereotyping to assume that allowing women to become voting members would by itself alter the Jaycees' message. Brennan dismissed the notion that young women would bring divergent views on a variety of public issues. As Brennan argued, "In claiming that [women] might have a different attitude about such issues as the federal budget, school prayer, voting rights, and foreign relations . . . the Jaycees relied solely on unsupported generalizations about the relative interests and perspectives of men and women." He then concluded, "We decline to indulge in the sexual stereotyping that underlies [the Jaycees] contention" (*Roberts*, 623).

Brennan implied that if the Jaycees' message supported discrimination, it would in fact fail to garner any protection. In other words, if a group's purpose is noxious, its rights are not safeguarded. Nancy L. Rosenblum in her critique of Brennan's opinion comments that this "comes perilously close to treading directly on viewpoint discrimination." Rosenblum argues, "Being legally required to admit a class of unwelcome members changes the group's voice, even if its impact on the group's actual public communications cannot be predicted, or does not occur at all. . . . Expression has to do with who we are and are perceived to be, not just what we say." She claims that if you change the membership of an organization, you alter its distinctive voice and perhaps its influence over others (Rosenblum 1998, 194). Douglas Linder takes issue with Brennan whether the exclusion of women is simply sexual stereotyping: "The experiences of women in American society today, as a group, differ in significant ways from the experiences of men as a group. Polling results support the prediction that gender does indeed correlate with certain attitudes towards issues ranging from abortion to war and peace" (Linder 1984, 1878).

THE O'CONNOR PERSPECTIVE

In her concurring opinion Justice Sandra Day O'Connor argued that the Court had both weakened freedom of association with its "insufficient protection to expressive associations" and "had cast doubt on the power of States to pursue the profoundly important goal of ensuring nondiscriminatory access to commercial opportunities in our society" (*Roberts,* 631). Although both Justices Brennan and O'Connor recognized that the First Amendment did offer protection for expressive association, O'Connor took far more seriously the relationship between membership and voice. According to O'Connor, the threshold question was whether the Jaycees were a predominantly commercial enterprise or an expressive one. She decided they were largely a commercial association. Consequently, they lacked full constitutional protection of freedom of expressive association and in the face of reasonable state regulations lost absolute control over their own membership.

O'Connor acknowledged that the distinction between commercial and expressive associations could not be determined with simple precision. It would require looking at all of an association's activities to see whether more than half were devoted to such matters as recruitment and the collection of dues or to such expressive activities as ritual, worship, debate, or lobbying. She indicated, however, that she might give greater weight to an association's commercial activities. "Once it enters the marketplace of commerce," O'Connor suggested, "in any substantial degree, it loses the complete control over its membership that it would otherwise enjoy if it confined its affairs to the marketplace of ideas." O'Connor found the Jaycees "a relatively easy case for application of the expressive-commercial dichotomy," since they recruited and sold memberships and members developed their "management and solicitation skills, primarily under the direction and supervision of the organization, primarily through their active recruitment of new members" (*Roberts,* 636).

The closer one looks at O'Connor's dichotomy, the vaguer it appears. The Jaycees also engaged in a considerable amount of expressive activity. For example, they passed resolutions that supported a balanced budget and a voluntary prayer in schools and opposed the distribution of pornography and federal funds for teachers' salaries. Political parties, clearly expressive associations, also recruit members and collect dues or contributions. Are labor unions, law firms, and trade associations commercial or expressive associations? Although the distinction between commercial and expressive associations is hard to draw, it matters a great deal for First Amendment analysis. The Court has developed sharply different standards for judging commercial speech and political speech about public issues—so-called core political speech. Content-based restrictions on core political speech are subject to strict scrutiny, demanding a compelling state interest narrowly tailored. Restrictions on commercial speech need only stand intermediate scrutiny. Under this doctrine the states can regulate solicitations by business. The Court has, however, protected solicitation for political advocacy groups because it is not primarily about providing information concerning characteristics and costs of goods and services (*Schaumberg v. Citizens for a Better Environment*, 444 U.S. 620; 1980 and Carpenter 2001, 1515). Given these different standards of review and judicial scrutiny, it follows that the membership policies of a commercial association would be subject to far greater state regulations than would those of an expressive association.

Despite limiting freedom of association for commercial enterprises and joining the Court in slamming the door on the Jaycees' claim, O'Connor was willing to go much further than Brennan in protecting noncommercial, expressive association. Once an association is defined as expressive, O'Connor would grant it broad control over its message and its membership. She believed that an association's right to define its membership is related to the creation of its voice and that selection of members in turn helps to define that voice. In establishing a clear nexus between membership and voice, O'Connor would grant greater protection for noncommercial associations to control their own membership against state antidiscrimination laws. She did not feel it was the place of the courts to determine what an association's message was. The First Amendment protected that. "Whether an association is or is not constitutionally protected in the selection of its membership should not depend on what the association says or why its members say it," she wrote (*Roberts*, 632). Her implication was that no matter how odious an expressive organization's message may be, it must be allowed to control its membership. Altering an organization's membership has the effect of altering its message.

Both Brennan's majority opinion and O'Connor's concurrence in *Roberts* left important questions unanswered. Brennan had not made clear under what circumstances an association's ability to control its membership could be related to its message. O'Connor left open the question of what precisely determined a commercial association, since her definition of such a group could include many expressive associations. Neither approach left freedom of expressive association with solid constitutional footing, particularly when weighed against the state's interest in ending discrimination. In his assertion that antidiscrimination laws generally served a compelling state interest, Brennan indicated it would be a rare occasion when freedom of association claims could trump such an interest.

THE *ROBERTS* TRILOGY

In the two cases that followed *Roberts* (and with it make up the so-called *Roberts* trilogy), the Supreme Court continued to give greater weight to the antidiscrimination claims against those of expressive association. *Rotary International v. Rotary Club of Duarte, California* (481 U.S. 537; 1987) became the second part of the *Roberts* trilogy. The Duarte club had admitted three women into active membership, and as a result Rotary International threatened to revoke its charter. The Duarte Rotary Club and two of its female members filed suit under the California antidiscrimination law, known as the Unruh Act. The California Superior Court held that Rotary did not qualify as a business establishment under the Unruh Act and was not subject to its antidiscrimination provisions. The California court of appeal reversed, and the California Supreme Court denied a petition for review.

The Supreme Court, however, granted certiorari. In its brief opinion the Court held that Rotary was not an intimate association and that "the evidence fails to demonstrate that admitting women to Rotary will affect in any significant way the existing members' ability to carry out their various purposes"(*Rotary*, 548). As in *Roberts*, the Court placed the burden on Rotary to justify its exclusion of women against the state's compelling interest in eliminating discrimination. Justice O'Connor did not participate in the case and thus had no opportunity to elaborate upon the commercial/noncommercial analysis she had developed in *Roberts*.

The third part of the *Roberts* trilogy was *New York State Club Association v. City of New York* (487 U.S. 1; 1988). The Court rejected a challenge to a city ordinance that applied its antidiscrimination provisions to any club with "more than four hundred members, [which] provides regular meal service and regularly received payments for dues, fees, use of space, facilities, services, meals or beverages directly or indirectly from or on behalf of nonmembers for the furtherance of trade or business" (*New York Clubs*, 8). The ordinance was an amendment to New York City's Human Rights Law of 1965 that was designed to eliminate "discriminatory practices of certain membership organizations where business deals are often made and personal contacts valuable for business purposes, employment and professional advancements are formed" (*New York City Administration Code*, 8–107). The Court, elaborating upon *Roberts*, upheld the ordinance since it would not require clubs to "abandon or alter" many of their activities. The Court did open the door to future freedom of association claims against antidiscrimination laws if an organization could show that it was organized specifically for expressive purposes. The Court stated, "It is conceivable . . . that an association might be able to show that it is organized for specific expressive purposes and that it will not be able to advocate its desired viewpoints nearly as effectively if it cannot confine its membership to those who share the same sex, for example, or the same religion" (*New York Clubs*, 13).

Justice O'Connor in her concurrence affirmed her commercial/expressive distinction. She suggested that there could be organizations with more than 400 members whose expressive purposes would be compromised "if they were unable to confine their membership to those of the same sex, race, religion, or ethnic background." She repeated that "predominantly commercial organizations are not entitled to claim a First Amendment associational or expressive right" regardless of size (*New York Clubs*, 18–19). Nonetheless, she was unable to persuade any of her colleagues on the court to join in her concurrence. The Brennan view remained at the heart of the *Roberts* trilogy.

The *Roberts* trilogy set narrow boundaries for a freedom of association claim, making it difficult to trump the state's interest in antidiscrimination. An organization would have to prove that its expressive purposes would be compromised if it admitted minorities, women, or gays. Embedded in this effort to protect the interests of women and minorities was a puzzling irony: such an approach would give the greatest protections to openly bigoted groups whose expressive purposes were clear and unambiguous, such as the Ku Klux Klan. Groups whose views were more balanced would have a more difficult time justifying controls over the membership against state antidiscrimination claims. Thus, mainstream groups could have far less constitutional protection against state interference than extremist societies.

HURLEY AND PARADES

The *Roberts* doctrine heavily influenced the state proceedings in *Hurley v. Irish-American Gay, Lesbian and Bisexual Group of*

Boston (515 U.S. 557; 1995) as it made its way to the Supreme Court. The Irish-American Gay, Lesbian and Bisexual Group of Boston (GLIB) was purportedly formed to march in the annual Boston St. Patrick's Day parade. In 1992 GLIB's application was rejected by the parade organizers, the South Boston Allied War Veterans Council. GLIB eventually obtained a court order allowing it to participate in the march. The next year the Veterans Council again denied GLIB the right to take part in the parade. GLIB then filed a lawsuit against the council and John J. Hurley, a member. The state trial court held for GLIB, ruling that the parade was covered by the state public accommodation law, that the expressive purpose of the parade was not discernible, and that there was no infringement of the War Veterans Council's First Amendment right of freedom of expressive association. The Massachusetts Supreme Court affirmed, also holding that the parade had no specific expressive purpose. In his dissent Judge Nolan raised a free speech issue, arguing that regardless of whether the council's parade had any message, it could not be forced to accept GLIB's message as its own.

When the case came to the U.S. Supreme Court, the justices took a cue from Judge Nolan's dissent and framed the question as a free speech issue, not an expressive association question. Speaking through Justice David Souter, the Court unanimously reversed the Massachusetts Supreme Court and stated that parades are "a form of expression." This cast the organizers of the parade as the speakers, who had the right not to have their message altered, whether or not it was a "particularized message." Parades, the Court elaborated, need not have "a narrow, succinctly articulable message [as] a condition of constitutional protection." Gay and lesbian individuals were not prohibited from marching in the parade as a part of other groups. GLIB did not desire to march under a particular gay rights banner but only under a simple sign that would carry the group's name. The parade organizers argued that allowing a gay and lesbian group to participate with such a sign indicating their presence would have signaled the organizers' acceptance of homosexuals. The Supreme Court agreed and stated, "The presence of the organized marchers would suggest their view that people of their sexual orientations have as much claim to unqualified social acceptance as heterosexuals and indeed as members of parade units organized around other identifying characteristics. The parade's organizers may not believe these facts about Irish sexuality to be so, or they may object to unqualified social acceptance of gays and lesbians or have some other reason for wishing to keep GLIB's message out of the parade. But whatever the reason, it boils down to the choice of a speaker not to propound a particular point of view, and that choice is presumed to lie beyond the government's power to control" (*Hurley*, 10).

Hurley established an uneasy relationship with the *Roberts* trilogy. If the Hurley Court had relied upon *Roberts,* it would have required that the parade organizers explain how GLIB's participation altered their message. As the Court framed the issue in *Hurley,* it was a question of imposing an unwanted position on the group, not contradicting an explicit position on an issue. Advocates of broader constitutional protection for freedom of association could find some solace in *Hurley,* as it gave groups greater control over their own message than did the *Roberts* trilogy. Unlike *Roberts, Hurley* did not put the burden of proof on the parade organizers to show that GLIB's participation would compromise their essential message. For the *Hurley* Court, it was the very identity of GLIB, not its specific message, that changed the parade organizers' own message.

What would be the impact of *Hurley?* Was it a purely speech case, or did it have freedom of association implications? The answer was hazy. A parade could be considered both a form of speech and a form of association. By leaving open the possibility that a future court might well conflate free speech and expressive association law, *Hurley* did place the *Roberts* trilogy in some doubt. If that were to happen, the protections for freedom of association could be far more secure.

Advocates of freedom of association found some comfort in *Hurley,* whereas gay rights advocates found the decision troubling. As one commentator put it, "The most damning question left in the wake of *Hurley* is how the homosexual group could have ever participated? The answer is that they could only participate if they communicated no message at all or at least communicated a message that parade organizers would tolerate. Neither of these is a possible answer under the Court's analysis in *Hurley.* If the presence of a group infers a message of requested acceptance, that group can never not communicate that message" (Hargis 2000, 1189). If the very participation of uncloseted gays in an expressive association implies support of gay rights, can an openly gay person be required under state antidiscrimination statutes to participate only in those organizations that clearly support gay rights? The Court would at the beginning of the twenty-first century give a sharper, although not a definitive, answer to these questions.

FREEDOM OF ASSOCIATION AND THE RIGHTS OF POLITICAL PARTIES

How does freedom of association apply to political parties? Are they private associations to be given the latitude over their membership that the Court has granted to other such organizations? They certainly are expressive associations that exist to advance an ideological agenda and nominate and elect supporters of that program. Yet political parties are not simply private actors as are service clubs and other voluntary organizations. Party primaries are part of the state-regulated election process, and state laws determine the process of membership in a party—whether or not one must formally declare a party affiliation to vote in a primary and how close to the primary date must one declare such an affiliation, if at all. No state election law allows a voter to be a member of two parties simultaneously. Some states require party affiliation to vote in that party's primary, and some states require no party affiliation to participate.

Since party primaries are an integral part of the election process, the constitutional provisions that affect the right to vote apply to them. These include protection against racial discrimination in the Fifteenth Amendment; prohibition against gender discrimination in the Nineteenth Amendment; the outlawing of federal poll taxes in the Twenty-Fourth Amendment; and the age of eligibility, set at eighteen years in the Twenty-Sixth Amendment. Parties may have associational rights, but these specific provisions of the Constitution trump them.

THE WHITE PRIMARY CASES

Despite the passage of the Fifteenth Amendment prohibiting racial discrimination in voting, the white South soon after Reconstruction engaged in a systematic policy of African American disenfranchisement. These devilish devices included white primaries, poll taxes, grandfather clauses, unfairly administered literacy tests, and social, economic, and even physical coercion. In the one-party South of that era, the Democratic Party primaries usually settled elections.

Eventually this history of blatant discrimination awakened the interest of the Supreme Court and brought about a degree of judicial intervention in the primary election process. From 1927 to 1953 the Court struck down the most insidious state statutes that prevented African Americans from participating in Democratic Party primaries, the so-called white primary laws (*Terry v. Adams*, 345 U.S. 461; 1953; *Smith v. Allwright*, 321 U.S. 649; 1944; *Nixon v. Condon*, 286 U.S. 73; 1932; *Nixon v. Herndon*, 273 U.S. 536; 1927). In *Smith v. Allwright*, the most widely cited of the white primary cases, the Court held that "the recognition of the place of the primary in the electoral scheme makes clear that state delegation to a party of the power to fix the qualifications of primary elections is delegation of a state function that may make the party's action the action of the state"(*Allwright*, 660). Given this degree of state action in the primary process, the Court concluded that the Fifteenth Amendment prohibited a state from "casting its electoral process in a form which permits a private organization to practice racial discrimination in the election" (*Allwright*, 664).

What do these white primary cases tell us about the limits on the associational freedom of political parties? Were they sui generis, reflecting the outrageous practices of the white South and the one-party monopoly of the southern Democrats, practices that the Fifteenth Amendment was designed to prevent? Or did these cases have a greater meaning, limiting party rights beyond racial discrimination? The answer is complex. Party primaries do exhibit strong attributes of state action. States can specify qualifications for getting on the ballot, when the election is to be held, and whether or not a simple majority or an absolute majority determines the winner, requiring a possible runoff. The actual administration of the election, setting the form of the ballot and counting the votes, is the responsibility of the state. Yet parties do, as Nathaniel Persily puts it, "exhibit features identical to other private associations or interest groups: they meet to discuss issues of collective action, they formulate policy programs, and in a literal sense they 'speak,' 'print,' 'assemble,' 'petition for redress of grievances' in ways identical to other collections of individuals"(Persily 2001, 759, 764).

Given how essential political parties have become to our democratic system, it is impossible to imagine that they do not have substantial constitutional protections under the right of expressive association. A free and competitive democracy would be seriously compromised in a system in which the state regulates the internal affairs of political parties. State laws that might control membership by forcing the inclusion of outsiders would disrupt a party's freedom of association. The question is, How does one balance the state's authority to regulate primary elections against the party organization's right to include or exclude certain voters from the nomination process? Any law that regulates who is eligible to vote in a party affects how a party runs its internal affairs, including the selection of leadership and the development of a platform. Few events are more important to a party's identity and voice than the nomination of its candidates for office. The major objective of a political party above all else is to nominate and elect candidates for public office.

PARTIES GAIN ASSOCIATIONAL RIGHTS

Although the Court had made clear that any associational rights that a party may claim did not justify procedures designed to mask racial disenfranchisement, the Court has in the past several decades granted parties a large degree of associational freedom.

In *Nader v. Schaffer* (429 U.S. 989; 1976), the Court affirmed a lower court ruling that closed primary laws requiring party membership to vote in a primary did not violate the rights of other voters. The lower court had ruled that a party's right to limit primary participation is inherent in its associational rights (417 F. Supp. 837; D. Conn. 1976). In *Democratic Party of the United States v. Wisconsin ex rel. La Follette et al.* (450 U.S. 107; 1981), the Court adjudicated a case involving a conflict between Wisconsin's open primary law and the rules of the Democratic National Convention. An open primary allows any voter, regardless of party, to vote in a primary. The Wisconsin law required that the delegates to the National Convention vote in accordance with the results of the open primary. The rules of the Democratic Convention prohibited the seating of delegates selected in primary elections that permitted the participation of nonparty members. The Court ruled in favor of the Democratic Party. In the majority opinion

Justice Potter Stewart declared that the freedom of association "presupposes the freedom to identify the people who constitute the association, and to limit the association to those people only." A party may protect itself against "those with adverse principles." A national convention is an essential form of a party's association, helping its members unite to select candidates and write a platform. The interests of the state, which included increasing voter participation and providing secrecy on the ballot, were not considered compelling and did not justify this "substantial intrusion into the associational freedom of members of the National Party" (*La Follette*, 122, 124). In his dissenting opinion Justice Lewis Powell observed that the Democratic Party is "not organized around the achievement of defined ideological goals," and that as a major party it is "characterized by a fluidity and overlap of philosophy and membership." The Democratic Party does not have "a monolithic ideological identity [excluding] all those with differing views." Therefore, Powell concluded, "it is hard to see what the Democratic Party has to fear from an open primary plan" (*La Follette*, 131).

The Court did not rule in *La Follette* on the constitutionality of an open primary per se but rather on the right of a national party to set conditions for the selection of its convention delegates. The language of Justice Stewart's opinion indicated that political parties would be given broad protection under freedom of association. This would involve the right to exclude non–party members from participating in the presidential nomination process. Conversely, what if a party wanted to include nonmembers in its primary elections and state law prevented it? In *Tashjian v. Republican Party* (479 U.S. 208; 1986), the Court held that a Connecticut law preventing a party from opening up its primary to independent voters violated a party's associational rights. The state of Connecticut had claimed its interests in having such a law included "administrability of the primary system, preventing raiding, avoiding voter confusion, and protecting the responsibility of party government" (*Tashjian*, 217). Since Connecticut was at that time dominated by the Democratic Party, the Court found the law to be a subterfuge that allowed the majority party to tell the minority Republican Party how to run its affairs. Even if the law were designed to help the Republican Party (an unlikely motivation), Justice Thurgood Marshall, writing the Court's opinion and citing *La Follette*, explained that a state cannot substitute its judgment for that of a party: "The Party's determination of the boundaries of its own association, and of the structure which best allows it to pursue its political goals, is protected by the Constitution" (*Tashjian*, 225).

The Court continued to uphold party autonomy under freedom of association. In *Eu v. San Francisco County Democratic Central Committee* (489 U.S. 214; 1989), a California state law prohibited a party organization from endorsing a candidate in a primary. In addition the law limited the terms of office for the state parties' central committees and required the rotation of party chairs between northern and southern California. The *Eu* Court required that a statute infringing on associational freedoms can survive constitutional scrutiny only if it serves a compelling state interest and is narrowly tailored to serve those interests. The state claimed it had two compelling interests: stable government and protecting voters from confusion. The Court recognized that stable government was a compelling interest but did not buy the argument that banning parties from endorsing primary candidates advanced that interest. Protecting voters from confusion was also considered a compelling interest, but the ban did not advance that interest and restricted the flow of information to voters. The Court declared the antiendorsement provision a clear violation of core political speech. Writing for the Court, Justice Marshall declared, "Because the ban on party endorsements by political parties burdens political speech while serving no compelling governmental interest, we hold that [those provisions] of the California Election Code violate the First and Fourteenth Amendments"

(*Eu*, 228). The Court ruled that the regulation of party structure infringed upon the party's freedom of association. "By regulating the identity of the parties' leaders," the Court ruled, "the challenged statutes may also color the parties' message and interfere with the parties' decisions as to the best means to promote that message" (*Eu*, 231). The Court quoted its decision in *Tashjian:* "The State has no interest in protecting the integrity of the Party against the Party itself" (*Eu*, 224).

The precedents established in *Nader, La Follette, Tashjian,* and *Eu* went a long way in providing parties the protection of freedom of association. They established that a state cannot regulate the organization or the message of a party and cannot dictate that certain people must be included in or excluded from party primaries. The state could regulate elections in ways that do not impose severe burdens on a party's associational rights. In *Timmons v. Twin Cities Area New Party* (520 U.S. 351; 1997), a minor political party challenged a law that prevented candidates from appearing on the ballots of more than one political party. In this case the Court declared, that "the burdens of the antifusion law imposed on the New Party's associational rights were justified by the correspondingly weighty valid state interests in ballot integrity and political stability." The law did not affect the New Party's message or its membership and thus burden its freedom of association. This antifusion law did not "restrict the ability of the New Party and its members to endorse, support, or vote for anyone they supported ... [or] directly limit the party's access to the ballot" (*Timmons*, 365, 364).

By the end of the twentieth century, the Court had protected freedom of association from government intrusion in several ways: (1) the government must show that an organization is actively engaged in prohibited conduct before making it illegal; (2) in order for an individual to be punished for membership in such an organization, the government must show that such a person is affiliated with the knowledge of its illegality and with the specific intent to further its purposes; (3) the government cannot inquire into the membership of any organization without a compelling reason; (4) the "right not to associate" gives individuals the right not to support expressive activities of organizations they do not approve of and gives associations the right not to accept unwanted members; (5) the government cannot interfere with an organization's internal structure without a compelling reason.

REFERENCES AND FURTHER READING

Association of American University Professors. 1953. "The Rights and Responsibilities of Universities and Their Faculties." In *McCarthyism: The Great American Red Scare,* edited by Albert Fried. New York: Oxford University Press, 1997.

Brody, Evelyn. 2002. "Entrance, Voice, and Exit: The Constitutional Bounds of the Right of Association." *University of California–Davis Law Review* 35 (April): 821–901.

Carpenter, Dale. 2001. "Expressive Association and Anti-Discrimination Law After *Dale:* A Tripartite Approach." *Minnesota Law Review* 85 (June): 1515–1589.

Cogley, John. 1971. *Blacklisting: Two Key Documents.* New York: Arno Press and the *New York Times.*

Emerson, Thomas I. 1970. *The System of Freedom of Expression.* New York: Random House.

Fried, Albert, ed. 1997. *McCarthyism: The Great American Red Scare.* New York: Oxford University Press.

Goodman, Walter. 1964. *The Committee: The Extraordinary Career of the House Committee on Un-American Activities.* London: History Book Club.

Hargis, Christopher S. 2000. "*Romer, Hurley,* and *Dale:* How the Supreme Court Languishes with 'Special Rights.'" *Kentucky Law Journal* 89 (Summer): 1189–1225.

Haynes, John Earl, and Harvey Klehr. 2000. *Venona: Decoding Soviet Espionage in America.* New Haven, CT: Yale University Press.

Hook, Sidney. 1952. "Not Mindful Enough." *Journal of Philosophy* 49 (February 14): 112–121.

———. 1953. *Heresy, Yes, Conspiracy, No.* New York: John Day and Company.

Kateb, George. 1998. "The Value of Assoication." In *Freedom of Association.* Edited by Amy Guttman. Princeton, NJ: Princton University Press.

Kirk, Russell. 1964. *John Randolph of Roanoke: A Study in American Politics.* Chicago: Henry Regnery.

Klehr, Harvey, John Earl Haynes, and Fridrikch Igorevich Firsov. 1995. *The Secret World of American Communism.* New Haven, CT: Yale University Press.

Kramer, Hilton. 1999. *The Twilight of the Intellectuals: Culture and Politics in the Era of the Cold War.* Chicago: Ivan Dee.

Linder, Douglas O. 1984. "Freedom of Association after *Roberts v. United States Jaycees.*" *Michigan Law Review* 82: 1878–1903.

Lowe, Victor. 1952. "In Defense of Individualistic Empiricism." *Journal of Philosophy* 49 (February 14): 100–111.

McGinnis, John O. 2002. "Reviving Tocqueville's America: The Rehnquist Court's Jurisprudence of Social Discovery." *California Law Review* 90 (March): 530–571.

Meiklejohn, Alexander. 1948. *Free Speech and Its Relation to Self Government.* New York: Harper Brothers.

New York City Human Rights Law, Chapter I, Section 107.

O'Neill, Robert M. 2001. "Tribute: The Neglected First Amendment Jurisprudence of the Second Justice Harlan." *New York University Annual Survey of American Law* 58: 57–66.

Persily, Nathaniel. 2001. "Toward a Functional Defense of Political Party Autonomy." *New York University Law Review* 76: 750–824.

Redish, Martin H., and Christopher R. McFadden. 2001. "HUAC, the Hollywood Ten and the First Amendment Right of Non-Association." *Minnesota Law Review* 85 (June): 1669–1728.

Rosenblum, Nancy L. 1998. *Membership and Morals: The Personal Uses of Pluralism in America.* Princeton, NJ: Princeton University Press.

Rovere, Richard. 1957. "Arthur Miller's Conscience." *New Republic,* June 17: 13–15.

Schrecker, Ellen. 1994. *The Age of McCarthyism: A Brief History with Documents.* Boston: St. Martin's Press.

———. 1998. *Many Are the Crimes: McCarthyism in America.* Princeton, NJ: Princeton University Press.

Tocqueville, Alexis de. 2000. *Democracy in America.* Edited by Harvey C. Mansfield and Delba Winthrop. Chicago: University of Chicago Press.

Tribe, Laurence H. *American Constitutional Law.* 2d ed. Mineola, NY: Foundation Press, 1998.

4

TWENTY-FIRST
CENTURY ISSUES

The twenty-first century began with the Supreme Court's deciding two cases that indicated a greater interest in protecting freedom of association. This reflected the more conservative perspective of the Rehnquist Court, particularly with the addition of Justices Antonin Scalia and Clarence Thomas. Inasmuch as constitutional protection of associational rights limits the power of the state to regulate the private sphere, a conservative Court found much to value in more fully protecting that right. Whether future Courts will continue to strengthen associational rights will depend upon whether the political consensus becomes more egalitarian or more libertarian. The dramatic 2000 presidential election was a reminder that at the beginning of this new century both the country and the Court were closely divided.

JAMES DALE CHALLENGES THE BOY SCOUTS

In 2000 the Supreme Court ruled on a case that tested the capacity of that body to find a balance between the imperatives of associational freedom and antidiscrimination. *Boy Scouts of America v. Dale* (530 U.S. 640) involved a clash between an American institution that embodied many traditional values and gay and lesbian groups who wished to be granted the protection of the state against social exclusion.

At the age of eleven, James Dale joined the Monmouth Council in New Jersey, a division of the Boy Scouts of America (BSA). He remained in the Scouts until he was eighteen, during which time he earned twenty-five merit badges, was admitted into the prestigious Order of the Arrow, and earned the rank of Eagle Scout, an award given to only 3 percent of all Scouts. He applied for adult membership and was approved as an assistant scoutmaster of Troop 73 of the Monmouth Council. During that same time he entered Rutgers University, where he became copresident of the Rutgers University Lesbian/Gay Alliance. In 1990 he attended a seminar about the health needs of lesbian and gay teenagers and was interviewed by a local newspaper about his advocacy of the need of homosexual teenagers for gay role models. The newspaper published the article over a caption identifying Dale as the copresident of the Lesbian/Gay Alliance.

Soon after the article's appearance Dale received a letter from James Kay, the Monmouth Council executive, revoking Dale's membership in the Boy Scouts. When Dale replied asking for an explanation, Kay informed him that membership in the Boy Scouts was a privilege and could be withdrawn "whenever there is a concern that an individual may not meet the high standards of members which BSA seeks to provide for American youth." When Dale sent another letter asking for the specific reason for his dismissal, Kay informed him that the grounds for the decision "are the standards of leadership established by the Boy Scouts of America, which specifically forbid membership to homosexuals."

THE NEW JERSEY COURTS RESPOND

In 1992 Dale filed a complaint against the Boy Scouts in New Jersey Superior Court's chancery division, alleging that the organization had violated New Jersey's public accommodations law that prohibited, among other things, discrimination on the basis of sexual orientation in places of public accommodation. Upon filing the complaint, Dale gave an interview to the *New York Times* in which he asserted, "I owe it to the organization to point out to them how bad and wrong this policy is. . . . Being proud about who I am is something the Boy Scouts taught me." He later stated on television, "Yes, I am gay, and I'm proud of who I am. . . . I have pride, I stand up for what I believe in, I mean what you see is what you get. I'm not hiding anything. But the Scouts don't like that" (quoted in *Dale*, Stevens dissent, fn. 20).

The chancery court granted summary judgment in favor of the Boy Scouts, ruling that New Jersey's public accommodations law was not applicable because BSA was a distinctly private group and not a place of public accommodation. The court found that "since its inception Scouting has sincerely and unswervingly held to the view that an 'avowed' sexually-active homosexual is engaging in immoral behavior which violates the Scout Oath (in which the person promises to be 'morally straight') and the Scout law (whereby the person promises to be keep himself 'clean')." Thus, the chancery court held that the Boy Scouts' position on active homosexuality was protected by the First Amendment's freedom of expressive association that prevented the government from forcing the Scouts to accept Dale as an adult leader.

The New Jersey Superior Court's appellate division reversed and held that the BSA was a place of public accommodation and not an exclusively private group under the New Jersey Law Against Discrimination (LAD). It rejected the Boy Scouts' federal constitutional claims because Dale was "not asserting a right under LAD to alter the content of the BSA's viewpoint" (706 A.2d 270, 293 N.J. Super. Ct. App. Div. 1998).

The New Jersey Supreme Court affirmed the appellate division's decision, agreeing that the BSA is a place of public accommodation. The New Jersey Supreme Court held that the Boy

Scouts was a large organization, engaged in broad public solicitation for members, advertised for members, received a federal charter, maintained relationships with the federal and local governments, and was frequently partners with public schools. The New Jersey Supreme Court ruled that the LAD did not violate the Boy Scouts' federal constitutional rights "to enter into and maintain . . . intimate or private relationships . . . [and] to associate for the purpose of engaging in protected speech."

The court concluded that the expulsion of Dale was based more on prejudice than a unified Boy Scout position and that his reinstatement would not compel the Boy Scouts to express any message. The BSA had argued that the "clean" provision of the Scout law and the "morally straight" provision of the Scout oath were evidence that BSA condemned homosexuality. The New Jersey Supreme Court rejected this argument, claiming, "The words 'morally straight' and 'clean' do not, on their face express anything about sexuality, much less that homosexuality, in particular, is immoral." The court failed to see how Dale's membership in the Boy Scouts would impair "in any significant way" BSA's ability to accomplish its purposes. The Boy Scouts appealed the case to the U.S. Supreme Court and were granted certiorari.

THE BOY SCOUTS SUPREME COURT BRIEF

In their legal brief to the Supreme Court, the Boy Scouts challenged the New Jersey Supreme Court ruling on several grounds. They disputed the court's interpretation of what constitutes a public accommodation under the New Jersey statute. In doing so, they pointed out that if any organization that solicits members, uses public facilities, or has any connection to the state could be considered a public accommodation, then numerous organizations would have to change their character and membership. The Boy Scouts would have to admit girls, and the Girl Scouts would have to admit boys. The BSA brief insisted that freedom of association must presuppose the freedom not to associate. Equally important, it must also presuppose the freedom to select leaders who would play an important role in articulating and transmitting the group's values. This would have to include adult leaders of the Scouts.

The BSA brief insisted that the New Jersey court had misread the meaning of the *Roberts* trilogy. The organizations involved in those cases differed markedly from the Boy Scouts. They were quasi-commercial organizations; they did not have a moral code logically related to membership criteria; and they did not have goals exclusively related to personal, moral, and physical development. The Boy Scouts was an inherently expressive organization with a clear moral code, and courts must give deference to an expressive organization's characterization of its own beliefs. For example, accepting a Ku Klux Klan member as a leader would interfere with the Boy Scouts' message of the importance of racial harmony, just as the B'nai B'rith could not be forced to accept an anti-Semite.

At the heart of the BSA brief was the claim that *Hurley* controlled the case and that freedom of expressive association included the right to be silent about issues. As the brief put it, "Boy Scouting does not convey an explicit 'anti-gay' message to the boys under its care; but it does not wish to convey approval of homosexual conduct either. . . . Dale cannot force Boy Scouting to grant him a platform upon which to expound those beliefs, or to garb him in the uniform of a Scoutmaster when he does so. . . . *Hurley* established that the organization has the right to exclude those who wish to proclaim their sexual identity as a part of the organization's message"(Brief for Petitioner, 21). The Boy Scouts was claiming that the government cannot decide what a private association's message is or force its own interpretation on any organization's moral message. Should an organization decide to alter its message, it can do so at any time without any involvement of the state.

The BAS brief also argued that the relationship of Scouts to their leaders constituted an intimate association. The characteristics of such an association were defined by Justice Brennan in *Roberts* as "deep attachments and commitments to the necessarily few other individuals with whom one shares not only a special community of thoughts, experiences, and beliefs but also distinctly personal aspects of one's life" (*Roberts,* 620). The Scouts is a large national organization, but they are organized into troops of typically fifteen to thirty boys and in small patrols that are composed of three to eight boys. The adult leader is to serve as a role model and friend, providing a close personal relationship with an adult outside of the family (Brief for Petitioner, 39–41).

In its amicus brief with the conservative women's group Eagle Forum supporting the Boy Scouts, the libertarian Cato Institute argued that private organizations need to be protected against "government's tendency toward self-aggrandizement . . . and to expand the public sphere in order to enforce the latest prescribed orthodoxy." The state's interest in nondiscriminatory access to publicly offered goods and services, the original purpose of most public accommodation laws, the brief argued, should not extend into unlimited access to noncommercial, private, expressive associations. Such groups should be allowed to define their own messages and their own qualifications for members. Private expressive associations should include "all nonprofit, noncommercial organizations that have some expressive purpose . . . and . . . the burden should be on the state to prove compelling evidence that such entity can be categorized as a public accommodation." The Boy Scouts' expressive purpose was at the heart of its educational mission to inculcate young Scouts with certain values. Should the Boy Scouts be forced to accept James Dale, who had made his sexuality a public matter, they would be placing its imprimatur "on a person who exemplifies particular values and behaviors that the Boy Scouts rejects." It would be similar to *Hurley* in that having Dale as an adult leader suggests a public and explicit position on homosexuality that the Boy Scouts would rather not assert or support (Amicus Brief for Cato Institute and Eagle Forum).

THE *DALE* SUPREME COURT BRIEF

The lawyers' brief for James Dale argued that the freedom of expressive association did not grant the BSA an unqualified right to select its leaders in defiance of a state civil rights law. The inclusion of a human being into an organization cannot be translated into speech; otherwise, the Dale brief asserted, "all discriminators could raise a First Amendment shield to any equal opportunity statute" (Brief for Respondent, 11). The brief contested the assertion that the Boy Scouts was a private organization, citing its federal charter granted in 1916 and other benefits from the federal government such as tax exemption and supplies and equipment from the Department of Defense. In addition the brief cited the nearly 500 public schools and school-affiliated groups in New Jersey that sponsor scouting units and the benefits the Scouts receive from the state—exemption from state taxes and the waiver of registration fees for motor vehicles owned by local BSA councils. Thus, the Boy Scouts was different from other private organizations such as a Jewish dating service, an Asian American theater company, or a Croatian Cultural Society and could come within the ambit of a state public accommodation law barring discrimination.

Even if one were to grant that the Boy Scouts was a private organization, the Dale brief cited the *Roberts* doctrine: that the freedom of association was not an absolute right, that the government can impose certain limits in order to serve a compelling state interest not related to the suppression of ideas so long as those interests cannot be achieved through means significantly less restrictive of associational freedoms. The Boy Scouts thus had, according to the Dale brief, no unqualified right to select its leaders in defiance of a civil rights law that served a compelling state

interest, namely, New Jersey's interest in eliminating discrimination. "Expressive associations," the Dale brief claimed, "have no
unqualified right to select their leaders in defiance of civil rights
prohibitions"(Brief for Respondent, 22). Relying heavily on
Roberts, Dale's lawyers asserted the Court should ask if ending
the policy of excluding gays would "affect in any significant way
the members' ability to carry out their expressive purposes [and]
if so whether New Jersey's interest [anti-discrimination] out-
weighs any such burden" (Brief for Respondent, 17). From Dale's
perspective, the New Jersey antidiscrimination law did not interfere with the Boy Scouts' core purposes. The Boy Scouts did not
associate for the purpose of disseminating the belief that homosexuality was wrong. The Dale brief rejected the BSA claim that
condemnation of homosexuality could be inferred from the requirements that Boy Scouts be "clean" and "morally straight."
The phrase "morally straight" could not be read as a code word
for an antigay policy. The Boy Scout Code allowed its members to
have divergent views on a variety of matters, and in fact the Boy
Scouts discouraged scoutmasters from disseminating any views on
sexual matters.

Both the Dale brief and an amicus brief (filed by the American
Civil Liberties Union, the NAACP Legal Defense Fund, the National Organization of Women, People for the American Way, and
other civil liberties groups) argued that *Hurley* was not controlling. In that case the parade was clearly a traditional form of expressive activity and its organizers could control the message they
wished to convey. James Dale was excluded simply because of his
sexual orientation and not because he wished to alter the Boy
Scouts' message. The amicus brief stated, "The Boy Scouts would
like to read *Hurley* for the proposition that the state can never enforce its civil rights laws over the opposition of any organization
that purports to represent a set of values that conflicts with the
states' antidiscrimination goals. But the holding of Hurley clearly
does not go so far" (ACLU Amicus Brief, section I.B.). The heart

of Dale's position was that his inclusion in the Boy Scouts was only an incidental burden on the organization's right of expressive association, since his simple membership could not alone alter the BSA's message. Dale had given no indication that he intended to teach anything about homosexuality and pledged that he would follow the Boy Scouts' guidance to refer to the boys' parents any of their questions about religion or sex. From Dale's perspective the most pressing constitutional claim was New Jersey's compelling interest in ensuring equal opportunity and equal access to goods and services. Gays and lesbians are among those who have been denied equal opportunity to participate in American life. New Jersey's interest in protecting the rights of gay people was a compelling interest placing only a slight burden on the BSA's right of free expression.

A DIVIDED COURT SPEAKS

On June 28, 2000, the U.S. Supreme Court announced its decision in *Boy Scouts of America v. Dale* (530 U.S. 640). By a vote of 5–4, the Court overturned the New Jersey Supreme Court decision and upheld the Boy Scouts' right to expel James Dale. Writing for the majority, Chief Justice William Rehnquist accepted the Boy Scouts' definition of their own message as being in opposition to homosexuality. Rehnquist concluded that no court should impose its own interpretation of an organization's message, which is the business of its leaders. "As we give deference to an association's assertions regarding the nature of its expression," Rehnquist asserted, "we must also give deference to an association's view of what would impair its expression." Rehnquist acknowledged that the rights of expressive association could not be used as a shield to claim that the "mere acceptance of a member from a particular group would impair its message" (*Dale*, 640). Dale was not merely gay; he was the copresident of his college gay and lesbian organization and remained a gay rights activist.

In reaching this conclusion, Rehnquist relied strongly on *Hurley*. GLIB, claimed Rehnquist, was not excluded from the St. Patrick's Day parade because its members were gay. Rather, it was because of their insistence on marching behind the GLIB banner and imposing their own message on the parade. Accepting a gay activist as an adult leader would have the same effect and would interfere with the Boy Scouts' message.

Rehnquist took issue with the New Jersey court's claim that Dale could not have interfered with the Scouts' message because Boy Scout members do not "associate for the purpose of disseminating the belief that homosexuality is immoral" (160 N.J. 612, 734 A.2d 1223, 1999). Associations are granted First Amendment protections even if their "purpose" is not to disseminate a certain message. Just as the Veterans Council had no wish to speak publicly on the question of sexual orientation, neither did the Boy Scouts have to put their policy on the subject in full public view.

As long as an organization engages in expressive activity that could be impaired, it is granted First Amendment protection. Every member of the Boy Scouts does not have to agree with the group's policy for it to be an expressive association. The fact that the Boy Scouts has an official position is enough, and Dale's presence would burden it. As Rehnquist put it, "The Boy Scouts has a First Amendment right to choose to send one message but not the other. The fact that the organization does not trumpet its views from the housetops, or that it tolerates dissent within its ranks, does not mean that it receives no First Amendment protection" (*Dale*, 640).

Rehnquist acknowledged that the Court in *Roberts* and *Duarte* had recognized a state's compelling interest in eliminating discrimination against women. However, in those cases the Court had concluded that the enforcement of antidiscrimination laws did not interfere with the ideas that the organization sought to express. Unlike the presence of women in the Jaycees or the Rotary, Dale's presence as a gay activist in the Boy Scouts would, Rehnquist concluded, interfere with their message or their desire to send a muted one.

Writing for the four dissenters, Justice John Paul Stevens argued the Boy Scouts had to meet a higher standard than the majority had imposed to establish a First Amendment claim. Citing *Roberts* and *Rotary,* Stevens claimed that to prevail on an assertion of expressive association against a state's antidiscrimination claim, an association must not simply engage in "some kind" of expressive activity. It must openly avow an exclusionary membership policy or assert some connection between the group's exclusionary policy and its expressive activities. The question should be, according to Stevens, whether the group was organized for the specific expressive purposes that it could be forced to abandon if its exclusionary policy was voided. The Boy Scouts' policies, as Stevens interpreted them, had never clearly articulated "a single particular religious or moral philosophy when it comes to sexual orientation." Its stated policy excluding homosexuals found in a 1978 statement on "policies and procedures relating to homosexuality and Scouting" was an internal memorandum and not circulated beyond the executive committee. It was written in the expectation that state antidiscrimination laws would someday protect homosexuals, but it also included a statement that it was a Scout's duty to "obey the laws."

The 1978 statement said only that homosexuality was not "appropriate." The memo made no effort, Stevens claimed, to connect homosexuality to "the myriad of publicly declared values and creeds of the BSA." Stevens dismissed other policy statements issued between 1991 and 1993. These were made after the Scouts had revoked Dale's membership and claimed that homosexuals do not provide a role model consistent with the expectations of scouting families. Stevens felt those statements taken together with their statements on tolerance and their view that sexual matters were not the Scouts' proper area made BSA's views on homosexuality "equivocal at best and incoherent at worst." In order to prevail in asserting the right of expressive association against a charge of violating an antidiscrimination law, "the organization must at least show it has adopted and advocated an unequivocal position inconsistent with a position advocacy or epitomized by the person whom the organization seeks to exclude." Stevens argued that the Court's review of whether an organization's views were sincerely held raised valid concerns. Nonetheless, he insisted, "unless one is prepared to turn the right to associate into a free pass out of antidiscrimination laws, an independent inquiry is a necessity" (*Dale*, S. Ct. 2446).

Stevens found the case clearly distinguishable from *Hurley*: "Unlike GLIB, Dale did not carry a banner or a sign; he did not distribute any fact sheet; and he expressed no intent to send any message. . . . The only apparent explanation for the majority holding, then," Stevens concluded, hinting at an ideological bias, "is that homosexuals are simply so different from the rest of society that their presence alone—unlike any other individual—should be singled out for special First Amendment treatment" (*Dale*, S. Ct. 2470, 2476).

In his dissent Justice David Souter pointed out that *Dale* was not a free speech case but an expressive association one. In free speech cases such as *Hurley,* the group's position must be taken at face value. An expressive association case, Souter argued, must be based upon "a clear position to be advocated over time in an unequivocal way." This distinction was far clearer to Souter and the dissenters than it was to Rehnquist and the majority.

The Court's decision in *Dale* was a significant departure from *Roberts.* In *Roberts* the Court took the responsibility of interpreting the Jaycees' message and found no reason why the inclusion of women would impair it; in *Dale* the Court accepted on face value exactly how Boy Scouts interpreted their own message. The influence of *Hurley* was quite apparent in the Rehnquist opinion. Dale's presence in the Boy Scouts had become the equivalent of the GLIB banner in the St. Patrick's Day parade. His very presence as a gay assistant scoutmaster was enough to cloud the Boy Scouts' position on homosexual behavior and to interfere with its desire to avoid discussion of sexual issues between the adult leaders and the young Scouts.

THE COURT'S CRITICS SPEAK

Some critics of the Court's decision in *Dale* claimed that the reliance on *Hurley* was misplaced. The parade organizers in Boston did not exclude marchers because they were gay; they excluded them because they insisted upon marching behind their own banner. It was the banner, not the individuals as gay people, that interfered with the parade organizers' right to control their own message. Dale was excluded not because of his insistence on bringing his message into the Scouts but as a consequence of being an openly gay man. The Court did not fully explain why the Scouts would not expel a heterosexual who supported gay rights and opposed the exclusionary policy yet would expel Dale, who had the same views but was gay himself. Thus, Dale was a walking billboard as a result of his homosexuality, and his exclusion was not based upon his message but his sexual identity. This kind of discrimination was exactly what the New Jersey statute was designed to prevent. Consequently, the critics felt that as a result of *Dale* any group professing a particular moral message could exclude gay members under the banner of expressive association. One critic imagined that *Dale* could open the floodgates for all kinds of organizations seeking to protect their discriminatory policies behind the banner of expressive association: "Almost all associations—every business, every apartment complex, every residential neighborhood—that wants to discriminate should now be able to file an action under the First Amendment and to demand strict scrutiny of virtually every discrimination law applied to it. . . . Why shouldn't states be obliged to accommodate discrimination—exemptions for, say, small businesses or small neighborhoods genuinely dedicated to expressing the belief that blacks, Jews, or women don't belong in the same places as whites, Christians, or men?" (Rubenfeld 2000, 767, 812).

Some argued that the decision was not merely a misreading of past precedents but a disparagement of gay rights. The Court in *Roberts* found a compelling need to eliminate gender discrimination, whereas in both *Hurley* and *Dale* the same weight was not granted to the claims of homosexuals. If antidiscrimination laws served a compelling state interest against the claims of expressive association, were the rights of women more compelling than the rights of gays (Hargis 2000, 1189)? It was not clear from *Dale* if the Court felt that it had only weak interest in protecting discrimination on the basis of anything other than race, gender, national origin, and illegitimacy.

THE DEFENDERS OF THE COURT SPEAK

Defenders of the *Dale* decision saw it as an important victory for freedom of association. They feared that if an organization "as potent as the Boy Scouts can be made to bend to the state's will, how much more likely is it that weak and unpopular groups might be forced to capitulate?" (Carpenter 2001, 1515). The doctrine of expressive association should allow unpopular and despised groups to bolster their strength and to gain a greater hearing for their message. State antidiscrimination laws could become a means to dampen such messages. A militant gay rights group may want to exclude all heterosexuals; a Black Nationalist group may want to exclude whites; a Muslim group may not invite non-Muslims.

Richard Epstein argues that the *Dale* dissenters' insistence that an expressive association claim must be based upon a clear and unequivocal message "restricts full protection for expressive liberties only to those organizations that adopt extreme social positions." Large mainstream organizations often must take nuanced and equivocal positions in order to avoid splits and possible disintegration. Expressive liberties must be afforded such groups, as they serve an important function in maintaining social cohesion. The Boy Scouts may realize the concerns of parents, justified or not, about placing their boys under the close supervision of avowed homosexuals on scouting trips. At the same time the Scouts may wish to avoid taking an unequivocal public position on homosexuality for fear of being seen as bigoted. As Epstein puts it, "In order to hold their complex coalition together, it may make sense for the Boy Scouts to gravitate toward a compromise that proves more stable in practice than coherent in theory. Go soft on the formal and explicit denunciations of gay practices, but nonetheless keep those practices out of the Scout troops in order to meet these parental demands" (Epstein 2000, 119). Why shouldn't freedom of association include First Amendment law in its suspicion of content-based distinctions? Freedom of association, Epstein says, should not protect only organizations with "more emphatic prejudiced and bigoted views" (Epstein 2000, 119).

Apart from the substantive philosophical and political concerns was the issue of whether *Dale* was consistent with *Roberts*. It is hard to argue that there wasn't an important break between the two cases. The *Dale* Court did shift the definition of what constitutes group expression in order to gain constitutional protection. Under *Roberts*, expressive association claims received close scrutiny and had to be based upon the views that brought the group together, that is, views that were at the core of the association's tenets. Under *Dale*, constitutional protection could broadly embrace "the ability of the group to express those, and only those, views that it intends to express" (*Dale*, 648). The *Dale* definition gives to associations much of the same protection afforded to individual expression under the First Amendment. *Dale* did grant to the leaders of expressive associations greater autonomy over the control of their message than was apparent in *Roberts*. Chief Justice Rehnquist simply accepted the Boy Scouts' assertion that homosexual conduct was inconsistent with its notion of what was "morally straight" and gave "deference to an association's assertions regarding the nature of its expression . . . [and to] an association's view of what would impair its expression." Was it simply Dale's gayness that impaired the Boy Scouts' message? Was Dale's homosexuality "so inherently expressive that admitting him to the Scouts would violate the organization's right against compelled association" (McGowan 2001, 121)? Yet the *Dale* Court did not dispute the finding in *Duarte* that antidiscrimination laws serve a compelling state interest and can apply to a private organization so long as they are unrelated to the suppression of ideas and are the least restrictive means of achieving that compelling interest.

The Legacy of the *Dale* Decision

Did the *Dale* Court develop a theory that balances the freedom of expressive association against the state's interest in antidiscrimination? Although the Court did say that expressive associations may not "erect a shield against antidiscrimination simply by asserting that mere acceptance of a member from a particular group would impair its message," it implied that this case was different because Dale was not simply gay but "openly gay" and a "gay rights activist." As Rehnquist put it, "The presence of an avowed homosexual and gay rights activist in an assistant scoutmaster's uniform sends a distinctly different message from the presence of a heterosexual assistant scoutmaster who is on record as disagreeing with Boy Scouts policy. The Boy Scouts has a First Amendment right to choose to send one message but not the other."

It is not clear from the Court's opinion whether the Scouts would have had the same First Amendment protection were they to exclude a gay who was not an activist. If Dale were merely "openly gay" or an "avowed" homosexual and not a gay activist, would the Boy Scouts have the same First Amendment claim? Despite Dale's statement that he would not use the Boy Scouts to proselytize for gay rights, would his very presence then send a message? Was any openly gay person, regardless of his views about the appropriateness or morality of homosexuality, a walking symbol so that groups that either abhor homosexuality or wish to say nothing about such issues could disassociate from him? The Court felt it did not have to address this question of whether being openly gay was a message in and of itself. Neither did the majority nor the dissenting opinion address the question whether the government had the same compelling interest in eradicating discrimination against homosexuals as it does on the basis of other characteristics such as race and gender.

The *Dale* Court did not present a coherent constitutional theory of expressive association, nor did it shed much light on the status of gay rights. The decision did interpret the right of expressive association more broadly than it had in the *Roberts* trilogy. Under *Dale*, the right is available for an organization that does not associate for the express purpose of disseminating a particular message. An organization can propound that message implicitly; it can tolerate dissenting views and yet continue an exclusionary policy.

The case represented another clash between social equality and free expression when both have claims on the same organization. In *Hurley* and *Dale* the claims for gay equality foundered on the assertion of expressive association. In the *Roberts* trilogy, the Court deferred to the state's compelling interest in general equality. Were the Boy Scouts that different from the Jaycees, the Rotary, or the New York Athletic Club? Or was it Dale's gayness that determined the outcome of his case? The case can be looked at as protection from the long arm of state-enforced orthodoxy or as a barrier to full social recognition of the status of gay people. As Kathleen Sullivan put it, "How one views the decision normatively will turn on how one regards a private sphere that deviates from public constitutional values of tolerance and equality: as a desirable safeguard against centralized homogenization and orthodoxy like the protection of abstinence from flag salutes in *West Virginia State Board of Education v. Barnette* (1943) or as a dangerous backwater likely to undermine the public values that depend upon the alteration of social norms" (Sullivan 2001, 723).

During the civil rights battles of the 1950s and 1960s, when public accommodation law extended racial integration to restaurants, hotels, theaters, and sports arenas, it was clear that racial minorities and African Americans in particular were to be protected from a hostile white majority in the South. Given, however, the social opprobrium the Boy Scouts have suffered as a consequence of their policy, it is not clear in the twenty-first century who is outside the prevailing orthodoxy, James Dale or the Boy Scouts of America. Neither is it clear what group over time would benefit from the Court's decision. As Sullivan reflects, "There is a good argument that the extension of equal protection to gay men and lesbians need not extend all the way down into every private association in New Jersey in order to be effective and that the right of expressive gay organizations to exclude homophobes is an important implicit corollary of the decision" (Sullivan 2001, 741).

The Boy Scouts, for its part, has found *Dale* to be a mixed blessing. According to *Newsweek* magazine, the national membership in the Scouts dropped 4.5 percent in 2000 and by 7.8 percent in the Northeast (August 6, 2001). The organization found itself in the middle of the culture wars. As a consequence of the attention given to their policy of barring gays, several state and local governments have found ways to shun them. Connecticut dropped the Boy Scouts from the State Employee Charitable Campaign because of the group's antigay policy. The Connecticut comptroller, who oversees the charitable campaigns, took the action to ensure the robust administration of the Connecticut Gay Rights Law, which prohibits the use of state facilities in furtherance of discrimination. In July 2003 a federal appeals court upheld the Connecticut policy. But other funding sources have remained steady or increased. According to the United Way national organization, only thirty-five to forty-five chapters out of 1,400 refused to put the Scouts on their funding list. In Minnesota the Twin Cities United Way chapter donations marked specifically for the Scouts went up $500,000 a year after the *Dale* decision.

The Broward County School Board in Florida, which had a policy forbidding the use of school facilities by any group that discriminated on the basis of sexual orientation, voted to ban the Scouts from using school property. The Boy Scouts successfully challenged the action in federal district court. The district court ruled that for the school board to deny the Scouts the use of their facilities on the same basis as other private groups would violate the First Amendment. Although the school board could express its own view on intolerance on homosexuality, it could not punish the Boy Scouts for a contrary view (*Boy Scouts of America v. Till,* 136 Supp. 2d 1308 [S.D. Fla. 2001]). New York City school chancellor Harold O. Levy announced in December 2000 that the Boy Scouts could no longer use the public schools as sites for recruiting new members and that the organization was barred from bidding on school contracts; soon after that announcement Boy Scout membership in New York City dropped by half (press release, cited in Brown 2002, 481).

Despite the public clamor, the Boy Scouts refused to alter their policy. In February 2002 they issued a public statement that "homosexual conduct is inconsistent with the traditional values espoused in the Scout Oath and Law and an avowed homosexual cannot serve as a role model for the values of the Oath and Law"(press release, Boy Scouts of America, February 2, 2002). This statement was also a message to any chapter that might be considering altering its policy, as was the case with local chapters in New York and Rhode Island (quoted in Brown 2002, 496).

Others came to the Boy Scouts' defense. In June 2001 the Senate approved a bill introduced by Senator Jesse Helms (R–NC) that would withhold federal funds from public schools that denied "equal access" to the Boy Scouts and any other group that expressed its "disapproval of homosexuality." The final bill, the Boy Scouts of America Equal Access Act (210 U.S.C. 7905), required schools to allow the Scouts to use facilities on the same terms as other groups. Schools were, however, free to withhold sponsorship of the Scouts.

The treatment of the Scouts after *Dale* is in some ways reminiscent of the treatment of the Communist Party in the 1950s. Many private groups shunned the party and its members. Universities, unions, bar associations, and the entertainment industry refused to hire its members. To be a member of the Communist Party was not necessarily illegal, but anyone so exposed would be treated as a pariah. People and institutions for various reasons did not want to be associated with Communists and asserted their right of nonassociation. Private groups who refuse to assist the Scouts may be asserting their own rights of nonassociation in the same way the entertainment industry refused to hire Communists.

What about the role of government? In *NAACP v. Alabama*, in order to protect NAACP members from private discrimination, the Court rejected Alabama's demand that the NAACP disclose its membership list. The Court claimed that disclosure would subject members to "economic reprisal, loss of employment, threat of physical coercion, and other manifestations of public hostility." The Court did not think it was crucial if the fear of punishment for unpopular association came "not from state action but from private community pressures." What mattered was "the interplay of governmental and private action, for it is only after the initial exertion of state power represented by the production order that private action takes hold" (*NAACP v. Alabama*, 462). Governmental intervention in the disclosure of members of the Communist Party served a sufficiently important interest, whereas disclosure of members of the NAACP did not. The distinction rested on the nature of the associations. The Communist Party constituted a potential threat to the political order; the NAACP did not.

Could government have any role in helping private citizens to support their right of nonassociation? During the Cold War, the FBI and HUAC routinely provided information to various businesses about the political associations of employees and potential employees. They could claim that by exposing Communists, they were pursuing a legitimate national security concern. Today, some agencies argue the government should shun the Boy Scouts in order to support equal protection. Critics of blacklisting argued that the practice had the effect of chilling free speech and forcing individuals to pay a price for their heretical views. Supporters of the Boy Scouts can claim that boycotts of the Scouts are forcing them indirectly to abandon the constitutional rights granted to them by the Court in *Dale*. Supporters of the blacklist argued that the Communist Party forfeited some its associational rights by its advocacy of forceful overthrow and its close ties to the Soviet Union. Today supporters of shunning or blacklisting the Boy Scouts would say if the Scouts have the right to determine their own membership, others have the right to shun them for excluding gays. Is this a moral equivalency? At what point is the state limited in restricting associational rights? Anticommunism was considered a compelling state interest in the 1950s. Is the protection of gay rights a similarly compelling interest in the twenty-first century that would justify some limits on associational freedom?

CALIFORNIA DEMOCRATIC PARTY V. JONES

Two days before the Supreme Court announced its decision in *Dale*, it decided another case related to the rights of political parties, expressive association, and the right not to associate: *California Democratic Party v. Jones* (530 U.S. 567; 2000). In this case the Court considered California's blanket primary rule, enacted in 1996 by referendum as Proposition 198. It changed California's closed primary system, whereby voters could vote only in the primary of the party for which they were registered. Under the blanket primary each voter's ballot listed candidates regardless of party affiliation and allowed the voter to choose among them. The candidate of each party who won the most votes would be that party's nominee for the general election. For example, a voter could vote for a Republican in the gubernatorial primary, a Democrat in the primary for attorney general, and a Green Party candidate for state treasurer. A voter's party affiliation had no bearing on what candidate he/she could select as that party's nominee.

The case represented conflict between the voters' right to associate with the party of their choice in a particular primary contest and the party's right to exclude voters not formally affiliated with them. All of California's political parties opposed the blanket primary, fearing that it would let outsiders select their nominees. As one opposition pamphlet put it, "Allowing members of one party a large voice in choosing another party's nominee—which is what Proposition 198 would do—is like letting UCLA's football team choose USC's head coach" (quoted in Persily 2001, 775). The parties were concerned that voters from one party would cross over and vote for the weaker candidate of another party hoping to defeat that candidate in the general election. They also feared that if one party had an uncontested primary, the voters of that party would enter another party's primary in order to nominate a candidate who was least offensive to them.

The state of California claimed seven compelling interests to justify Proposition 198. These were (1) producing elected officials who better represented the electorate; (2) expanding the candidate debate beyond partisan concerns; (3) enfranchising independents and voters in one-party districts; (4) allowing voters regardless of party affiliation an equal choice at the ballot box; (5) expanding the choices of all voters with a wider array of candidates; (6) increasing voter participation; (7) protecting privacy by not forcing voters to reveal their party affiliation.

The federal district court that initially heard the case concluded that the blanket primary did not impose a significant burden on the parties' associational rights. The district court found that California's interest in "enhancing the democratic nature of the election process and the representativeness of elected officials" was a compelling state interest. The district court argued that political parties' associational rights differ from those of private clubs and associations. States have substantial regulatory authority over parties in setting election and voter registration rules that they do not have over private associations. The district court did not find sufficient evidence of crossover voting, saying that only 10 to 25 percent of voters crossed over, which was not enough to change the outcome of the election. On the other hand, the state's interests in opening up the electoral process to more voters, granting more popular accountability, and increasing the chances of more moderate candidates were compelling (*California Democratic Party v. Jones*, 984, F. Supp. 1297–1301; 1997). The Ninth Circuit Court of Appeals affirmed the district court.

THE SCALIA OPINION

The Supreme Court overruled the lower court and declared this election law unconstitutional. Justice Scalia, writing for the majority, conceded that the states did have a role to play in structuring and monitoring elections. They could require parties to use primary elections in selecting candidates, could require parties to demonstrate a modicum of support before they could be on the ballot, and could require a reasonable period for party registration before a primary election. However, Scalia denied that party affairs are exclusively public affairs and that parties are afforded First Amendment associational rights. Proposition 198, as Scalia saw it, adulterated the candidate selection process, which is the basic function of a political party. Political parties had the right to allow only their members to participate in the selection of their party's nominees. The state of California had argued that the blanket primary required candidates to appeal to a larger segment of the electorate. Scalia claimed this interest "reduced to nothing more than a stark repudiation of freedom of political association: Parties should not be free to select their own nominees because these nominees, and the position taken by those nominees, will not be congenial to the majority." Scalia considered such an interest too weak against a claim of freedom of association. Relying on *Eu, Timmons,* and *La Follette,* Scalia stated that political parties have a constitutional right to limit that association to those with whom they share common goals and values. "In no area," Scalia stated, "is the political association's right to exclude more important than in the process of selecting its nominee. That process often determines the party's positions on the most significant public policy issues of the day, and even when those positions are predetermined it is the nominee who becomes the party's ambassador" (*Jones,* 2000, 575). Even if the state's interests were compelling, Scalia did not think the blanket primary was narrowly tailored to meet those interests. He suggests instead a nonpartisan blanket primary (used in Louisiana), in which the voters, regardless of party affiliation, could select any candidate, regardless of party. The top two (or however many the state prescribed) for each office would become candidates in the general election.

Although Scalia recognized that Jones did not "require us to determine the constitutionality of open primaries"(*Jones,* 2000, 578 fn. 8), he distinguished between the blanket primary and the open primary. In the open primary, where a voter can choose in which party's primary to vote, the vote at least affiliates the individual for the time he or she is in the voting booth. This distinction may be a bit parlous, and a future Court might find the open primary inconsistent with *Jones,* putting the primary systems of many states at risk.

THE STEVENS DISSENT

In his dissent Justice John Paul Stevens argued, "The so-called 'right not to associate' that the Court relies upon . . . is simply inapplicable to participation in a state election." Stevens distinguished a primary election, which he considered a public affair, from a caucus, convention, and other internal processes of a political party. He did not believe that the right not to associate should limit a state from broadening voter participation in "state-run, state-financed elections." Stevens distinguished this power from *Tashjian,* when the Republicans were prevented from having independents participate in their primaries. "When a State acts not to limit democratic participation, but to expand the ability of individuals to participate in the democratic process, it is acting not as foe for the First Amendment but as friend and ally" (*Jones,* 2000, 599). Scalia found Stevens's effort to reconcile *Tashjian* with his dissent in *Jones* unpersuasive: "Combining *Tashjian* with the dissent's rule affirms a party's constitutional right to allow outsiders to select its candidates, but denies a party's constitutional right to reserve candidate selection to its own members. The First Amendment would thus guarantee a party's right to lose its identity, but not to preserve it" (*Jones,* 2000, 576).

The debate between Scalia and Stevens in *Jones* represents more than judicial differences. It is a clash of democratic values. Scalia believes the associational rights of parties, their ability to preserve their autonomy and control their nomination process, to be far more important than the state's interest in broadening voter participation and choice. Stevens does not see associational rights of parties in elections as having the same constitutional claim as would a private association. For Stevens, the democratic rights of the electorate trump the associational rights of a group. Scalia's argument is more Tocquevillian in its concern about the dangers of majoritarianism. Scalia would not allow a majority (in this case the voters for Proposition 198) to determine how political parties can order their affairs. Scalia rejected the state's argument that the blanket primary would produce elected officials who better represent the electorate and would bring in disenfranchised independent voters. He found those interests "reduced to nothing more than a stark repudiation of freedom of political association" (*Jones,* 2000, 577). A majority of voters may wish to have the chance to jump into another party's primary at their own whim. Scalia would give much greater deference to a party's right to immunize itself from majority rule in its desire to shape its message and pick its nominees. Those who champion freedom of association see it as an important barrier to social and political standardization.

Stevens's argument is more consistent with the twentieth-century view that more democracy is generally more desirable than less democracy and that state intervention is often justified to secure the demands of a majority. Scalia, like Tocqueville, sees private associations as necessary buffers between the state and the individual. Proposition 198 gives the state substantial power to determine party affairs; Scalia would place serious limitations on that power. This debate is a variation on the tension between liberty and equality that we saw in the antidiscrimination cases. Opening up the political process to more voters and giving them greater choices is a form a greater equality, and it requires more intrusive state intervention into political association.

Critics of Scalia's opinion did not think its analysis could sustain the distinction among various primary systems. An open primary, for example, limits a voter to one party's ballot but to a party of the voter's choice. Thus, voters join a party for one election. What, then, is the distinction when a voter traverses a ballot in a blanket primary to affiliate moment by moment rather than for one day in an open primary?

In both *Jones* and *Dale*, decided in the first year of the twenty-first century, the Court breathed more life into freedom of association. What remains unclear is to what degree freedom of association is yoked to freedom of speech and to what degree it has its own properties. In *Jones* and its predecessor cases, the Court did not explicitly define freedom of association as granting the right of autonomy of political parties but as derived from the need for free speech in the political arena.

CONCLUSION

There is still much to be settled in this area. For example, it is difficult to reconcile *Jones* with *Roberts*. In *Roberts* the Court denied the Jaycees' claim to freedom of association because the local chapters were neither small nor selective, and "the maintenance of the association involves the participation of strangers to that relationship" (*Roberts*, 609). Political parties are far from being small and selective and can involve the participation of millions of strangers. What would give either the Jaycees or political parties any associational rights is linked to protection of their message. This is a rule much more suited to a First Amendment claim than one uniquely suited for associations. The Court in *Roberts* did look at the function and nature of the Jaycees as well as its message. In *Hurley*, *Dale*, and *Jones*, the emphasis was more upon the relationship between message and membership, not the function of the associations involved. If the Court were to make a functional analysis of an association, it would have to ask what comprises its purpose and what social interests would be advanced by any restrictions on its independence (Issacharoff 2001, 274).

The terrain of the freedom of association has been mapped out only in the broadest strokes. The Court will have to refine this doctrine in the twenty-first century and find the proper balance between society's competing values.

REFERENCES AND FURTHER READING

Barry, Seamus K. 2001. "Stealing the Covers: The Supreme Court's Ban on Blanket Primary Elections and Its Effect on a Citizen's First Amendment Right 'to Petition the Government for a Redress of Grievances.'" *Common Law Conspectus* 9: 71–85.

Bernstein, David E. 2001. "Perspectives on Constitutional Exemptions to Civil Rights Laws: *Boy Scouts of America v. Dale:* The Right of Expressive Association and Private Universities' Racial Preferences and Speech Codes." *William and Mary Bill of Rights Journal* 9 (April): 619–643.

Boop, James, Jr., and Richard E. Coleson. 2002. "The First Amendment Needs No Reform: Protecting Liberty from Campaign Finance 'Reformers.'" *Catholic University Law Review* 51 (Spring): 785–837.

Bronson, Brian Patrick. 2001. "The California Open Primary Act Unconstitutionally Burdens Political Parties' Associational Rights: *California Democratic Party v. Jones.*" *Duquesne Law Review* 39 (Summer): 845–863.

Brown, Jennifer Gerarda. 2002. "Facilitating Boycotts of Discriminatory Organizations through an Informed Association Statute." *Minnesota Law Review* 87 (December): 481–509.

Carpenter, Dale. 2001. "Expressive Association and Anti-Discrimination Law After *Dale:* A Tripartite Approach." *Minnesota Law Review* 85 (June): 1515–1589.

Chemerinsky, Erwin, and Catherine Fisk. 2001. "Perspectives on Constitutional Exemptions to Civil Rights Laws: *Boy Scouts of America v. Dale:* The Expressive Interest of Associations." *William and Mary Bill of Rights Journal* 9 (April): 595–617.

Endejann, N. Nicole. 2001. "Coming Out Is a Free Pass: *Boy Scouts of America v. Dale.*" *Akron Law Review* 34: 893–917.

Epstein, Richard A. 2000. "The Constitutional Perils of Moderation: The Case of the Boy Scouts." *Southern California Law Review* 74 (November): 119–143.

———. 2000. "Free Association: The Incoherence of Antidiscrimination Laws." *National Review* (9 October): 38–40.

Farber, Daniel A. 2001. "Speaking in the First Person Plural: Expressive Associations and the First Amendment." *Minnesota Law Review* 85 (June): 1483–1513.

Flynn, Taylor. 2001. "Don't Ask Us to Explain Ourselves, Don't Tell Us What to Do: The Boy Scouts' Exclusion of Gay Members and the Necessity of Independent Judicial Review." *Stanford Law and Policy Review* 12 (Winter): 87–96.

Fowler, Christopher C. 2001. "The Supreme Court Endorses 'Invidious Discrimination': *Boy Scouts of America v. Dale* Creates a Constitutional Right to Exclude Gay Men." *Journal of Law and Policy* 9: 929–1000.

Garnett, Richard. 2001. "The Story of Henry Adams' Soul: Education and the Expression of Associations." *Minnesota Law Review* 85 (June): 1841–1883.

Hargis, Christopher S. 2000. "*Romer, Hurley,* and *Dale:* How the Supreme Court Languishes with 'Special Rights.'" *Kentucky Law Journal* 89 (Summer): 1189–1225.

Hills, Roderick M., Jr. 2003. "The Constitutional Rights of Private Governments." *New York University Law Review* 78 (April): 144–238.

Issacharoff, Samuel. 2001. "Private Parties with Public Purposes: Political Parties, Associational Freedoms, and Partisan Competition." *Columbia Law Review* 101 (March): 274–313.

MacDonald, Teresa. 2002. "*California Democratic Party v. Jones:* Invalidation of the Blanket Primary." *Pepperdine Law Review* 29: 319–341.

Madigan, James P. 2001. "Questioning the Coercive Effect of Self-Identifying Speech." *Iowa Law Review* 87 (October): 75–144.

McGowan, David. 2001. "Making Sense of *Dale.*" *Constitutional Commentary* 18 (Spring): 121–175.

McGuire, Daniel E. 2002. "*Boy Scouts of America v. Dale* and Its Implications in and out of the Courtroom." *Villanova Law Review* 47: 387–421.

O'Quinn, John C. 2000. "How Solemn Is the Duty of the Mighty Chief: Mediating the Conflict in *Boy Scouts of America v. Dale.*" *Harvard Journal of Law and Public Policy* 34: 319–367.

Patrick, Jeremy. 2001. "A Merit Badge for Homophobia? The Boy Scouts Earn the Right to Exclude Gays in *Boy Scouts of America v. Dale.*" *Law and Sexuality: A Review of Lesbian, Gay, Bisexual, and Transgender Legal Issues* 10: 93–121.

Paulsen, Michael Stokes. 2001. "Scouts, Families, and Schools." *Minnesota Law Review* 85 (June): 1917–1955.

Persily, Nathaniel. 2001. "Toward a Functional Defense of Political Party Autonomy." *New York University Law Review* 76: 750–824.

Powers, Elizabeth A. 2001. "The Freedom of Expressive Association, an Organization's Right to Choose What Not to Say: *Boy Scouts of America v. Dale.*" *Florida Law Review* 53 (April): 399–408.

Rubenfeld, Jed. 2000. "The First Amendment's Purpose." *Stanford Law Review* 53 (April): 767–832.

Sullivan, Kathleen M. 2001. "Sex, Money, and Groups: Free Speech and Association Decisions in the October 1999 Term." *Pepperdine Law Review* 28: 723–746.

Tribe, Laurence H. 2001. "Disentangling Symmetries: Speech, Association, Parenthood." *Pepperdine Law Review* 28: 641–665.

Udell, Colin O'Connor. 1998. "Intimate Association: Resurrecting a Hybrid Right." *Texas Journal of Women and the Law* 7 (Spring): 231–285.

5

KEY PEOPLE,
CASES, AND EVENTS

Adler v. Board of Education (1952)

In the early 1950s most public institutions required that employees take a loyalty oath swearing not only fidelity to the Constitution but also denial of any membership in the Communist Party or any other subversive organization. Reflecting the strong anticommunist consensus of those years, the Supreme Court in *Adler* upheld a loyalty oath for teachers. It accepted the argument that membership in the Communist Party could make someone unfit for a teaching position or a government job. The Supreme Court later overruled the case in *Keyishian v. Board of Regents* (1967).

American Civil Liberties Union (ACLU)

One of the leading legal defense organizations in the United States to champion the cause of civil liberties. In the *Dale* case, however, the ACLU felt that the imperatives of antidiscrimination trumped freedom of association. It joined other groups in an amicus brief arguing that "any incidental burden on the Boy Scouts' freedom of expressive association is outweighed by the state's compelling interest in ensuring equality. In banning sexual orientation discrimination, New Jersey sought to include in ordinary life a group of Americans unfairly excluded from much of it."

Aptheker v. Secretary of State (1964)

One of several Supreme Court decisions in the 1960s that reflected greater skepticism over the government's power to restrict the liberty of individuals in the name of national security. In this case the Court struck down as a restriction on the right to travel a provision of the Internal Security Act of 1950 that denied passports to members of the Communist Party. Although not an explicit freedom of association case, the decision does limit the power of the government to punish mere membership in an unpopular organization.

Barenblatt v. United States (1959)

In this case the Court backed away from its criticism of the charter of the House Un-American Activities Committee and its concern about exposure for exposure's sake. Taking a more cautionary approach to the rights of the congressional committee, the Court denied that Barenblatt had a First Amendment right not to discuss his association with the Communist Party. The Court granted Congress the right to inquire into activities of the Communist Party and to Barenblatt's membership in it, since the party advocated the right to overthrow the government by any means possible.

Bates v. City of Little Rock (1960)

A case that followed the Court's groundbreaking freedom of association decision in *NAACP v. Alabama* (1958). As in that earlier case, the Court upheld the right of the NAACP not to disclose its membership list as a requirement of a local licensing tax, since exposing membership in this civil rights organization during that period could subject someone to serious economic, social, or even physical harm. In writing for the majority, Justice Potter Stewart sounded a loud tocsin for freedom of association. Stewart announced that "it is now beyond dispute that freedom of association for the purpose of advancing ideas and airing grievances is protected by the Due Process Clause from invasion by the States."

Blacklisting

The policy of blacklisting, practiced largely in the entertainment industry during the 1950s, prohibited the employment of persons thought to be members of the Communist Party or its sympathizers. People could have their names removed from the blacklist if they came forward to the House Un-American Activities Committee, confessed that they were not members of the Communist Party, and revealed the names of those whom they knew in the party. The blacklist was broken in 1959 when Kirk Douglas hired onetime Communist Dalton Trumbo to write the screenplay for the film *Spartacus* without any reprisals at the box office.

Blanket Primary

A primary rule adopted by California in 1998 whereby voters can select among a party's candidates on an office-by-office basis. Consequently, a voter might decide to vote for a Democrat in a gubernatorial primary and a Republican in a primary for attorney general. The Supreme Court declared in *California Democratic Party v. Jones* (see below) that the system violated a party's autonomy and its freedom of association.

Boy Scout Oath

The Boy Scouts of America justified their refusal to hire gay scoutmasters on the basis that to do so violated the organization's oath and its right of expressive association. The oath read: "On my honor I will do my best; To do my duty to God and my country and to obey the Scout Law; To help other people at all times; To keep myself physically strong, mentally awake, and morally straight." The Scouts claimed that homosexual conduct was inconsistent with the phrase "morally straight." This was a central issue in *Boy Scouts of America v. Dale* (see below).

Boy Scouts of America v. Dale (2000)

Landmark Supreme Court decision on freedom of association. The Court, by a 5–4 vote, declared that the New Jersey public accommodation law forbidding discrimination on the basis of sexual orientation violated the Scouts' freedom of association. The Court accepted the Scouts' right to define their own message and their own definition of "morally straight." The Court reaffirmed that control of membership was related to control over message and that both were essential to freedom of association.

Brennan, William J.

Associate justice of the Supreme Court (1956–1990) appointed by President Dwight D. Eisenhower. Brennan was one of the most influential justices of his era, a close colleague of Chief Justice Earl Warren, and a strong liberal voice on the Court. As the author of the Court's opinion in *Roberts v. United States Jaycees*, Brennan wrote one of the most important opinions in freedom of association law. He constructed the distinction between intimate association and expressive association. In the *Roberts* case he made it clear that freedom of association was not absolute and that compelling government interests such as gender discrimination could override it.

California Democratic Party v. Jones (2000)

Landmark Supreme Court decision decided two days before *Dale*. In this case the Court declared that California's blanket primary system was unconstitutional. Writing for the majority, Justice Antonin Scalia pointed out that the system did not serve a compelling state interest and violated the associational rights of a political party to control its decisions and membership. The ruling is considered a large step in granting associational freedom to political parties and protecting party identity against state laws that may hinder it.

Cato Institute

Libertarian think tank that filed with other groups an important amicus curiae brief in the *Dale* case. The brief argued for a broad definition of private expressive associations and feared the use of antidiscrimination laws that restrict the membership choices of any noncommercial expressive association. The brief argued that the burden of proof should be on the states to prove that any entity was a public accommodation with restricted associational rights.

Civic Associations

A vast array of nongovernmental organizations, from those with a global reach such as Amnesty International to churches and neighborhood organizations. Civic associations are considered essential to developing the habits of self-government in a free society. These are also voluntary organizations where people are free to join and participate or not. Many have a loose formal structure and no restrictions on membership; others may require specific qualification for membership and adherence to a set of rules and policies.

Civil Rights Act of 1964

A landmark piece of legislation in the struggle for civil rights, initiated by President John F. Kennedy and eventually signed by President Lyndon B. Johnson. Section II of this law prohibits discrimination on the basis of race in places of public accommodation even though they are privately owned. This was largely directed at restaurants, stores, hotels and motels, theaters, and sports arenas in the South that discriminated against African Americans. The law did not apply to private and other organizations closed to the public.

Civil Society

A network of intimate, expressive, and associational institutions that serve as a buffer between the individual and the state. Some consider their freedom from government interference essential to a democracy. Others argue that certain compelling public interests, such as nondiscrimination, justify government intervention and regulation of this aspect of community life. In the debates over freedom of association, there is great division over when the internal lives of private associations should be subject to public norms.

Closed Primary

A primary in which only registered members of a particular party can vote. Party leaders often prefer this system. It is designed to maintain party unity and coherence by keeping independents and members of other parties from participating in the party's nominating process.

Communist Party of the United States of America

Founded in 1919, soon after the Russian revolution, the American Communist Party maintained close ties to the Soviet Union, endorsed the principle of forceful revolution, and unfailingly supported Soviet foreign policy. During the Cold War it was subject to numerous prosecutions under the Smith Act and the Internal Security Act. Although the Supreme Court upheld the convictions of its top leaders under the Smith Act in *Dennis v. United States* (1951), the Court eventually ruled in subsequent cases that mere membership in the party was not a crime. One had to be actively engaged in an organization's illegal activities to be legally liable. By the early 1960s, the government ceased most of its legal attacks on the party, which was by then a shattered organization.

Communist Party of the United States v. Subversive Activities Control Board (1961)

A divided Supreme Court by a 5–4 vote upheld a SACB rule requiring the Communist Party to register with the attorney general as a "Communist-action organization." The Court ruled that the freedom of speech and association did not prevent Congress "from requiring the filing of membership lists by organizations substantially dominated or controlled by foreign powers controlling the world Communist movement." This ruling, however, was never enforced, since future Court decisions ruled that such registration would violate the privilege of self-incrimination protected by the Fifth Amendment.

Dale, James

A longtime member of the Boy Scouts, who, when he came out as a gay man while attending college, was dismissed from his job as an assistant scoutmaster. Dale brought suit under a New Jersey law that prohibited discrimination on the basis of sexual orientation. Although he was successful in the New Jersey state court, in the landmark case *Boy Scouts of America v. Dale* (see above) the U.S. Supreme Court in 2000 upheld the right of the Boy Scouts to dismiss Dale under their right of expressive association.

De Jonge v. State of Oregon (1937)

This case was an early watershed in the development of freedom of association jurisprudence. De Jonge was charged with violating Oregon's criminal syndicalism law by participating in a meeting called by the Communist Party. In a unanimous decision written by Chief Justice Charles Evans Hughes, the Court declared the "right of peaceable assembly is a right cognate to those of free speech and press and is equally fundamental." Many have found that the seeds of freedom of association are found in the First Amendment's freedom of assembly.

Democratic Party of the United States v. Wisconsin ex rel. La Follette et al. (1981)

This was an important decision in establishing that the autonomy of political parties was embraced under freedom of association. The Court sided with the Democratic National Convention in its refusal to seat delegates selected in open primary elections. In the majority opinion written by Justice Potter Stewart, the Court ruled that under freedom of association a political party could protect itself from the participation of non–party members. Stewart declared that freedom of association "presupposes the freedom to identify with the people who constitute the association." Although this decision cast doubt on the future of all open primary elections, the Court ruled only on the right of a national party to set conditions for selection of convention delegates.

Due Process Clause

The Fourteenth Amendment declares that no state shall "deprive any person of life, liberty or property, without due process of law." The Court has interpreted the due process clause as incorporating the commands of the First Amendment and applying them to the states. In *NAACP v. Alabama*, freedom of association, considered instrumental to the First Amendment, was also incorporated into due process and made binding upon state and local law.

Emerson, Thomas I.

Political theorist and constitutional scholar Thomas I. Emerson raised serious doubts that freedom of association was an independent constitutional right. He thought that the concept was too vague and could be "stretched to cover so many things, and be limited by so many qualifications, as to be meaningless." He argued that the right should be clearly enveloped in the First Amendment as an extension of the right of expression. His concept was later adopted by the Supreme Court as expressive association and has become the most important and well-developed dimension of associational freedom.

Eu v. San Francisco County Democratic Central Committee (1989)

An important Supreme Court decision linking the autonomy of political parties to freedom of association. In this case the Court struck down a California law prohibiting party organizations from endorsing candidates in a primary. The Court held that the law served no compelling state interest, interfered with the parties' right to color their own messages, and infringed upon their freedom of association. The case was important in the development of constitutional doctrine that primary elections had to respect the autonomy of parties and were not exclusively matters of state power.

Expressive Association

The dimension of freedom of association most closely linked to freedom of speech. Expressive association is the right to associate with others in pursuit of common social, economic, educational, religious, and cultural ends. The right to associate with others for expressive purposes makes freedom of association instrumental to First Amendment rights of free speech and does not define the right of association as having its own intrinsic value apart from the First Amendment. The right of expressive association was central to the Court's decision in *Dale* to allow the Boy Scouts to define their own message and membership policy in regard to homosexual members.

Federalist No. 10

Written by James Madison, *Federalist* No. 10 includes his famous warning against the "mischiefs of faction." This was a suspicion also shared by George Washington about the dangers of private associations. Madison feared that some factions could be united "by some common impulse of passion, or of interest, adverse to the rights of other citizens, or to the permanent and aggregate interests of the community." Madison argued that such factions could be less likely to cause a problem in the United States than in a smaller polity.

First Amendment

The First Amendment guarantee that "Congress shall make no law . . . abridging the freedom of speech, or of the press, or the right of the people peaceably to assemble, to petition the Government for a redress of grievances" has been interpreted by the Supreme Court as implicitly protecting freedom of association. The rights of free speech and assembly, so the argument goes, cannot simply be a guarantee to individuals; they must also allow people to associate in order to advance their arguments and illuminate their thoughts.

Freedom of Association

A constitutionally protected right that has grown out of the First Amendment's guarantee of the right to peaceably assemble and to petition the government and out of the due process clause of the Fourteenth Amendment. It involves both the right of expressive association, which has First Amendment origins, and the right of intimate association, which is a part of the liberty protected by the due process clause.

Galston, William A.

Distinguished political philosopher and author of many works on associational life, including *Liberal Pluralism*. A strong defender of associational rights, Galston has argued that networks of civic engagement, protected by freedom of association, strengthen the mediating institutions of civil society and build social trust, which is essential to a democracy.

Gay Rights

Some argue that the right of intimate association includes the rights of homosexuals to be free from any state sanction on their behavior as consenting adults and not to be discriminated against on the basis of sexual orientation. Yet some defenders of associational rights argued successfully in the *Dale* case that the Boy

Scouts' right of expressive association trumped the state's interest in protecting homosexuals from discrimination.

Gibson v. Florida Legislative Investigation Committee (1963)

In this case the Court held that the Miami branch of the NAACP could not be forced to disclose its lists of members and contributors simply because a legislative committee was investigating alleged Communist infiltration of the organization. The Court found no link between the Communists or any subversive activity and the NAACP. This was one of several cases in which the Court took a far more generous view of the NAACP's associational rights than it did of the rights of the Communist Party and the Ku Klux Klan.

Guilt by Association

A term that gained great currency in the 1950s, guilt by association was the practice of ostracizing people for their political associations. Many who were associated with left-wing causes in the 1930s and 1940s and refused to disclose to various government committees and agencies these activities and those of their associates often suffered loss of jobs, careers, and social standing. In several cases the Supreme Court declared that simple membership in an organization did not make an individual responsible for whatever illegal activities in which the group was involved. The concept is considered odious since it discourages free political association and strongly implies collective guilt.

Guttman, Amy

Political scientist, provost of Princeton University, and editor of a leading collection of essays entitled *Freedom of Association*. The collection is a serious discussion of the relationship of associational freedom to other important values such as nondiscrimination, civic equality, and economic opportunity.

Harlan, John Marshall

Associate justice of the Supreme Court (1955–1971) appointed by President Dwight D. Eisenhower. Marshall's opinion in *NAACP v. Alabama* (see below) was the first to include freedom of association within the scope of the First and Fourteenth Amendments. In his decisions in *Yates v. United States* (1957) and *Scales v. United States* (1961), he made the prosecution for simple membership in the Communist Party quite difficult by requiring that the government prove that an individual was an active and willing participant in its illegal activities. At the same time Harlan often gave considerable deference to governmental power and in *Barenblatt v. United States* (1959) upheld the right of congressional committees to investigate the activities of Communist Party members.

Helms, Jesse

Conservative Republican senator from North Carolina (1973–2003). Helms was a staunch defender of the Boy Scouts' right to exclude homosexual scoutmasters and defended them against government retaliation. He sponsored a Senate bill that would withhold federal funds from public schools that denied "equal access" to the Boy Scouts and any other group that expressed its "disapproval of homosexuality." The final bill, the Boy Scouts of America Equal Access Act, required schools to allow the Scouts to use facilities on the same terms as other groups, though schools were free to withhold sponsorship of the Scouts.

The Hollywood Ten

A group of prominent Hollywood screenwriters and directors who were called before the House Un-American Activities Committee in 1947 to testify about their association with the Communist Party. All refused to disclose such information on First Amendment (free speech) rather than Fifth Amendment (self-incrimination) grounds. They were all charged with contempt of Congress and sentenced to prison. The film studios suspended them without pay and announced that they would no longer hire any known Communists. Several of the Hollywood Ten, including Dalton Trumbo and Ring Lardner Jr., did return to work in the 1960s.

Hook, Sidney

Sidney Hook was born in New York in 1902 and died in 1989. An outspoken participant in many of the principal political debates of his time, he was best known for his vigorous defense of political and academic freedom and his stand against totalitarianism in all forms. His book *Heresy Yes, Conspiracy, No* was a defense of the idea that active Communists were part of a conspiratorial organization controlled by the Soviet Union and designed to subvert democracy and thus were not entitled to broad associational rights.

House Un-American Activities Committee (HUAC)

A committee of the U.S. House of Representatives, chartered in 1938 to investigate "the diffusion within the United States of subversive and un-American propaganda that it instigated from foreign countries not of a democratic origin." Its initial work was to look into the participation of German Americans in pro-Nazi activities. During the late 1940s and 1950s, the committee investigated Communist activities and influence in unions, educational institutions, and the entertainment industry. It gained great notoriety and public support in its 1948 investigation of Alger Hiss, a former high-level State Department official who was later charged with lying about his espionage activities on behalf of the Soviet Union. Some supported the committee's work in isolating and exposing the efforts of the Communist Party to penetrate various institutions; others objected to its prying into the political associations of Americans who had engaged in no illegal activities. In the 1970s the committee lost much of its political support, and the House abolished it in 1975.

Hurley v. Irish-American Gay, Lesbian, and Bisexual Group of Boston (1995)

In this case the Supreme Court upheld the right of the organizers of the annual Boston St. Patrick's Day parade to exclude the Irish-American Gay, Lesbian, and Bisexual Group of Boston (GLIB) from participating, though gays and lesbians were allowed to march in the parade as individuals. The Court agreed that having a group march under a gay rights banner could be seen as forcing the parade organizers to take a position on the issue. The Court considered a parade a form of speech whose message or lack thereof was for its organizers to determine. Although it was not a freedom of association case, in giving parade organizers the right to control their message and to disassociate from those who could alter it, *Hurley* had important implications for the rights of all private groups.

Internal Security Act of 1950

Passed in 1950 over President Harry Truman's veto, the Internal Security Act established the Subversive Activities Control Board (SACB; see below) and declared that members of the Communist Party had repudiated their allegiance to the United States and transferred it to a foreign policy. The law required that all organizations deemed by the board to be "Communist action" or "Communist front" must register its officers, members, and funds received and spent. It also denied members of the Communist Party the right to apply for a passport and to hold government and defense jobs. The Supreme Court declared most of these provisions unconstitutional, and the law has had little if any effect.

The Irish-American Gay, Lesbian, and Bisexual Group of Boston (GLIB)

This gay rights group was purportedly formed to march in the annual Boston St. Patrick's Day parade. In 1992 GLIB's application was rejected by the parade organizers, the South Boston Allied War Veterans Council. GLIB eventually obtained a court order allowing it to participate in the march. The next year the Veterans Council again denied GLIB the right to take part in the parade. GLIB then filed a lawsuit against the council and John J. Hurley, a member. The state trial court held for GLIB, ruling that the parade was covered by the state public accommodation law, that the expressive purpose of the parade was not discernible, and that there was no infringement of the War Veterans Council's First Amendment right of freedom of expressive association. The case was eventually appealed to the Supreme Court in *Hurley v. Irish-American Gay, Lesbian, and Bisexual Group of Boston* (see above), where GLIB lost its case.

Kateb, George

Political philosopher who argues that the freedom of association should be defined beyond expressive association and intimate association and be given much broader constitutional protection than the Supreme Court has thus far granted. According to Kateb, freedom of association should protect most voluntary arrangements to allow individuals "a life of decent adventure."

Keyishian v. Board of Regents (1967)

In *Keyishian* the Court struck down a requirement that obligated state employees to sign a certificate that they were not Communists. By not distinguishing between active and passive membership, the Court said, the requirement would "sweep over broadly into association which may not be proscribed."

Ku Klux Klan

A secret racist society formed in the South after the Civil War. Since the Ku Klux Klan was often associated with violent and illegal actions, the Court did not grant it the same deference and associational rights in *Bryant v. Zimmerman* (1928) that it later granted to the NAACP and other organizations.

Lawrence v. Texas (2003)

Supreme Court decision overturning a Texas statute outlawing homosexual sodomy. In his majority opinion Justice Anthony Kennedy came close to a definition of freedom that included intimate association without using the term. He stated, "Freedom extends beyond spatial bounds. Liberty presumes an autonomy of self that includes freedom of thought, belief, expressions, and certain intimate conduct. The instant case involves liberty of the person both in its spatial and more transcendent dimensions."

Liberal Pluralism

A concept of associational freedom developed by William Galston that would limit the power of the state to interfere with the internal affairs of civic associations. Since the world has many competing values, the government should be careful about interfering with legitimate individual and associational practices.

Madison, James

One of the major architects of the U.S. Constitution, one of three authors of *The Federalist*, sponsor of the Bill of Rights as a member of the First Congress, secretary of state under Thomas Jefferson, the fourth president of the United States. As author of *Federalist* Nos. 10 and 51, he was concerned that private associations and ambitions pursuing narrow self-interest could undermine the health of this new Republic. He felt the cure would be the inevitable multiplicity of associations in a large republic such as the United States and separation of powers within the formal structure of government. Although never a champion of freedom of association, he, along with Thomas Jefferson, was a founder of one of America's oldest political associations—the Democratic Party.

McCarran-Walter Immigration Act of 1952

Passed during the height of the Cold War, this act contained language delineating the exclusion of and right to deport "any alien who has engaged or has had purpose to engage in activities prejudicial to the public interest" or "subversive to national security."

McCarthy, Joseph R.

Republican senator from Wisconsin (1947–1957). McCarthy became a household name in 1950 when he charged that there were numerous Communists in the State Department known to the secretary of state. He later charged that Communist influence in the State Department was responsible for our failure to support the Nationalist Chinese against the Communists. The term *McCarthyism* was soon coined to mean the practice of making unsubstantiated accusations of disloyalty or Communist leanings and the use of unsupported accusations for any purpose.

Meiklejohn, Alexander

Leading educator, philosopher of free speech, and author of the landmark book *Free Speech and Its Relation to Self Government* (1948). Meiklejohn argued that freedom of speech is not just an individual right but one that enriches both the audience and the speaker. His interpretation yokes free speech to freedom of association. He once said, "In the field of public discussion, when citizens and their fellow thinkers 'peaceably assemble' to listen to a speaker, whether he be American or foreign, conservative or radical, safe or dangerous, the First Amendment is not, in the first instance, concerned with the 'right' of the speaker to this or that. It is concerned with the authority of the hearers to meet together, to discuss, and to hear discussion by speakers of their own choice, whatever they may deem worthy of their consideration."

NAACP v. Alabama ex rel. Patterson (1958)

Considered the landmark case in the establishment of freedom of association as a protected constitutional right, *NAACP v. Alabama* was the first time the Supreme Court explicitly recognized the right. The Court struck down an Alabama statute that demanded the membership lists of the NAACP. In a memorable and historical passage, Justice John M. Harlan wrote for a unanimous Court, "Effective advocacy of both public and private points of view, particularly controversial ones, is undeniably enhanced by group association, as this Court has more than once recognized by remarking upon the close nexus between freedoms of speech and assembly. It is beyond debate that freedom to engage in association for the advancement of beliefs and ideas is an inseparable aspect of the 'liberty' assured by the Due Process Clause of the Fourteenth Amendment, which embraces freedom of speech."

NAACP v. Button (1963)

One of a series of cases in the late 1950s and early 1960s in which the Supreme Court reaffirmed freedom of association as protected by the First and Fourteenth Amendments. This case involved a Virginia law that prohibited the NAACP from urging its members to institute litigation through the association's legal staff. Justice William Brennan, writing for the majority, began by declaring that litigation could be a form of speech. Brennan found protection for this activity not "under a narrow, literal conception of freedom of speech, petition or assembly. For there is no longer any doubt that the First and Fourteenth Amendments protect certain forms of orderly group activity. Thus we have affirmed the right 'to engage in association for the advancement of beliefs and ideas.'"

Nader v. Schaffer (1976)

A case that marked the Supreme Court's inclination to grant associational freedom to political parties in primary elections. The Court affirmed a lower court ruling that held that closed primary laws requiring party membership to vote in a primary did not violate the rights of other voters. The lower court had ruled that a party's right to limit primary participation is inherent in its associational rights.

Naming Names

A practice of informing on colleagues with whom you had participated in Communist or other left-wing activities, encouraged by the House Un-American Activities Committee. Many on the left considered "naming names" to be a cardinal sin since it could cause grave problems for those mentioned. Others considered working for the Communists to be a much more significant offense and believed that not all informing was evil. The question of naming names involved how seriously one took the issue of domestic communism.

Noto v. United States (1961)

A Supreme Court case that made it increasingly difficult for the federal government to prosecute the Communist Party. The Court reversed a conviction for membership in the Communist Party because the evidence did not suffice to establish that the party had engaged in unlawful behavior. Writing for the Court, Justice John M. Harlan declared, "There must be some substantial direct or circumstantial evidence of a call to violence now or in the future which is both sufficiently strong and sufficiently pervasive to lend color to the otherwise ambiguous theoretical material regarding Communist Party teaching, and to justify the inference that such a call to violence may fairly be imputed to the Party as a whole, and not merely to some narrow segment of it."

O'Connor, Sandra Day

Associate justice of the Supreme Court (1981–) and the first woman appointed to the high court. Her concurrent opinion in the *Roberts* case made the important distinction between the rights of expressive associations and commercial associations. O'Connor would give commercial associations far less leeway in choosing their membership than she would expressive associations. This distinction has yet to be adopted by a majority of the Court.

Open Primary

A primary in which any registered voter may participate in any party's primary. By its decision in *California Democratic Party v. Jones* (2000), the Court cast doubt on whether such primaries, by allowing non–party members to participate, are a violation of a party's autonomy and associational freedom.

Primary Associations

Associations of family and other intimates. Justice William Brennan deemed such associations worthy of constitutional protection under the doctrine of freedom of intimate association. These relationships are considered essential to establishing a person's identity, fostering diversity, and developing crucial buffers between an individual and the state.

Proposition 198

A rule established in 1996 by referendum that changed California's closed primary system, whereby voters could vote only in the primary of the party for which they were registered, and established instead a blanket primary (see above). It was designed to encourage greater voter participation in primary elections and reduce the likelihood of highly partisan candidates. The Supreme Court declared the rule unconstitutional in *California Democratic Party v. Jones* (2000; see above), calling it a violation of party autonomy and of a party's associational rights.

Public Accommodation Laws

Laws that historically have prevented businesses open to the public, such as restaurants, theaters, and sports arenas, from discriminating on the basis of race, ethnicity, and gender. The New Jersey Law against Discrimination also prevented discrimination on the basis of sexual orientation and was the law upon which James Dale brought his suit against the Boy Scouts. One of the major questions in public accommodation law is, When does a private organization take on the color of a public accommodation?

Putnam, Robert D.

Author of *Bowling Alone: The Collapse and Revival of American Community* (2000), an important work on the decline of social capital and civic engagement in the United States. Putnam makes a strong case for the importance of associational life for the functioning of a healthy democracy.

"Red Channels"

In 1950 "Red Channels" was published by *Counterattack: The Newsletter of Facts to Combat Communism*. It contained a list of entertainers and the organizations with which they were or had once been affiliated that were now considered subversive. This, in essence, is the blacklist.

Rehnquist, William H.

Appointed to the Supreme Court as an associate justice by President Richard M. Nixon in 1972 and then named chief justice by President Ronald Reagan in 1986. Generally considered an important conservative voice on the Court, Rehnquist often gives deference to legislative decisions, but as a believer in state-centered federalism and private property rights he has often overruled a legislative judgment. His most important contribution to freedom of association law was his majority opinion in *Boy Scouts of America v. Dale* (2000). In supporting the Boy Scouts' right to exclude a homosexual scoutmaster, Rehnquist gave great deference to the Boy Scouts' right to define its message and membership rules consistent with that message.

Right of Intimate Association

Derived, according to Justice William Brennan, from the general concept of liberty found in the Fourteenth Amendment. As Brennan defined it in *Roberts v. United States Jaycees* (1984), this concept includes "the formation and preservation of certain kinds of highly personal relationships"—such as marriage, childbirth, raising and educating children, and cohabitation with one's relatives—that warrant "a substantial measure of sanctuary from unjustified interference by the State." Brennan listed among the characteristics of such associations "relative smallness, a high degree of selectivity in decisions to begin and maintain the affiliation, and seclusion from others in critical aspects of the relationship, and he said that these relationships alone "are likely to reflect the considerations that have led to an understanding of freedom of association as an intrinsic element of personal liberty."

The *Roberts* Trilogy

A series of three Supreme Court decisions in the mid-1980s— *Roberts v. United States Jaycees* (1984), *Rotary International v. Rotary Club of Duarte, California* (1987), and *New York State Club Association v. City of New York* (1988)—that dealt with the issues of associational freedom and antidiscrimination laws. It was in these cases that the Court developed a framework for analyzing the question. In the *Roberts* case, Justice William Brennan defined two dimensions of associational freedom, freedom of intimate association and freedom of expressive association, as well as the freedom to disassociate.

Rosenblum, Nancy

Political theorist who has written extensively on civil society and associational rights. In her book *Membership and Morals: The Personal Uses of Pluralism in America* (1998), she argues that associations are essential to liberal pluralism, temper individual self-interest, and integrate otherwise disconnected individuals into society. Rosenblum would grant associations a broad degree of autonomy from state regulation to promote freedom and pluralism.

Runyon v. McCrary (1976)

A Supreme Court case involving the practice in several southern states of providing funding for whites-only private academies. The Court held that the schools were "more public than private" and denied the schools' claim of freedom of association on fairly narrow grounds. Although the Court affirmed the schools' right to promote the notion of segregation, it ruled that ending its discriminatory practices would not interfere with its teaching "of any ideas or dogma." *Runyon* did not call into question "the right of a private social organization to limit its membership on racial or any other grounds [or] the right of a private school to limit its student body to boys, to girls, or to adherents of a particular religious faith," nor did it challenge "private sectarian schools that practice racial exclusion on religious grounds."

Rutledge, Wiley

Associate justice of the Supreme Court (1943–1949), the last of President Franklin D. Roosevelt's nine Court appointments. During his brief tenure on the Court, Rutledge was a strong defender of First Amendment rights. He believed along with the majority of his colleagues on the Court that the First Amendment was in a preferred position in the Constitution and entitled to great deference. His opinion in *Thomas v. Collins* (1945) not only restated that view but also the concept that freedom of speech protected the speaker as well as his audience. This was considered one of the foundation stones of freedom of association.

Scales v. United States (1961)

In this case the Supreme Court upheld the conviction of Communist Party member Junius Scales under the Smith Act, which outlawed membership in "any society, group, or assembly of persons who teach, advocate, or encourage the overthrow or destruction of any government in the United States by force or violence." But in so doing, the Court made an important distinction between active and nominal membership. According to Justice John Marshall Harlan, who wrote the majority opinion, individuals were in defiance of the law if they specifically intended "to accomplish [the goals of the organization] by resort to violence." Scales was the last defendant convicted under the Smith Act.

Scalia, Antonin

Associate justice of the Supreme Court, appointed by President Ronald Reagan in 1986. Known for his strongly worded opinions and conservative judicial philosophy, Scalia is an advocate of freedom of association and the right of political parties to a large degree of autonomy. He joined the majority in *Boy Scouts of America v. Dale* (2000) and was author of the majority opinion in *California Democratic Party v. Jones* (2000). In *Jones* he stated, "In no area is the political association's right to exclude more important than in the process of selecting its nominee."

Secondary Associations

Large membership organizations of people who may never see each other, including political parties and special interest groups such as the American Association of Retired People (AARP) and the National Rifle Association (NRA). The *Encyclopedia of Associations* lists 23,000 nonprofit membership organizations of national scope. These organizations allow individuals to amplify their own self-interests and to have an impact upon the political system. Since many of them are expressive associations, they would have broad constitutional protections under freedom of association.

Smith v. Allwright (1944)

From 1927 to 1953 the Court struck down state statutes that prevented African Americans from participating in Democratic Party primaries, the so-called white primary laws. *Smith v. Allwright* is perhaps the most widely cited of the white primary cases. In it the Court held that "the recognition of the place of the primary in the electoral scheme makes clear that state delegation to a party of the power to fix the qualifications of primary elections is delegation of a state function that may make the party's action the action of the state." Some interpreted these decisions as granting the state broad authority over party autonomy in primary elections. In subsequent cases the Court did not carry the logic of the white primary cases that far and granted political parties considerable associational freedom against laws dictating who can participate in primaries, unless those laws dealt with racial discrimination.

Social Capital

A concept used frequently in Robert Putnam's *Bowling Alone* (see above) that describes the social benefits of associational life. Putnam distinguishes between bridging social capital, which generates broader identities and reciprocity, and bonding social capital, which creates strong group loyalties. Both are important in developing social cohesion and invigorating political life.

Stevens, John Paul

Associate justice of the Supreme Court (1975–) appointed by President Gerald Ford. Although initially a somewhat conservative justice, he later became a leader of the Court's liberal bloc. He was suspicious of freedom of association claims against the state's interest in antidiscrimination and in the regulation of elections. He wrote strong dissenting opinions in both *Boy Scouts of America v. Dale* (2000) and *California Democratic Party v. Jones* (2000). In *Jones* he wrote, "The so-called 'right not to associate' that the Court relies upon, then, is simply inapplicable to participation in a state election."

Subversive Activities Control Board (SACB)

A government agency established by the Internal Security Act with broad authority to hold hearings and identify so-called subversive groups. These groups would then be required to register with the attorney general, and their members could be denied the right to hold a government job, a defense position, or a passport. A series of Supreme Court decisions (*Yates, Robel, Scales, Aptheker*) weakened the authority of the board, and in 1973 Congress abolished it with little public notice or opposition.

Tashjian v. Republican Party (1986)

In this case the Supreme Court held that a Connecticut law preventing a party from opening up its primary to independent voters violated a party's associational rights. The Court found the law to be a subterfuge that allowed the majority Democratic Party to tell the minority Republican Party how to run its affairs. Justice Thurgood Marshall, writing the Court's opinion, explained that a state cannot substitute its judgment for that of a party: "The Party's determination of the boundaries of its own association, and of the structure which best allows it to pursue its political goals, is protected by the Constitution." This case became an important precedent for *California Democratic Party v. Jones* (see above).

Thomas v. Collins (1945)

In this case a union leader had been cited for contempt for ignoring a court order that he obtain a license for union organizers. Writing for the Court, Justice Wiley Rutledge saw this as a prior restraint on Thomas's right to speak as well as upon his audience's right to hold a public meeting. Although Rutledge did not explicitly mention freedom of association, by acknowledging that the rights of the speaker and the audience were "necessarily correlative," he established a basis for freedom of association as an extension of the First Amendment.

Timmons v. Twin Cities Area New Party (1997)

In this case a minor political party, the New Party, challenged a law that prevented candidates from appearing on the ballots of more than one political party. The Court did not find for the New Party and declared that the burdens the law imposed were justified by the correspondingly weighty valid state interests in ballot integrity and political stability. The New Party's associational rights were not compromised since the law did not affect the party's message or its membership. The case makes clear that there are limits, beyond racial discrimination, to a party's autonomy in a primary election.

Tocqueville, Alexis de

A French aristocrat who traveled to America in 1830 to discover and write about "what a great republic is." He later published in two volumes what many to this day consider to be the best book ever written about the United States, *Democracy in America.* Tocqueville observed that democracy is both an expression of a culture as well as the reflection of certain constitutional forms. Although he found much to admire in the young republic, he was concerned about the "tyranny of the majority." Tocqueville believed the American genius for developing voluntary associations was essential to the health of the democracy and to the prevention of such a tyranny. Such associations keep individuals from being isolated and develop habits of self-government and cooperation. He wrote, "In democratic countries the science of association is the mother science; the progress of all the others depends on the progress of that one." Many of the arguments for freedom of association are found in Tocqueville's classic study.

United States v. Cruikshank (1875)

This case involved the Enforcement Act, a Reconstruction law that made it a crime to "band or conspire together to oppress any citizen or hinder his free exercise . . . of any right . . . secured to him by the Constitution" or federal law. A group of white defendants had conspired to deprive a number of black citizens their right to assemble for peaceful and lawful purposes. Although the Supreme Court declared the indictment too broad (the black group was not meeting to petition to the federal government), the Court did declare that "the very idea of a government, republican in form, implies a right on the part of its citizens to meet peaceably for consultation in respect to public affairs and to petition for a redress of grievances." In his interpretation of *Cruikshank,* David Cole has argued, "If the right of assembly is implicit in a republican government, so too is the right of association, since the very reason assembly was considered implicit was that it made association possible." In its emphasis upon the right of assembly as implicit in republican government, *Cruikshank* implies as well that associations are central to republican government. Thus, the constitutional doctrine of freedom of association originates with *Cruikshank.*

United States v. Robel (1967)

One of the Supreme Court decisions that weakened the Internal Security Act and strengthened freedom of association. In this case the Court struck down a provision of the Internal Security Act that denied employment in any defense industry to members of the Communist Party. The Court ruled that the statute infringed upon freedom of association by reaching too broadly in its inclusion of inactive members and those employed in nonsensitive positions.

Voting Rights Act of 1965

A landmark piece of legislation that eliminated most of the barriers to the enfranchisement of African American voters in the South and realized the promise of the Fifteenth Amendment guarantee against racial barriers to voting. It also gave the Justice Department and the federal courts greater influence over the drawing of congressional districts so as to protect minority interests. It represents the view expressed in the white primary cases that party autonomy cannot be a justification for racial discrimination.

Waldorf Statement

Issued by the heads of the major film studios at a meeting at the Waldorf-Astoria Hotel in New York City on November 25, 1947, in response to the Hollywood Ten's refusal to cooperate with the House Un-American Activities Committee. The statement was part of an effort to purge the film industry of Communists and began what was to become the blacklist. It read in part, "We will not knowingly employ a Communist or a member of any party or group which advocates the overthrow of the government of the United States by force or by any illegal or unconstitutional methods. In pursuing this policy, we are not going to be swayed by hysteria or intimidation from any source. We are frank to recognize that such a policy involves dangers and risks. There is the danger of hurting innocent people. There is the risk of creating an atmosphere of fear. Creative work at its best cannot be carried on in an atmosphere of fear. We will guard against this danger, this risk, this fear. To this end we will invite the Hollywood talent guilds to work with us to eliminate any subversives, to protect the innocent, and to safeguard free speech and a free screen wherever threatened."

Warren, Earl

Chief justice of the United States (1953–1969) who presided over one of the most important eras in the history of the Supreme Court, in which numerous rights, including freedom of association, were more explicitly developed. He was the author of the majority opinion in *Watkins v. United States* (1957), in which he warned the House Un-American Activities Committee against "exposure for exposure's sake." Although Warren's opinion in *Watkins* was modified in *Barenblatt v. United States* (1959), the Court during his tenure moved slowly but persistently in assuring that freedom of association was embedded in the meaning of the First and Fourteenth Amendments.

Washington, George

One of the founding fathers, hero of the Revolutionary War, and first U.S. president (1789–1797). Washington, like Madison, harbored great suspicions about political associations and political parties in particular. In his farewell address he warned against "ill-concerted and incongruous projects of factions" that would conflict with the common interests of the country.

Watkins v. United States (1957)

In this decision the Court challenged the right of congressional committees to examine an individual's political beliefs and associations. Chief Justice Earl Warren cast doubt on the constitutionality of the House Un-American Activities Committee's charter, which authorized it to investigate "un-American" propaganda. Warren stated, "It would be difficult to imagine a less explicit authorizing resolution. Who can define the meaning of 'un-American'?" He also declared that there was no power to "expose for the sake of exposure." Two years later, in *Barenblatt v. United States* (see above), the Court backed away from any direct challenge to the House Un-American Activities Committee and upheld the right of the Congress to investigate the activities of the Communist Party and its members.

6

DOCUMENTS

GEORGE WASHINGTON'S
FAREWELL ADDRESS (1796)

This is one of the great state papers in our history and one of the most memorable presidential addresses. It was issued on 17 September 1796, six months before Washington actually retired from office. He did it to commemorate the ninth anniversary of the completion and signing of the Constitution and expressed the wish that "the Constitution be sacredly maintained." He also warned against political parties and factions that would place their own interests over those of the country. Washington's suspicions of faction, shared by James Madison, did not persuade his fellow citizens, who became a nation of joiners.

To the People of the United States.

FRIENDS AND FELLOW-CITIZENS:

1. The period for a new election of a citizen, to administer the executive government of the United States, being not far distant, and the time actually arrived, when your thoughts must be employed designating the person, who is to be clothed with that important trust, it appears to me proper, especially as it may conduce to a more distinct expression of the public voice, that I should now apprize you of the resolution I have formed, to decline being considered among the number of those out of whom a choice is to be made.

2. I beg you at the same time to do me the justice to be assured that this resolution has not been taken without a strict regard to all the considerations appertaining to the relation which binds a dutiful citizen to his country; and that in withdrawing the tender of service, which silence in my situation might imply, I am influenced by no diminution of zeal for your future interest, no deficiency of grateful respect for your past kindness, but am supported by a full conviction that the step is compatible with both.

3. The acceptance of, and continuance hitherto in, the office to which your suffrages have twice called me, have been a uniform sacrifice of inclination to the opinion of duty, and to a deference for what appeared to be your desire. I constantly hoped, that it would have been much earlier in my power, consistently with motives, which I was not at liberty to disregard, to return to that retirement, from which I had been reluctantly drawn. The strength of my inclination to do this, previous to the last election, had even led to the preparation of an address to declare it to you; but mature reflection on the then perplexed and critical posture of our affairs with foreign nations, and the unanimous advice of persons entitled to my confidence impelled me to abandon the idea.

4. I rejoice, that the state of your concerns, external as well as internal, no longer renders the pursuit of inclination incompatible with the sentiment of duty, or propriety; and am persuaded, whatever partiality may be retained for my services, that, in the present circumstances of our country, you will not disapprove my determination to retire.

5. The impressions, with which I first undertook the arduous trust, were explained on the proper occasion. In the discharge of this trust, I will only say, that I have, with good intentions, contributed towards the organization and administration of the government the best exertions of which a very fallible judgment was capable. Not unconscious, in the outset, of the inferiority of my qualifications, experience in my own eyes, perhaps still more in the eyes of others, has strengthened the motives to diffidence of myself; and every day the increasing weight of years admonishes me more and more, that the shade of retirement is as necessary to me as it will be welcome. Satisfied, that, if any circumstances have given peculiar value to my services, they were temporary, I have the consolation to believe, that, while choice and prudence invite me to quit the political scene, patriotism does not forbid it. . . .The basis of our political systems is the right of the people to make and to alter

their constitutions of government. But the Constitution which at any time exists, till changed by an explicit and authentic act of the whole people, is sacredly obligatory upon all. The very idea of the power and the right of the people to establish government presupposes the duty of every individual to obey the established government. . . .

17. All obstructions to the execution of the Laws, all combinations and associations, under whatever plausible character, with the real design to direct, control, counteract, or awe the regular deliberation and action of the constituted authorities, are destructive of this fundamental principle, and of fatal tendency. They serve to organize faction, to give it an artificial and extraordinary force; to put, in the place of the delegated will of the nation, the will of a party, often a small but artful and enterprising minority of the community; and, according to the alternate triumphs of different parties, to make the public administration the mirror of the ill-concerted and incongruous projects of faction, rather than the organ of consistent and wholesome plans digested by common counsels, and modified by mutual interests.

18. However combinations or associations of the above description may now and then answer popular ends, they are likely, in the course of time and things, to become potent engines, by which cunning, ambitious, and unprincipled men will be enabled to subvert the power of the people, and to usurp for themselves the reins of government; destroying afterwards the very engines, which have lifted them to unjust dominion.

19. Towards the preservation of your government, and the permanency of your present happy state, it is requisite, not only that you steadily discountenance irregular oppositions to its acknowledged authority, but also that you resist with care the spirit of innovation upon its principles, however specious the pretexts. One method of assault may be to effect, in the forms of the constitution, alterations, which will impair the energy of the system, and thus to undermine what cannot be directly overthrown. In all the changes to which you may be invited, remember that time and habit are at least as necessary to fix the true character of governments, as of other human institutions; that experience is the surest standard, by which to test the real tendency of the existing constitution of a country; that facility in changes, upon the credit of mere hypothesis and opinion, exposes to perpetual change, from the endless variety of hypothesis and opinion; and remember, especially, that, for the efficient management of our common interests, in a country

so extensive as ours, a government of as much vigor as is consistent with the perfect security of liberty is indispensable. Liberty itself will find in such a government, with powers properly distributed and adjusted, its surest guardian. It is, indeed, little else than a name, where the government is too feeble to withstand the enterprises of faction, to confine each member of the society within the limits prescribed by the laws, and to maintain all in the secure and tranquil enjoyment of the rights of person and property.

20. I have already intimated to you the danger of parties in the state, with particular reference to the founding of them on geographical discriminations. Let me now take a more comprehensive view, and warn you in the most solemn manner against the baneful effects of the spirit of party, generally.

21. This spirit, unfortunately, is inseparable from our nature, having its root in the strongest passions of the human mind. It exists under different shapes in all governments, more or less stifled, controlled, or repressed; but, in those of the popular form, it is seen in its greatest rankness, and is truly their worst enemy.

22. The alternate domination of one faction over another, sharpened by the spirit of revenge, natural to party dissension, which in different ages and countries has perpetrated the most horrid enormities, is itself a frightful despotism. But this leads at length to a more formal and permanent despotism. The disorders and miseries, which result, gradually incline the minds of men to seek security and repose in the absolute power of an individual; and sooner or later the chief of some prevailing faction, more able or more fortunate than his competitors, turns this disposition to the purposes of his own elevation, on the ruins of Public Liberty.

23. Without looking forward to an extremity of this kind (which nevertheless ought not to be entirely out of sight), the common and continual mischiefs of the spirit of party are sufficient to make it the interest and duty of a wise people to discourage and restrain it.

24. It serves always to distract the Public Councils, and enfeeble the Public Administration. It agitates the Community with ill-founded jealousies and false alarms; kindles the animosity of one part against another, foments occasionally riot and insurrection. It opens the door to foreign influence and corruption, which find a facilitated access to the government itself through the channels of party passions. Thus the pol-

icy and the will of one country are subjected to the policy and will of another.

25. There is an opinion, that parties in free countries are useful checks upon the administration of the Government, and serve to keep alive the spirit of Liberty. This within certain limits is probably true; and in Governments of a Monarchical cast, Patriotism may look with indulgence, if not with favor, upon the spirit of party. But in those of the popular character, in Governments purely elective, it is a spirit not to be encouraged. From their natural tendency, it is certain there will always be enough of that spirit for every salutary purpose. And, there being constant danger of excess, the effort ought to be, by force of public opinion, to mitigate and assuage it. A fire not to be quenched, it demands a uniform vigilance to prevent its bursting into a flame, lest, instead of warming, it should consume.

26. It is important, likewise, that the habits of thinking in a free country should inspire caution, in those intrusted with its administration, to confine themselves within their respective constitutional spheres, avoiding in the exercise of the powers of one department to encroach upon another. The spirit of encroachment tends to consolidate the powers of all the departments in one, and thus to create, whatever the form of government, a real despotism. A just estimate of that love of power, and proneness to abuse it, which predominates in the human heart, is sufficient to satisfy us of the truth of this position. The necessity of reciprocal checks in the exercise of political power, by dividing and distributing it into different depositories, and constituting each the Guardian of the Public Weal against invasions by the others, has been evinced by experiments ancient and modern; some of them in our country and under our own eyes. To preserve them must be as necessary as to institute them. If, in the opinion of the people, the distribution or modification of the constitutional powers be in any particular wrong, let it be corrected by an amendment in the way, which the constitution designates. But let there be no change by usurpation; for, though this, in one instance, may be the instrument of good, it is the customary weapon by which free governments are destroyed. The precedent must always greatly overbalance in permanent evil any partial or transient benefit, which the use can at any time yield.

27. Of all the dispositions and habits, which lead to political prosperity, Religion and Morality are indispensable supports. In vain would that

man claim the tribute of Patriotism, who should labor to subvert these great pillars of human happiness, these firmest props of the duties of Men and Citizens. The mere Politician, equally with the pious man, ought to respect and to cherish them. A volume could not trace all their connexions with private and public felicity. Let it simply be asked, Where is the security for property, for reputation, for life, if the sense of religious obligation desert the oaths, which are the instruments of investigation in Courts of Justice? And let us with caution indulge the supposition, that morality can be maintained without religion. Whatever may be conceded to the influence of refined education on minds of peculiar structure, reason and experience both forbid us to expect, that national morality can prevail in exclusion of religious principle.

28. It is substantially true, that virtue or morality is a necessary spring of popular government. The rule, indeed, extends with more or less force to every species of free government. Who, that is a sincere friend to it, can look with indifference upon attempts to shake the foundation of the fabric?

29. Promote, then, as an object of primary importance, institutions for the general diffusion of knowledge. In proportion as the structure of a government gives force to public opinion, it is essential that public opinion should be enlightened.

30. Relying on its kindness in this as in other things, and actuated by that fervent love towards it, which is so natural to a man, who views it in the native soil of himself and his progenitors for several generations; I anticipate with pleasing expectation that retreat, in which I promise myself to realize, without alloy, the sweet enjoyment of partaking, in the midst of my fellow-citizens, the benign influence of good laws under a free government, the ever favorite object of my heart, and the happy reward, as I trust, of our mutual cares, labors, and dangers.

George Washington
United States, September 17, 1796

BRYANT V. ZIMMERMAN (1928)

Under a New York statute, every membership corporation of twenty or more persons that requires an oath as a prerequisite or condition of membership, other than a labor union or a benevolent order, must file a sworn copy of its constitution, bylaws, rules, regulations, and oath of member-

ship, together with a roster of its membership and a list of its officers for the current year.

The law stated that any member of such an association that knew the association had failed to comply with any provision of that article would be guilty of a misdemeanor. The statute was clearly directed at the Ku Klux Klan. The Klan contended that under the equal protection clause the statute discriminated against them, since it excepted from its requirements several associations having oath-bound membership, such as labor unions, the Masonic fraternity, the Independent Order of Odd Fellows, the Grand Army of the Republic, and the Knights of Columbus. Freedom of association was a dormant concept, and the Court did not resolve the case on that basis. It did, however, make it clear that the character of the organization would have some bearing on its rights.

Decided November 19, 1928.

Mr. Justice VAN DEVANTER delivered the opinion of the Court.

The offense charged against the relator is that he attended meetings and remained a member of the Buffalo Provisional Klan of the Knights of the Ku Klux Klan, an unincorporated association—but neither a labor union nor a benevolent order mentioned in the benevolent orders law—having a membership of more than 20 persons and requiring an oath as a prerequisite or condition of membership, he then having knowledge that such association had wholly failed to comply with the requirement in section 53.

There are various privileges and immunities which under our dual system of government belong to citizens of the United States solely by reason of such citizenship. It is against their abridgement by state laws that the privilege and immunity clause in the Fourteenth Amendment is directed. But no such privilege or immunity is in question here. If to be and remain a member of a secret, oath-bound association within a state be a privilege arising out of citizenship at all, it is an incident of state rather than United States citizenship; and such protection as is thrown about it by the Constitution is in no wise affected by its possessor being a citizen of the United States. Thus there is no basis here for invoking the privilege and immunity clause.

The relator's contention under the due process clause is that the statute deprives him of liberty in that it prevents him from exercising his right of membership in the association. But his liberty in this regard, like most other personal rights, must yield to the rightful exertion of the police power. There can be no doubt that under that power the state may prescribe and apply to associations having an oath-bound membership any reasonable regulation calculated to confine their purposes and activities within limits which are consistent with the rights of others and the public welfare. The requirement in section 53 that each association shall file with the secretary of state a sworn copy of its constitution, oath of membership, etc., with a list of members and officers is such a regulation. It proceeds on the two-fold theory that the state within whose territory and under whose protection the association exists is entitled to be informed of its nature and purpose, of whom it is composed and by whom its activities are conducted, and that requiring this information to be supplied for the public files will operate as an effective or substantial deterrent from the violations of public and private right to which the association might be tempted if such a disclosure were not required. The requirement is not arbitrary or oppressive, but reasonable and likely to be of real effect. Of course, power to require the disclosure includes authority to prevent individual members of an association which has failed to comply from attending meetings or retaining membership with knowledge of its default. We conclude that the due process clause is not violated.

The main contention made under the equal protection clause is that the statute discriminates against the Knights of the Ku Klux Klan and other associations in that it excepts from its requirements several associations having oath-bound membership, such as labor unions, the Masonic fraternity, the Independent Order of Odd Fellows, the Grand Army of the Republic, and the Knights of Columbus—all named in another statute, which provides for their incorporation and requires the names of their officers as elected from time to time to be reported to the secretary of state.

The courts below recognized the principle . . . and reached the conclusion that the classification was justified by a difference between the two classes of associations shown by experience, and that the difference consisted (a) in a manifest tendency on the part of one class to make the secrecy surrounding its purposes and membership a cloak for acts and conduct inimical to personal rights and public welfare, and (b) in the absence of such a tendency on the part of the other class. In pointing out this difference one of the courts (123 Misc. Rep. 859, 206 N. Y. S. 533) said of the Ku Klux Klan, the principal association in the included class:

"It is a matter of common knowledge that this organization functions largely at night, its members disguised by hoods and gowns and doing things calculated to strike terror into the minds of the people,"

—and later said of the other class:

"These organizations and their purposes are well known, many of them having been in existence for many years. Many of them are oath-bound and secret. But we hear of no complaints against them regarding violation of the peace or interfering with the rights of others."

Another of the courts (213 App. Div. 414, 210 N. Y. S. 269) said: "It is a matter of common knowledge that the association or organization of which relator is concededly a member exercises activities tending to the prejudice and intimidation of sundry classes of our citizens. But the legislation is not confined to this society,"—and later said of the other class:

"Labor unions have a recognized lawful purpose. The benevolent orders mentioned in the Benevolent Orders Law have already received legislative scrutiny and been granted special privileges so that the legislature may well consider them beneficent rather than harmful agencies."

The third court (241 N. Y. 405, 150 N. E. 497, 43 A. L. R. 909), after recognizing "the potentialities of evil in secret societies" and observing that "the danger of certain organizations has been judicially demonstrated"—meaning in that state—said:

"Benevolent orders, labor, unions and college fraternities have existed for many years, and, while not immune from hostile criticism, have on the whole justified their existence."

We assume that the Legislature had before it such information as was readily available, including the published report of a hearing before a committee of the House of Representatives of the Fifty-Seventh Congress relating to the formation, purposes, and activities of the Ku Klux Klan. If so it was advised—putting aside controverted evidence— that the order was a revival of the Ku Klux Klan of an earlier time, with additional features borrowed from the Know Nothing and the A. P. A. orders of other periods; that its membership was limited to native-born, gentile, Protestant whites; that in part of its constitution and printed creed it proclaimed the widest freedom for all and full adherence to the Constitution of the United States, in another exacted of its members an oath to shield and preserve "white supremacy," and in still another declared any person actively opposing its principles to be "a dangerous ingredient in the body politic of our country and an enemy to the weal of our national commonwealth"; that it was conducting a crusade against Catholics, Jews, and negroes, and stimulating hurtful religious and race prejudices; that it was striving for political power, and assuming a sort of guardianship over the administration of local, state, and national affairs; and that at times it was taking into its own hands the punishment of what some of its members conceived to be crimes.

We think it plain that the action of the courts below in holding that there was a real and substantial basis for the distinction made between the two sets of associations or orders was right and should not be disturbed.

We conclude that all the objections urged against the statute are untenable as held by the courts below.

Judgment affirmed.

DE JONGE V. STATE OF OREGON (1937)

De Jonge was convicted under the Oregon criminal syndicalism law. This law made it a crime to participate in a meeting of an organization that advocated the unlawful use of force as a means of accomplishing political change. De Jonge, who was a member of the Communist Party, had presided over a public meeting of the party to protest against acts of police brutality. The meeting was orderly, and there was no call for violence.

Decided January 4, 1937.

Mr. Chief Justice HUGHES delivered the opinion of the Court.

It thus appears that, while defendant was a member of the Communist Party, he was not indicted for participating in its organization, or for joining it, or for soliciting members or for distributing its literature. He was not charged with teaching or advocating criminal syndicalism or sabotage or any unlawful acts, either at the meeting or elsewhere. He was accordingly deprived of the benefit of evidence as to the orderly and lawful conduct of the meeting and that it was not called or used for the advocacy of criminal syndicalism or sabotage or any unlawful action. His sole offense as charged, and for which he was convicted and sentenced to imprisonment for seven years, was that he had assisted in the conduct of a public meeting, albeit otherwise lawful, which was held under the auspices of the Communist Party.

The broad reach of the statute as thus applied is plain. While defendant was a member of the Communist Party, that membership was not necessary to conviction on such a charge. A like fate might have attended any speaker, although not a member who "assisted in the conduct" of the meeting. However innocuous the object of the meeting, however lawful the subjects and tenor of the addresses, however reasonable and timely the discussion, all those assisting in the conduct of the meeting would be subject to imprisonment as felons if the meeting were held by the Communist Party. This manifest result was brought out sharply at this bar by the concessions which the Attorney General made, and could not avoid, in the light of the decision of the state court. Thus, if the Communist Party had called a public meeting in Portland to discuss the tariff, or the foreign policy of the government, or taxation, or relief, or candidacies for the offices of President, members of Congress, Governor, or state legislators, every speaker who assisted in the conduct of the meeting would be equally guilty with the defendant in this case, upon the charge as here defined and sustained. The list of illustrations might be indefinitely extended to every variety of meetings under the auspices of the Communist Party although held for the discussion of political issues or to adopt protests and pass resolutions of an entirely innocent and proper character.

While the States are entitled to protect themselves from the abuse of the privileges of our institutions through an attempted substitution of force and violence in the place of peaceful political action in order to effect revolutionary changes in government, none of our decisions go to the length of sustaining such a curtailment of the right of free speech and assembly as the Oregon statute demands in its present application. In *Gitlow v. People of State of New York,* under the New York statute defining criminal anarchy, the defendant was found to be responsible for a "manifesto" advocating the overthrow of the government by violence and unlawful means. In *Whitney v. People of State of California* under the California statute relating to criminal syndicalism, the defendant was found guilty of willfully and deliberately assisting in the forming of an organization for the purpose of carrying on a revolutionary class struggle by criminal methods. . . .

The case of *Burns v. United States* involved a similar ruling under the California statute as extended to the Yosemite National Park. On the other hand, in *Fiske v. Kansas,* the criminal syndicalism act of that State was held to have been applied unconstitutionally and the judgment of conviction was reversed, where it was not shown that unlawful methods had been advocated.

Freedom of speech and of the press are fundamental rights which are safeguarded by the due process clause of the Fourteenth Amendment of the Federal Constitution. The right of peaceable assembly is a right cognate to those of free speech and free press and is equally fundamental. As this Court said in *United States v. Cruikshank:* "The very idea of a government, republican in form, implies a right on the part of its citizens to meet peaceably for consultation in respect to public affairs and to petition for a redress of grievances." The First Amendment of the Federal Constitution expressly guarantees that right against abridgment by Congress. But explicit mention there does not argue exclusion elsewhere. For the right is one that cannot be denied without violating those fundamental principles of liberty and justice which lie at the base of all civil and political institutions—principles which the Fourteenth Amendment embodies in the general terms of its due process clause.

These rights may be abused by using speech or press or assembly in order to incite to violence and crime. The people through their Legislatures may protect themselves against that abuse. But the legislative intervention can find constitutional justification only by dealing with the abuse. The rights themselves must not be curtailed. The greater the importance of safeguarding the community from incitements to the overthrow of our institutions by force and violence, the more imperative is the need to preserve inviolate the constitutional rights of free speech, free press and free assembly in order to maintain the opportunity for free political discussion, to the end that government may be responsive to the will of the people and that changes, if desired, may be obtained by peaceful means. Therein lies the security of the Republic, the very foundation of constitutional government.

It follows from these considerations that, consistently with the Federal Constitution, peaceable assembly for lawful discussion cannot be made a crime. The holding of meetings for peaceable political action cannot be proscribed. Those who assist in the conduct of such meetings cannot be branded as criminals on that score. The question, if the rights of free speech and peaceable assembly are to be preserved, is not as to the auspices under which the meeting is held but as to its purpose; not as to the relations of the speakers, but whether their utterances transcend the bounds of the freedom of speech which the Constitution protects. If the persons assembling have committed crimes elsewhere, if they have formed or are engaged in a conspiracy against the public peace and order, they may be prosecuted for their conspiracy or other violation of valid laws. But it is a different matter when the State, instead of prosecuting them for such offenses, seizes upon mere participation in a peaceable assembly and a lawful public discussion as the basis for a criminal charge.

We are not called upon to review the findings of the state court as to the objectives of the Communist Party. Notwithstanding those objectives, the defendant still enjoyed his personal right of free speech and to take part in a peaceable assembly having a lawful purpose, although called by that party. The defendant was none the less entitled to discuss the public issues of the day and thus in a lawful manner, without incitement to violence or crime, to seek redress of alleged grievances. That was of the essence of his guaranteed personal liberty.

We hold that the Oregon statute as applied to the particular charge as defined by the state court is repugnant to the due process clause of the Fourteenth Amendment. The judgment of conviction is reversed and the cause is remanded for further proceedings not inconsistent with this opinion.

Reversed.

THE SMITH ACT (1940)

This law, named after Representative Howard W. Smith (D–VA), was passed as a rider to the Alien Registration Bill and received very little attention at the time. The law punished not only seditious activity but also associations with seditious organizations, with the Communist Party very much in mind. Since the Communist Party was a full supporter of the American effort in World War II, prosecutions were not brought against it during the war. There were, however, two other wartime prosecutions, one against the Socialist Workers Party and a failed attempt to prosecute twenty-eight alleged pro-Nazis. During the Cold War the federal government brought charges against twelve members of the Central Committee of the Communist Party.

Whoever knowingly or willfully advocates, abets, advises, or teaches the duty, necessity, desirability, or propriety of overthrowing or destroying the government of the United States or the government of any State, Territory, District or Possession thereof, or the government of any political subdivision therein, by force or violence, or by the assassination of any officer of any such government; or

Whoever, with intent to cause the overthrow or destruction of any such government, prints, publishes, edits, issues, circulates, sells, distributes, or publicly displays any written or printed matter advocating, advising, or teaching the duty, necessity, desirability, or propriety of overthrowing or destroying any government in the United States by force or violence, or attempts to do so; or

Whoever organizes or helps or attempts to organize any society, group, or assembly of persons who teach, advocate, or encourage the overthrow or destruction of any such government by force or violence; or becomes or is a member of, or affiliates with, any such society, group, or assembly of persons, knowing the purposes thereof—

Shall be fined under this title or imprisoned not more than twenty years, or both, and shall be ineligible for employment by the United States or any department or agency thereof, for the five years next following his conviction.

If two or more persons conspire to commit any offense named in this section, each shall be fined under this title or imprisoned not more than twenty years, or both, and shall be ineligible for employment by the United States or any department or agency thereof, for the five years next following his conviction.

As used in this section, the terms "organizes" and "organize," with respect to any society, group, or assembly of persons, include the recruiting of new members, the forming of new units, and the regrouping or expansion of existing clubs, classes, and other units of such society, group, or assembly of persons.

THOMAS V. COLLINS (1945)

Texas had passed a law requiring that any labor organizer "before soliciting any members for his organization" must file be with the state, giving his name and affiliation, and obtain an organizer's card. Thomas, a United Automobile Workers Union official, went to Texas with the in-

tention of testing the law and addressed a mass meeting without having fulfilled state requirements, asking persons present to join the union. He was convicted of contempt for violating a restraining order that had been issued against him prior to the address. Texas argued that the statute was a valid exercise of the police power to protect "laborers from imposture when approached by an alleged organizer. The Supreme Court reversed, five to four.

Decided January 8, 1945.

Mr. Justice RUTLEDGE delivered the opinion of the Court.

The case confronts us again with the duty our system places on this Court to say where the individual's freedom ends and the State's power begins. Choice on that border, now as always delicate, is perhaps more so where the usual presumption supporting legislation is balanced by the preferred place given in our scheme to the great, the indispensable democratic freedoms secured by the First Amendment. That priority gives these liberties a sanctity and a sanction not permitting dubious intrusions. And it is the character of the right, not of the limitation, which determines what standard governs the choice.

For these reasons any attempt to restrict those liberties must be justified by clear public interest, threatened not doubtfully or remotely, but by clear and present danger. The rational connection between the remedy provided and the evil to be curbed, which in other contexts might support legislation against attack on due process grounds, will not suffice. These rights rest on firmer foundation. Accordingly, whatever occasion would restrain orderly discussion and persuasion, at appropriate time and place, must have clear support in public danger, actual or impending. Only the gravest abuses, endangering paramount interests, give occasion for permissible limitation. It is therefore in our tradition to allow the widest room for discussion, the narrowest range for its restriction, particularly when this right is exercised in conjunction with peaceable assembly. It was not by accident or coincidence that the rights to freedom in speech and press were coupled in a single guaranty with the rights of the people peaceably to assemble and to petition for redress of grievances. All these, though not identical, are inseparable. They are cognate rights, cf. *De Jonge v. Oregon.*

This conjunction of liberties is not peculiar to religious activity and institutions alone. The First Amendment gives freedom of mind the same security as freedom of conscience. Great secular causes, with small ones, are guarded. The grievances for redress of which the right of petition was insured, and with it the right of assembly, are not solely religious or political ones. And the rights of free speech and a free press are not confined to any field of human interest.

The idea is not sound therefore that the First Amendment's safeguards are wholly inapplicable to business or economic activity. And it does not resolve where the line shall be drawn in a particular case merely to urge, as Texas does, that an organization for which the rights of free speech and free assembly are claimed is one "engaged in business activities" or that the individual who leads it in exercising these rights receives compensation for doing so. Nor, on the other hand, is the answer given, whether what is done is an exercise of those rights and the restriction a forbidden impairment, by ignoring the organization's economic function, because those interests of workingmen are involved or because they have the general liberties of the citizen, as appellant would do.

These comparisons are at once too simple, too general, and too inaccurate to be determinative. Where the line shall be placed in a particular application rests, not on such generalities, but on the concrete clash of particular interests and the community's relative evaluation both of them and of how the one will be affected by the specific restriction, the other by its absence. That judgment in the first instance is for the legislative body. But in our system where the line can constitutionally be placed presents a question this Court cannot escape answering independently, whatever the legislative judgment, in the light of our constitutional tradition. And the answer, under that tradition, can be affirmative, to support an intrusion upon this domain, only if grave and impending public danger requires this.

Thomas went to Texas for one purpose and one only—to make the speech in question. Its whole object was publicly to proclaim the advantages of workers' organizations and to persuade workmen to join Local No. 1002 as part of a campaign for members. These also were the sole objects of the meeting. The campaign, and the meeting, were incidents of an impending election for a collective bargaining agent, previously ordered by national authority pursuant to the guaranties of national law. Those guaranties include the workers' right to organize freely for collective bargaining. And this comprehends whatever may be appropriate and lawful to accomplish and maintain such organization. It included, in this case, the right to designate Local No. 1002 or any other union or agency as the employees' representative. It included their right fully and freely to discuss and be informed concerning this choice, privately or in public assembly. Necessarily correlative was the right of the union, its members and officials, whether residents or nonresidents of Texas and, if the latter, whether there for a single occasion or sojourning longer, to discuss with and inform the employees concerning matters involved in their choice. These rights of assembly and discussion are protected by the First Amendment. Whatever would restrict them, without sufficient occasion, would infringe its safeguards. The occasion was clearly protected. The speech was an essential part of the occasion, unless all meaning and purpose were to be taken from it. And the invitations, both general and particular, were parts of the speech, inseparable incidents of the occasion and of all that was said or done.

That there was restriction upon Thomas' right to speak and the rights of the workers to hear what he had to say, there can be no doubt. The threat of the restraining order, backed by the power of contempt, and of arrest for crime, hung over every word. A speaker in such circumstances could avoid the words "solicit," "invite," "join." It would be impossible to avoid the idea. The statute requires no specific formula. It is not contended that only the use of the word "solicit" would violate the prohibition. Without such a limitation, the statute forbids any language which conveys, or reasonably could be found to convey, the meaning of invitation. That Thomas chose to meet the issue squarely, not to hide in ambiguous phrasing, does not counteract this fact. General words create different and often particular impressions on different minds. No speaker, however careful, can convey exactly his meaning, or the same meaning, to the different members of an audience. How one might "laud unionism," as the State and the State Supreme Court concede Thomas was free to do, yet in these circumstances not imply an invitation is hard to conceive. This is the nub of the case, which the State fails to meet because it cannot do so. Workingmen do not lack capacity for making rational connections. They would understand, or some would, that the president of U.A.W. and vice president of C.I.O., addressing an organization meeting, was not urging merely a philosophic attachment to abstract principles of unionism, disconnected from the business immediately at hand. The feat would be incredible for a national leader, addressing such a meeting, lauding unions and their principles, urging adherence to union philosophy, not also and thereby to suggest attachment to the union by becoming a member.

Furthermore, whether words intended and designed to fall short of invitation would miss that mark is a question both of intent and of effect. No speaker, in such circumstances, safely could assume that anything he might say upon the general subject would not be understood by some as an invitation. In short, the supposedly clear-cut distinction between discussion, laudation, general advocacy, and solicitation puts the speaker in these circumstances wholly at the mercy of the varied understanding of his hearers and consequently of whatever inference may be drawn as to his intent and meaning.

Such a distinction offers no security for free discussion. In these conditions it blankets with uncertainty whatever may be said. It compels the speaker to hedge and trim. He must take care in every word to create no impression that he means, in advocating unionism's most central principle, namely, that workingmen should unite for collective bargaining, to urge those present to do so. The vice is not merely that invitation, in the circumstances shown here, is speech. It is also that its prohibition forbids or restrains discussion which is not or may not be invitation. The sharp line cannot be drawn surely or securely. The effort to observe it could not be free speech, free press, or free assembly, in any sense of free advocacy of principle or cause. The restriction's effect, as applied, in a very practical sense was to prohibit Thomas not only to solicit members and memberships, but also to speak in advocacy of the cause of trade unionism in Texas, without having first procured the card. Thomas knew this and faced the alternatives it presented. When served with the order he had three choices: (1) To stand on his right and speak freely; (2) to quit, refusing entirely to speak; (3) to trim, and even thus to risk the penalty. He chose the first alternative. We think he was within his rights in doing so.

The assembly was entirely peaceable, and had no other than a wholly lawful purpose. The statements forbidden were not in themselves unlawful, had no tendency to incite to unlawful action, involved no element of clear and present, grave and immediate danger to the public welfare. Moreover, the State has shown no justification for placing restrictions on the use of the word "solicit." We have here nothing comparable to the case where use of the word "fire" in a crowded theater creates a clear and present danger which the State may undertake to avoid or against which it may protect. We cannot say that "solicit" in this setting is such a dangerous word. So far as free speech alone is concerned, there can be no ban or restriction or burden placed on the use of such a word except on showing of exceptional circumstances where the public safety, morality or health is involved or some other substantial interest of the community is at stake.

If therefore use of the word or language equivalent in meaning was illegal here, it was so only because the statute and the order forbade the particular speaker to utter it. When legislation or its application can confine labor leaders on such occasions to innocuous and abstract discussion of the virtues of trade unions and so becloud even this with doubt, uncertainty and the risk of penalty, freedom of speech for them will be at an end. A restriction so destructive of the right of public discussion, without greater or more imminent danger to the public interest than existed in this case, is incompatible with the freedoms secured by the First Amendment.

We do not mean to say there is not, in many circumstances, a difference between urging a course of action and merely giving and acquiring information. On the other hand, history has not been without periods when the search for knowledge alone was banned. Of this we may assume the men who wrote the Bill of Rights were aware. But the protection they sought was not solely for persons in intellectual pursuits. It extends to more than abstract discussion, unrelated to action. The First Amendment is a charter for government, not for an institution of learning. "Free trade in ideas" means free trade in the opportunity to persuade to action, not merely to describe facts. Indeed, the whole history of the problem shows it is to the end of preventing action that repression is primarily directed and to preserving the right to urge it that the protections are given.

Accordingly, decision here has recognized that employers' attempts to persuade to action with respect to joining or not joining unions are within the First Amendment's guaranty. Decisions of other courts have done likewise. When to this persuasion other things are added which bring about coercion, or give it that character, the limit of the right has been passed. Cf. *National Labor Relations Board v. Virginia Electric & Power Co., supra.* But short of that limit the employer's freedom cannot be impaired. The Constitution protects no less the employees' converse right. Of course espousal of the cause of labor is entitled to no higher constitutional protection than the espousal of any other lawful cause. It is entitled to the same protection.

VI.

Apart from its "business practice" theory, the State contends that Section 5 is not inconsistent with freedom of speech and assembly, since this is merely a previous identification requirement which, according to the State court's decision, gives the Secretary of State only "ministerial, not discretionary" authority.

How far the State can require previous identification by one who undertakes to exercise the rights secured by the First Amendment has been largely undetermined. It has arisen here chiefly, though only tangentially, in connection with license requirements involving the solicitation of funds, and other activities upon the public streets or in public places or house-to-house canvassing, cf. *Schneider v. State, supra*. In these cases, however, the license requirements were for more than mere identification or previous registration and were held invalid because they vested discretion in the issuing authorities to censor the activity involved. Nevertheless, it was indicated by dictum in *Cantwell v. Connecticut* that a statute going no further than merely to require previous identification would be sustained in respect to the activities mentioned. Although those activities are not involved in this case, that dictum and the decision in *People of State of New York ex rel. Bryant v. Zimmerman* furnish perhaps the instances of pronouncement or decision here nearest this phase of the question now presented.

As a matter of principle a requirement of registration in order to make a public speech would seem generally incompatible with an exercise of the rights of free speech and free assembly. Lawful public assemblies, involving no element of grave and immediate danger to an interest the state is entitled to protect, are not instruments of harm which require previous identification of the speakers. And the right either of workmen or of unions under these conditions to assemble and discuss their own affairs is as fully protected by the Constitution as the right of businessmen, farmers, educators, political party members or others to assemble and discuss their affairs and to enlist the support of others.

We think the controlling principle is stated in *De Jonge v. Oregon*. In that case this Court held that "consistently with the Federal Constitution, peaceable assembly for lawful discussion cannot be made a crime." And "those who assist in the conduct of such meetings cannot be branded as criminals on that score. The question, if the rights of free speech and peaceable assembly are to be preserved, is not as to the auspices under which the meeting is held but as to its purpose; not as to the relations of the speakers, but whether their utterances transcend the bounds of the freedom of speech which the Constitution protects. If the persons assembling have committed crimes elsewhere, if they have formed or are engaged in a conspiracy against the public peace and order, they may be prosecuted for their conspiracy or other violation of valid laws. But it is a different matter when the State, instead of prosecuting them for such offenses, seizes upon mere participation in a peaceable assembly and a lawful public discussion as the basis for a criminal charge."

If the exercise of the rights of free speech and free assembly cannot be made a crime, we do not think this can be accomplished by the device of requiring previous registration as a condition for exercising them and making such a condition the foundation for restraining in advance their exercise and for imposing a penalty for violating such a restraining order. So long as no more is involved than exercise of the rights of free speech and free assembly, it is immune to such a restriction. If one who solicits support for the cause of labor may be required to register as a condition to the exercise of his right to make a public speech, so may he who seeks to rally support for any social, business, religious or political cause. We think a requirement that one must register before he undertakes to make a public speech to enlist support for a lawful movement is quite incompatible with the requirements of the First Amendment.

WALDORF STATEMENT (1947)

On November 24, 1947, fifty leaders of the motion picture industry, including studio heads and Eric Johnston, the head of the Association of Motion Picture Producers, met in Manhattan's famed Waldorf-Astoria Hotel and issued a statement the next day that many consider the beginning of the Hollywood blacklist. The statement made it the clear that the film studios would not hire any of the Hollywood Ten or any members of the Communist Party. The Screen Writers Guild and the Screen Actors Guild later adopted a similar policy excluding Communists from their membership. The blacklist lasted until the early 1960s.

Members of the Association of Motion Picture Producers deplore the action of the 10 Hollywood men who have been cited for contempt by the House of Representatives. We do not desire to prejudge their legal rights, but their actions have been a disservice to their employers and have impaired their usefulness to the industry.

We will forthwith discharge or suspend without compensation those in our employ, and we will not re-employ any of the 10 until such time as he is acquitted or has purged himself of contempt and declares under oath that he is not a Communist.

On the broader issue of alleged subversive and disloyal elements in Hollywood, our members are likewise prepared to take positive action.

We will not knowingly employ a Communist or a member of any party or group which advocates the overthrow of the government of the United States by force or by any illegal or unconstitutional methods.

In pursuing this policy, we are not going to be swayed by hysteria or intimidation from any source. We are frank to recognize that such a policy involves danger and risks. There is the danger of hurting innocent people. There is the risk of creating an atmosphere of fear. Creative work at its best cannot be carried on in an atmosphere of fear. We will guard against this danger, this risk, this fear.

To this end we will invite the Hollywood talent guilds to work with us to eliminate any subversives, to protect the innocent, and to safeguard free speech and a free screen wherever threatened.

The absence of a national policy, established by Congress, with respect to the employment of Communists in private industry makes our task difficult. Ours is a nation of laws. We request Congress to enact legislation to assist American industry to rid itself of subversive, disloyal elements.

Nothing subversive or un-American has appeared on the screen, nor can any number of Hollywood investigations obscure the patriotic services of the 30,000 loyal Americans employed in Hollywood who have given our government invaluable aid to war and peace.

WATKINS V. UNITED STATES (1957)

Watkins testified before the House Un-American Activities Committee that was investigating Communist activity in the labor unions. He freely discussed his own relationship to the Communist Party but refused to an-

swer questions concerning others. He was later convicted in federal district court for his refusal to answer questions pertinent to a congressional inquiry. The Court in a controversial decision reversed the conviction and asserted that First Amendment rights, including freedom of association, apply to congressional investigations.

Decided June 17, 1957.

Mr. Chief Justice WARREN delivered the opinion of the Court.

In the decade following World War II, there appeared a new kind of congressional inquiry unknown in prior periods of American history. Principally this was the result of the various investigations into the threat of subversion of the United States Government, but other subjects of congressional interest also contributed to the changed scene. This new phase of legislative inquiry involved a broad-scale intrusion into the lives and affairs of private citizens. It brought before the courts novel questions of the appropriate limits of congressional inquiry. Prior cases, like *Kilbourn, McGrain* and *Sinclair,* had defined the scope of investigative power in terms of the inherent limitations of the sources of that power. In the more recent cases, the emphasis shifted to problems of accommodating the interest of the Government with the rights and privileges of individuals. The central theme was the application of the Bill of Rights as a restraint upon the assertion of governmental power in this form.

It was during this period that the Fifth Amendment privilege against self-incrimination was frequently invoked and recognized as a legal limit upon the authority of a committee to require that a witness answer its questions. Some early doubts as to the applicability of that privilege before a legislative committee never matured. When the matter reached this Court, the Government did not challenge in any way that the Fifth Amendment protection was available to the witness, and such a challenge could not have prevailed. It confined its argument to the character of the answers sought and to the adequacy of the claim of privilege.

A far more difficult task evolved from the claim by witnesses that the committees' interrogations were infringements upon the freedoms of the First Amendment. Clearly, an investigation is subject to the command that the Congress shall make no law abridging freedom of speech or press or assembly. While it is true that there is no statute to be reviewed, and that an investigation is not a law, nevertheless an investigation is part of lawmaking. It is justified solely as an adjunct to the legislative process. The First Amendment may be invoked against infringement of the protected freedoms by law or by lawmaking.

Abuses of the investigative process may imperceptibly lead to abridgment of protected freedoms. The mere summoning of a witness and compelling him to testify, against his will, about his beliefs, expressions or associations is a measure of governmental interference. And when those forced revelations concern matters that are unorthodox, unpopular, or even hateful to the general public, the reaction in the life of the witness may be disastrous. This effect is even more harsh when it is past beliefs, expressions or associations that are disclosed and judged by current standards rather than those contemporary with the matters exposed. Nor does the witness alone suffer the consequences. Those who are identified by witnesses and thereby placed in the same glare of publicity are equally subject to public stigma, scorn and obloquy. Beyond that, there is the more subtle and immeasurable effect upon those who tend to adhere to the most orthodox and uncontroversial views and associations in order to avoid a similar fate at some future time. That this impact is partly the result of non-governmental activity by private persons cannot relieve the investigators of their responsibility for initiating the reaction.

The Court recognized the restraints of the Bill of Rights upon congressional investigations in *United States v. Rumely.* The magnitude and complexity of the problem of applying the First Amendment to that case led the Court to construe narrowly the resolution describing the committee's authority. It was concluded that, when First Amendment rights are threatened, the delegation of power to the committee must be clearly revealed in its charter.

Accommodation of the congressional need for particular information with the individual and personal interest in privacy is an arduous and delicate task for any court. We do not underestimate the difficulties that would attend such an undertaking. It is manifest that despite the adverse effects which follow upon compelled disclosure of private matters, not all such inquiries are barred. *Kilbourn v. Thompson* teaches that such an investigation into individual affairs is invalid if unrelated to any legislative purpose. That is beyond the powers conferred upon the Congress in the Constitution. *United States v. Rumely* makes it plain that the mere semblance of legislative purpose would not justify an inquiry in the face of the Bill of Rights. The critical element is the existence of, and the weight to be ascribed to, the interest of the Congress in demanding disclosures from an unwilling witness. We cannot simply assume, however, that every congressional investigation is justified by a public need that overbalances any private rights affected. To do so would be to abdicate the responsibility placed by the Constitution upon the judiciary to insure that the Congress does not unjustifiably encroach upon an individual's right to privacy nor abridge his liberty of speech, press, religion or assembly.

Petitioner has earnestly suggested that the difficult questions of protecting these rights from infringement by legislative inquiries can be surmounted in this case because there was no public purpose served in his interrogation. His conclusion is based upon the thesis that the Subcommittee was engaged in a program of exposure for the sake of exposure. The sole purpose of the inquiry, he contends, was to bring down upon himself and others the violence of public reaction because of their past beliefs, expressions and associations. In support of this argument, petitioner has marshalled an impressive array of evidence that some Congressmen have believed that such was their duty, or part of it.

We have no doubt that there is no congressional power to expose for the sake of exposure. The public is, of course, entitled to be informed concerning the workings of its government. That cannot be inflated into a general power to expose where the predominant result can only be an invasion of the private rights of individuals. But a solution to our problem is not to be found in testing the motives of committee members for this purpose. Such is not our function. Their motives alone would not vitiate an investigation which had been instituted by a House of Congress if that assembly's legislative purpose is being served.

Petitioner's contentions do point to a situation of particular significance from the standpoint of the constitutional limitations upon congressional investigations. The theory of a committee inquiry is that the committee members are serving as the representatives of the parent assembly in collecting information for a legislative purpose. Their function is to act as the eyes and ears of the Congress in obtaining facts upon which the full legislature can act. To carry out this mission, committees and subcommittees, sometimes one Congressman are endowed with the full power of the Congress to compel testimony. In this case, only two men exercised that authority in demanding information over petitioner's protest.

An essential premise in this situation is that the House or Senate shall have instructed the committee members on what they are to do with the power delegated to them. It is the responsibility of the Congress, in the first instance, to insure that compulsory process is used only in further-ance of a legislative purpose. That requires that the instructions to an in-vestigating committee spell out that group's jurisdiction and purpose with sufficient particularity. Those instructions are embodied in the au-thorizing resolution. That document is the committee's charter. Broadly drafted and loosely worded, however, such resolutions can leave tremendous latitude to the discretion of the investigators. The more vague the committee's charter is, the greater becomes the possibility that the committee's specific actions are not in conformity with the will of the parent House of Congress.

The authorizing resolution of the Un-American Activities Commit-tee was adopted in 1938 when a select committee, under the chairman-ship of Representative Dies, was created. Several years later, the Com-mittee was made a standing organ of the House with the same mandate. It defines the Committee's authority as follows:

"The Committee on Un-American Activities, as a whole or by sub-committee, is authorized to make from time to time investigations of (1) the extent, character, and objects of un-American propaganda activities in the United States, (2) the diffusion within the United States of sub-versive and un-American propaganda that is instigated from foreign countries or of a domestic origin and attacks the principle of the form of government as guaranteed by our Constitution, and (3) all other ques-tions in relation thereto that would aid Congress in any necessary reme-dial legislation."

It would be difficult to imagine a less explicit authorizing resolution. Who can define the meaning of "un-American"? What is that single, solitary "principle of the form of government as guaranteed by our Constitution"? There is no need to dwell upon the language, however. At one time, perhaps, the resolution might have been read narrowly to confine the Committee to the subject of propaganda. The events that have transpired in the fifteen years before the interrogation of petitioner make such a construction impossible at this date.

The members of the Committee have clearly demonstrated that they did not feel themselves restricted in any way to propaganda in the nar-row sense of the word. Unquestionably the Committee conceived of its task in the grand view of its name. Un-American activities were its target, no matter how or where manifested. Notwithstanding the broad purview of the Committee's experience, the House of Representatives repeatedly approved its continuation. Five times it extended the life of the special committee. Then it made the group a standing committee of the House. A year later, the Committee's charter was embodied in the Legislative Reorganization Act. On five occasions, at the beginning of sessions of Congress, it has made the authorizing resolution part of the rules of the House. On innumerable occasions, it has passed appropriation bills to allow the Committee to continue its efforts.

Combining the language of the resolution with the construction it has been given, it is evident that the preliminary control of the Committee exercised by the House of Representatives is slight or non-existent. No one could reasonably deduce from the charter the kind of investigation that the Committee was directed to make. As a result, we are asked to engage in a process of retroactive rationalization. Looking backward from the events that transpired, we are asked to uphold the Committee's actions unless it appears that they were clearly not authorized by the charter. As a corollary to this inverse approach, the Government urges that we must view the matter hospitably to the power of the Congress— that if there is any legislative purpose which might have been furthered by the kind of disclosure sought, the witness must be punished for withholding it. No doubt every reasonable indulgence of legality must be accorded to the actions of a coordinate branch of our Government. But such deference cannot yield to an unnecessary and unreasonable dissipation of precious constitutional freedoms.

The Government contends that the public interest at the core of the investigations of the Un-American Activities Committee is the need by the Congress to be informed of efforts to overthrow the Government by force and violence so that adequate legislative safeguards can be erected. From this core, however, the Committee can radiate outward infinitely to any topic thought to be related in some way to armed insurrection. The outer reaches of this domain are known only by the content of "un-American activities." Remoteness of subject can be aggravated by a probe for a depth of detail even farther removed from any basis of legislative action. A third dimension is added when the investigators turn their attention to the past to collect minutiae on remote topics, on the hypothesis that the past may reflect upon the present.

The consequences that flow from this situation are manifold. In the first place, a reviewing court is unable to make the kind of judgment made by the Court in *United States v. Rumely, supra.* The Committee is allowed, in essence, to define its own authority, to choose the direction and focus of its activities. In deciding what to do with the power that has been conferred upon them, members of the Committee may act pursuant to motives that seem to them to be the highest. Their decisions, nevertheless, can lead to ruthless exposure of private lives in order to gather data that is neither desired by the Congress nor useful to it. Yet it is impossible in this circumstance, with constitutional freedoms in jeopardy, to declare that the Committee has ranged beyond the area committed to it by its parent assembly because the boundaries are so nebulous.

More important and more fundamental than that, however, it insulates the House that has authorized the investigation from the witnesses who are subjected to the sanctions of compulsory process. There is a wide gulf between the responsibility for the use of investigative power and the actual exercise of that power. This is an especially vital consideration in assuring respect for constitutional liberties. Protected freedoms should not be placed in danger in the absence of a clear determination by the House or the Senate that a particular inquiry is justified by a specific legislative need.

An excessively broad charter, like that of the House Un-American Activities Committee, places the courts in an untenable position if they are to strike a balance between the public need for a particular interrogation and the right of citizens to carry on their affairs free from unnecessary governmental interference. It is impossible in such a situation to ascertain whether any legislative purpose justifies the disclosures sought and, if so, the importance of that information to the Congress in furtherance of its legislative function. The reason no court can make this critical judgment is that the House of Representatives itself has never made it. Only the legislative assembly initiating an investigation can assay the relative necessity of specific disclosures.

Absence of the qualitative consideration of petitioner's questioning by the House of Representatives aggravates a serious problem, revealed in this case, in the relationship of congressional investigating committees and the witnesses who appear before them. Plainly these committees are restricted to the missions delegated to them, i.e., to acquire certain data to be used by the House or the Senate in coping with a problem that falls within its legislative sphere. No witness can be compelled to make disclosures on matters outside that area. This is a jurisdictional concept of pertinency drawn from the nature of a congressional committee's source of authority. It is not wholly different from nor unrelated to the element of pertinency embodied in the criminal statute under which petitioner was prosecuted. When the definition of jurisdictional pertinency is as uncertain and wavering as in the case of the Un-American Activities Committee, it becomes extremely difficult for the Committee to limit its inquiries to statutory pertinency.

In fulfillment of their obligation under this statute, the courts must accord to the defendants every right which is guaranteed to defendants in all other criminal cases. Among these is the right to have available, through a sufficiently precise statute, information revealing the standard of criminality before the commission of the alleged offense. Applied to persons prosecuted under this raises a special problem in that the statute defines the crime as refusal to answer "any question pertinent to the question under inquiry." Part of the standard of criminality, therefore, is the pertinency of the questions propounded to the witness.

The problem attains proportion when viewed from the standpoint of the witness who appears before a congressional committee. He must decide at the time the questions are propounded whether or not to answer.

It is obvious that a person compelled to make this choice is entitled to have knowledge of the subject to which the interrogation is deemed pertinent. That knowledge must be available with the same degree of explicitness and clarity that the Due Process Clause requires in the expression of any element of a criminal offense. The "vice of vagueness" must be avoided here as in all other crimes. There are several sources that can outline the "question under inquiry" in such a way that the rules against vagueness are satisfied. The authorizing resolution, the remarks of the chairman or members of the committee, or even the nature of the proceedings themselves, might sometimes make the topic clear. This case demonstrates, however, that these sources often leave the matter in grave doubt. . . .

The conclusions we have reached in this case will not prevent the Congress, through its committees, from obtaining any information it needs for the proper fulfillment of its role in our scheme of government. The legislature is free to determine the kinds of data that should be collected. It is only those investigations that are conducted by use of compulsory process that give rise to a need to protect the rights of individuals against illegal encroachment. That protection can be readily achieved through procedures which prevent the separation of power from responsibility and which provide the constitutional requisites of fairness for witnesses. A measure of added care on the part of the House and the Senate in authorizing the use of compulsory process and by their committees in exercising that power would suffice. That is a small price to pay if it serves to uphold the principles of limited, constitutional government without constricting the power of the Congress to inform itself.

The judgment of the Court of Appeals is reversed, and the case is remanded to the District Court with instructions to dismiss the indictment.

NAACP v. Alabama (1958)

An Alabama statute had required that an out-of-state corporation doing business in Alabama had to file its charter and designate its place of business. The NAACP had refused to comply, and the attorney general of Alabama brought a suit enjoining them from conducting further activities in Alabama. He also sought a court order requiring the NAACP to produce various records, including a list of its members and their addresses. Upon its refusal, the NAACP was held in contempt of court. The Supreme Court unanimously reversed the conviction.

Decided June 30, 1958.
Mr. Justice HARLAN delivered the opinion of the Court.
We thus reach petitioner's claim that the production order in the state litigation trespasses upon fundamental freedoms protected by the Due Process Clause of the Fourteenth Amendment. Petitioner argues that in view of the facts and circumstances shown in the record, the effect of compelled disclosure of the membership lists will be to abridge the rights of its rank-and-file members to engage in lawful association in support of their common beliefs. It contends that governmental action which, although not directly suppressing association, nevertheless carries this consequence, can be justified only upon some overriding valid interest of the State.

Effective advocacy of both public and private points of view, particularly controversial ones, is undeniably enhanced by group association, as this Court has more than once recognized by remarking upon the close nexus between the freedoms of speech and assembly. It is beyond debate that freedom to engage in association for the advancement of beliefs and ideas is an inseparable aspect of the "liberty" assured by the Due Process Clause of the Fourteenth Amendment, which embraces freedom of speech. Of course, it is immaterial whether the beliefs sought to be advanced by association pertain to political, economic, religious or cultural matters, and state action which may have the effect of curtailing the freedom to associate is subject to the closest scrutiny.

The fact that Alabama, so far as is relevant to the validity of the contempt judgment presently under review, has taken no direct action to restrict the right of petitioner's members to associate freely, does not end inquiry into the effect of the production order. In the domain of these indispensable liberties, whether of speech, press, or association, the decisions of this Court recognize that abridgment of such rights, even though unintended, may inevitably follow from varied forms of governmental action. Thus in *Douds,* the Court stressed that the legislation there challenged, which on its face sought to regulate labor unions and to secure stability in interstate commerce, would have the practical effect "of discouraging" the exercise of constitutionally protected political rights, and it upheld the statute only after concluding that the reasons advanced for its enactment were constitutionally sufficient to justify its possible deterrent effect upon such freedoms. Similar recognition of possible unconstitutional intimidation of the free exercise of the right to advocate underlay this Court's narrow construction of the authority of a congressional committee investigating lobbying and of an Act regulating lobbying, although in neither case was there an effort to suppress speech. The governmental action challenged may appear to be totally unrelated to protected liberties. Statutes imposing taxes upon rather than prohibiting particular activity have been struck down when perceived to have the consequence of unduly curtailing the liberty of freedom of press assured under the Fourteenth Amendment.

It is hardly a novel perception that compelled disclosure of affiliation with groups engaged in advocacy may constitute as effective a restraint on freedom of association as the forms of governmental action in the cases above were thought likely to produce upon the particular consti-

tutional rights there involved. This Court has recognized the vital relationship between freedom to associate and privacy in one's associations.
When referring to the varied forms of governmental action which might
interfere with freedom of assembly, it said in *American Communications
Assn. v. Douds, supra,* at 402: "A requirement that adherents of particular religious faiths or political parties wear identifying arm-bands, for
example, is obviously of this nature." Compelled disclosure of membership in an organization engaged in advocacy of particular beliefs is of the
same order. Inviolability of privacy in group association may in many
circumstances be indispensable to preservation of freedom of association, particularly where a group espouses dissident beliefs. We think that
the production order, in the respects here drawn in question, must be re-
garded as entailing the likelihood of a substantial restraint upon the exercise by petitioner's members of their right to freedom of association.
Petitioner has made an uncontroverted showing that on past occasions
revelation of the identity of its rank-and-file members has exposed these
members to economic reprisal, loss of employment, threat of physical
coercion, and other manifestations of public hostility. Under these circumstances, we think it apparent that compelled disclosure of petitioner's Alabama membership is likely to affect adversely the ability of
petitioner and its members to pursue their collective effort to foster beliefs which they admittedly have the right to advocate, in that it may induce members to withdraw from the Association and dissuade others
from joining it because of fear of exposure of their beliefs shown
through their associations and of the consequences of this exposure.

It is not sufficient to answer, as the State does here, that whatever re-
pressive effect compulsory disclosure of names of petitioner's members
may have upon participation by Alabama citizens in petitioner's activities follows not from state action but from private community pressures.
The crucial factor is the interplay of governmental and private action, for
it is only after the initial exertion of state power represented by the production order that private action takes hold.

We turn to the final question whether Alabama has demonstrated an
interest in obtaining the disclosures it seeks from petitioner which is sufficient to justify the deterrent effect which we have concluded these disclosures may well have on the free exercise by petitioner's members of
their constitutionally protected right of association. It is not of moment
that the State has here acted solely through its judicial branch, for

whether legislative or judicial, it is still the application of state power which we are asked to scrutinize.

It is important to bear in mind that petitioner asserts no right to absolute immunity from state investigation, and no right to disregard Alabama's laws. As shown by its substantial compliance with the production order, petitioner does not deny Alabama's right to obtain from it such information as the State desires concerning the purposes of the Association and its activities within the State. Petitioner has not objected to divulging the identity of its members who are employed by or hold official positions with it. It has urged the rights solely of its ordinary rank-and-file members. This is therefore not analogous to a case involving the interest of a State in protecting its citizens in their dealings with paid solicitors or agents of foreign corporations by requiring identification.

Whether there was "justification" in this instance turns solely on the substantiality of Alabama's interest in obtaining the membership lists. During the course of a hearing before the Alabama Circuit Court on a motion of petitioner to set aside the production order, the State Attorney General presented at length, under examination by petitioner, the State's reason for requesting the membership lists. The exclusive purpose was to determine whether petitioner was conducting intrastate business in violation of the Alabama foreign corporation registration statute, and the membership lists were expected to help resolve this question. The issues in the litigation commenced by Alabama by its bill in equity were whether the character of petitioner and its activities in Alabama had been such as to make petitioner subject to the registration statute, and whether the extent of petitioner's activities without qualifying suggested its permanent ouster from the State. Without intimating the slightest view upon the merits of these issues, we are unable to perceive that the disclosure of the names of petitioner's rank-and-file members has a substantial bearing on either of them. As matters stand in the state court, petitioner (1) has admitted its presence and conduct of activities in Alabama since 1918; (2) has offered to comply in all respects with the state qualification statute, although preserving its contention that the statute does not apply to it; and (3) has apparently complied satisfactorily with the production order, except for the membership lists, by furnishing the Attorney General with varied business records, its charter and statement of purposes, the names of all of its directors and officers, and with the total number of its Alabama members and the amount of their dues. These last items would not on this record appear subject to constitutional challenge and have been furnished, but whatever interest the State may have in obtaining names of ordinary members has not been shown to be sufficient to overcome petitioner's constitutional objections to the production order.

From what has already been said, we think it apparent that *Bryant v. Zimmerman* cannot be relied on in support of the State's position, for that case involved markedly different considerations in terms of the interest of the State in obtaining disclosure. There, this Court upheld, as applied to a member of a local chapter of the Ku Klux Klan, a New York statute requiring any unincorporated association which demanded an oath as a condition to membership to file with state officials copies of its " ... constitution, by-laws, rules, regulations and oath of membership, together with a roster of its membership and a list of its officers for the current year." In its opinion, the Court took care to emphasize the nature of the organization which New York sought to regulate. The decision was based on the particular character of the Klan's activities, involving acts of unlawful intimidation and violence, which the Court assumed was before the state legislature when it enacted the statute, and of which the Court itself took judicial notice. Furthermore, the situation before us is significantly different from that in *Bryant,* because the organization there had made no effort to comply with any of the requirements of New York's statute but rather had refused to furnish the State with any information as to its local activities.

We hold that the immunity from state scrutiny of membership lists which the Association claims on behalf of its members is here so related to the right of the members to pursue their lawful private interests privately and to associate freely with others in so doing as to come within the protection of the Fourteenth Amendment. And we conclude that Alabama has fallen short of showing a controlling justification for the deterrent effect on the free enjoyment of the right to associate which disclosure of membership lists is likely to have. Accordingly, the judgment of civil contempt and the $100,000 fine which resulted from petitioner's refusal to comply with the production order in this respect must fall.

Reversed.

BARENBLATT V. UNITED STATES (1959)

In 1954 Lloyd Barenblatt, a former psychology instructor at Vassar College, was called before the House Un-American Activities Committee to answer questions about his associations with the Communist Party. Unlike Watkins, who had agreed to talk about his own associations, Barenblatt refused to answer any questions about either his own activities or those of others, claiming that the committee had no authority to inquire into his political beliefs and associations. He was convicted for contempt of Congress. The Court in this case granted much greater leeway for the Congress to inquire into the activities of those who may have been associated with the Communist Party.

Decided June 8, 1959.

Mr. Justice HARLAN delivered the opinion of the Court.

Our function, at this point, is purely one of constitutional adjudication in the particular case and upon the particular record before us, not to pass judgment upon the general wisdom or efficacy of the activities of this Committee in a vexing and complicated field. The precise constitutional issue confronting us is whether the Subcommittee's inquiry into petitioner's past or present membership in the Communist Party transgressed the provisions of the First Amendment, which of course reach and limit congressional investigations. *Watkins, supra,* at 197.

The Court's past cases establish sure guides to decision. Undeniably, the First Amendment in some circumstances protects an individual from being compelled to disclose his associational relationships. However, the protections of the First Amendment, unlike a proper claim of the privilege against self-incrimination under the Fifth Amendment, do not afford a witness the right to resist inquiry in all circumstances. Where First Amendment rights are asserted to bar governmental interrogation, resolution of the issue always involves a balancing by the courts of the competing private and public interests at stake in the particular circumstances shown. These principles were recognized in the *Watkins* case, where, in speaking of the First Amendment in relation to congressional inquiries, we said : "It is manifest that despite the adverse effects which follow upon compelled disclosure of private matters, not all such inquiries are barred. . . . The critical element is the existence of, and the weight to be ascribed to, the interest of the Congress in demanding disclosures from an unwilling witness. . . ." We applied the same principles in judging state action claimed to infringe rights of association assured by the Due Process Clause of the Fourteenth Amendment, and stated that the "subordinating interest of the State must be compelling" in order to overcome the individual constitutional rights at stake. In light of these principles we now consider petitioner's First Amendment claims.

The first question is whether this investigation was related to a valid legislative purpose, for Congress may not constitutionally require an individual to disclose his political relationships or other private affairs except in relation to such a purpose. See *Watkins v. United States, supra,* at 198.

That Congress has wide power to legislate in the field of Communist activity in this Country, and to conduct appropriate investigations in aid thereof, is hardly debatable. The existence of such power has never been questioned by this Court, and it is sufficient to say, without particularization, that Congress has enacted or considered in this field a wide range of legislative measures, not a few of which have stemmed from recommendations of the very Committee whose actions have been drawn in question here. In the last analysis this power rests on the right of self-preservation, "the ultimate value of any society." Justification for its exercise in turn rests on the long and widely accepted view that the tenets of the Communist Party include the ultimate overthrow of the Government of the United States by force and violence, a view which has been given formal expression by the Congress.

On these premises, this Court in its constitutional adjudications has consistently refused to view the Communist Party as an ordinary political party, and has upheld federal legislation aimed at the Communist problem which in a different context would certainly have raised constitutional issues of the gravest character. On the same premises, this Court has upheld under the Fourteenth Amendment state legislation requiring those occupying or seeking public office to disclaim knowing membership in any organization advocating overthrow of the Government by force and violence, which legislation none can avoid seeing was aimed at membership in the Communist Party. Similarly, in other areas, this Court has recognized the close nexus between the Communist Party and violent overthrow of government. To suggest that because the Communist Party may also sponsor peaceable political reforms the constitutional issues before us should now be judged as if that Party were just an ordinary political party from the standpoint of national security, is to ask this Court to blind itself to world affairs which have determined the whole course of our national policy since the close of World War II . . . and to the vast burdens which these conditions have entailed for the entire Nation.

We think that investigatory power in this domain is not to be denied Congress solely because the field of education is involved. Nothing in the prevailing opinions in *Sweezy v. New Hampshire, supra,* stands for a contrary view. The vice existing there was that the questioning of Sweezy, who had not been shown ever to have been connected with the Communist Party, as to the contents of a lecture he had given at the University of New Hampshire, and as to his connections with the Progressive Party, then on the ballot as a normal political party in some 26 States, was too far removed from the premises on which the constitutionality of the State's investigation had to depend to withstand attack under the Fourteenth Amendment. This is a very different thing from inquiring into the extent to which the Communist Party has succeeded in infiltrating into our universities, or elsewhere, persons and groups committed to furthering the objective of overthrow. Indeed we do not understand petitioner here to suggest that Congress in no circumstances may inquire into Communist activity in the field of education. Rather, his position is in effect that this particular investigation was aimed not at the revolutionary aspects but at the theoretical classroom discussion of communism.

In our opinion this position rests on a too constricted view of the nature of the investigatory process, and is not supported by a fair assessment of the record before us. An investigation of advocacy of or preparation for overthrow certainly embraces the right to identify a witness as a member of the Communist Party, and to inquire into the various manifestations of the Party's tenets. The strict requirements of a prosecution under the Smith Act are not the measure of the permissible scope of a congressional investigation into "overthrow," for of necessity the investigatory process must proceed step by step. Nor can it fairly be concluded that this investigation was directed at controlling what is being taught at our universities rather than at overthrow. The statement of the Subcommittee Chairman at the opening of the investigation evinces no such intention . . . and so far as this record reveals nothing thereafter transpired which would justify our holding that the thrust of the investigation later changed. The record discloses considerable testimony concerning the foreign domination and revolutionary purposes and efforts of the Communist Party.

Nor can we accept the further contention that this investigation should not be deemed to have been in furtherance of a legislative purpose because the true objective of the Committee and of the Congress was purely "exposure." So long as Congress acts in pursuance of its constitutional power, the Judiciary lacks authority to intervene on the basis of the motives which spurred the exercise of that power.

Finally, the record is barren of other factors which in themselves might sometimes lead to the conclusion that the individual interests at stake were not subordinate to those of the state. There is no indication in this record that the Subcommittee was attempting to pillory witnesses. Nor did petitioner's appearance as a witness follow from indiscriminate dragnet procedures, lacking in probable cause for belief that he possessed information which might be helpful to the Subcommittee. And the relevancy of the questions put to him by the Subcommittee is not open to doubt.

We conclude that the balance between the individual and the governmental interests here at stake must be struck in favor of the latter, and that therefore the provisions of the First Amendment have not been offended.

We hold that petitioner's conviction for contempt of Congress discloses no infirmity, and that the judgment of the Court of Appeals must be affirmed.

Mr. Justice BLACK, with whom the Chief Justice and Mr. Justice DOUGLAS concur, dissenting.

On May 28, 1954, petitioner Lloyd Barenblatt, then 31 years old, and a teacher of psychology at Vassar College, was summoned to appear before a Subcommittee of the House Committee on Un-American Activities. After service of the summons, but before Barenblatt appeared on June 28, his four-year contract with Vassar expired and was not renewed. He, therefore, came to the Committee as a private citizen without a job. Earlier that day, the Committee's interest in Barenblatt had been aroused by the testimony of an ex-Communist named Crowley. When Crowley had first appeared before the Un-American Activities Committee he had steadfastly refused to admit or deny Communist affiliations or to identify others as Communists. After the House reported this refusal to the United States Attorney for prosecution, Crowley "voluntarily" returned and asked to testify. He was sworn in and interrogated, but not before he was made aware by various Committee members of Committee policy to "make an appropriate recommendation" to protect any witness who "fully cooperates with the committee." He then talked at length, identifying by name, address and occupation, whenever possible, people he claimed had been Communists. One of these was Barenblatt, who, according to Crowley, had been a Communist during 1947–1950 while a graduate student and teaching fellow at the University of Michigan. Though Crowley testified in great detail about the small group of Communists who had been at Michigan at that time and though the Committee was very satisfied with his testimony, it sought repetition of much of the information from Barenblatt. Barenblatt, however, refused to answer their questions and filed a long statement outlining his constitutional objections. He asserted that the Committee was violating the Constitution by abridging freedom of speech, thought, press, and association, and by conducting legislative trials of known or suspected Communists which trespassed on the exclusive power of the judiciary. He argued that however he answered questions relating to membership in the Communist Party his position in society and his ability to earn a living would be seriously jeopardized; that he would, in effect, be subjected to a bill of attainder despite the twice-expressed constitutional mandate against such legislative punishments. This would occur, he pointed out, even if he did no more than invoke the protection of clearly applicable provisions of the Bill of Rights as a reason for refusing to answer.

II.

The First Amendment says in no equivocal language that Congress shall pass no law abridging freedom of speech, press, assembly or petition. The activities of this Committee, authorized by Congress, do precisely that, through exposure, obloquy and public scorn. The Court does not really deny this fact but relies on a combination of three reasons for permitting the infringement: (A) The notion that despite the First Amendment's command Congress can abridge speech and association if this Court decides that the governmental interest in abridging speech is greater than an individual's interest in exercising that freedom, (B) the Government's right to "preserve itself," (C) the fact that the

Committee is only after Communists or suspected Communists in this investigation.

(A) I do not agree that laws directly abridging First Amendment freedoms can be justified by a congressional or judicial balancing process.

But even assuming what I cannot assume, that some balancing is proper in this case, I feel that the Court after stating the test ignores it completely. At most it balances the right of the Government to preserve itself, against Barenblatt's right to refrain from revealing Communist affiliations. Such a balance, however, mistakes the factors to be weighed. In the first place, it completely leaves out the real interest in Barenblatt's silence, the interest of the people as a whole in being able to join organizations, advocate causes and make political "mistakes" without later being subjected to governmental penalties for having dared to think for themselves. It is this right, the right to err politically, which keeps us strong as a Nation. For no number of laws against communism can have as much effect as the personal conviction which comes from having heard its arguments and rejected them, or from having once accepted its tenets and later recognized their worthlessness. Instead, the obloquy which results from investigations such as this not only stifles "mistakes" but prevents all but the most courageous from hazarding any views which might at some later time become disfavored. This result, whose importance cannot be overestimated, is doubly crucial when it affects the universities, on which we must largely rely for the experimentation and development of new ideas essential to our country's welfare. It is these interests of society, rather than Barenblatt's own right to silence, which I think the Court should put on the balance against the demands of the Government, if any balancing process is to be tolerated.... Yet the Court styles this attenuated interest self-preservation and allows it to overcome the need our country has to let us all think, speak, and associate politically as we like and without fear of reprisal.

Moreover, I cannot agree with the Court's notion that First Amendment freedoms must be abridged in order to "preserve" our country. That notion rests on the unarticulated premise that this Nation's security hangs upon its power to punish people because of what they think, speak or write about, or because of those with whom they associate for political purposes. The Government, in its brief, virtually admits this position when it speaks of the "communication of unlawful ideas." I challenge this premise, and deny that ideas can be proscribed under our

Constitution. I agree that despotic governments cannot exist without stifling the voice of opposition to their oppressive practices. The First Amendment means to me, however, that the only constitutional way our Government can preserve itself is to leave its people the fullest possible freedom to praise, criticize or discuss, as they see fit, all governmental policies and to suggest, if they desire, that even its most fundamental postulates are bad and should be changed; "Therein lies the security of the Republic, the very foundation of constitutional government." On that premise this land was created, and on that premise it has grown to greatness. Our Constitution assumes that the common sense of the people and their attachment to our country will enable them, after free discussion, to withstand ideas that are wrong. To say that our patriotism must be protected against false ideas by means other than these is, I think, to make a baseless charge. Unless we can rely on these qualities— if, in short, we begin to punish speech—we cannot honestly proclaim ourselves to be a free Nation and we have lost what the Founders of this land risked their lives and their sacred honor to defend.

The Court implies, however, that the ordinary rules and requirements of the Constitution do not apply because the Committee is merely after Communists and they do not constitute a political party but only a criminal gang.

Of course it has always been recognized that members of the Party who, either individually or in combination, commit acts in violation of valid laws can be prosecuted. But the Party as a whole and innocent members of it could not be attainted merely because it had some illegal aims and because some of its members were lawbreakers. Thus in *De Jonge v. Oregon* (1937), on stipulated facts that the Communist Party advocated criminal syndicalism— "crime, physical violence, sabotage or any unlawful acts or methods as a means of accomplishing or effecting industrial or political change or revolution" —a unanimous Court, speaking through Chief Justice Hughes, held that a Communist addressing a Communist rally could be found guilty of no offense so long as no violence or crime was urged at the meeting. The Court absolutely refused to concede that either De Jonge or the Communist Party forfeited the protections of the First and Fourteenth Amendments because one of the Party's purposes was to effect a violent change of government. . . .

No matter how often or how quickly we repeat the claim that the Communist Party is not a political party, we cannot outlaw it, as a group, without endangering the liberty of all of us. The reason is not hard to find, for mixed among those aims of communism which are illegal are perfectly normal political and social goals. And muddled with its revolutionary tenets is a drive to achieve power through the ballot, if it can be done. These things necessarily make it a political party whatever other, illegal, aims it may have. Significantly until recently the Communist Party was on the ballot in many States. When that was so, many Communists undoubtedly hoped to accomplish its lawful goals through support of Communist candidates. Even now some such may still remain. To attribute to them, and to those who have left the Party, the taint of the group is to ignore both our traditions that guilt like belief is "personal and not a matter of mere association" and the obvious fact that "men adhering to a political party or other organization notoriously do not subscribe unqualifiedly to all of its platforms or asserted principles."

The fact is that once we allow any group which has some political aims or ideas to be driven from the ballot and from the battle for men's minds because some of its members are bad and some of its tenets are illegal, no group is safe.

GIBSON V. FLORIDA LEGISLATIVE INVESTIGATION COMMITTEE (1963)

The Florida legislature had authorized its Legislative Investigation Committee to look into Communist infiltration into various organizations, including the Miami branch of the NAACP. The committee had information that there were members of the branch who were also members of the Communist Party. The committee ordered Gibson, the president of the Miami branch, to appear before it and bring records showing the names of its members. He refused and was convicted of contempt. The Supreme Court reversed 5–4. The decision indicated that the Court was developing a more sympathetic approach toward freedom of association.

Decided March 25, 1963.
Mr. Justice GOLDBERG delivered the opinion of the Court.

We are here called upon once again to resolve a conflict between individual rights of free speech and association and governmental interest in conducting legislative investigations. Prior decisions illumine the contending principles.

This Court has repeatedly held that rights of association are within the ambit of the constitutional protections afforded by the First and Fourteenth Amendments.

At the same time, however, this Court's prior holdings demonstrate that there can be no question that the State has power adequately to inform itself—through legislative investigation, if it so desires—in order to act and protect its legitimate and vital interests. It is no less obvious, however, that the legislative power to investigate, broad as it may be, is not without limit. The fact that the general scope of the inquiry is authorized and permissible does not compel the conclusion that the investigatory body is free to inquire into or demand all forms of information. Validation of the broad subject matter under investigation does not necessarily carry with it automatic and wholesale validation of all individual questions, subpoenas, and documentary demands. When, as in this case, the claim is made that particular legislative inquiries and demands infringe substantially upon First and Fourteenth Amendment associational rights of individuals, the courts are called upon to, and must, determine the permissibility of the challenged actions. The interests here at stake are of significant magnitude, and neither their resolution nor impact is limited to, or dependent upon, the particular parties here involved. Freedom and viable government are both, for this purpose, indivisible concepts; whatever affects the rights of the parties here, affects all.

II.

Significantly, the parties are in substantial agreement as to the proper test to be applied to reconcile the competing claims of government and individual and to determine the propriety of the Committee's demands. As declared by the respondent Committee in its brief to this Court, "Basically, this case hinges entirely on the question of whether the evidence before the Committee [was] . . . sufficient to show probable cause or nexus between the NAACP Miami Branch, and Communist activities." We understand this to mean—regardless of the label applied, be it "nexus," "foundation," or whatever—that it is an essential prerequisite to the validity of an investigation which intrudes into the area of constitutionally protected rights of speech, press, association and petition that the State convincingly show a substantial relation between the information sought and a subject of overriding and compelling state interest.

Absent such a relation between the NAACP and conduct in which the State may have a compelling regulatory concern, the Committee has not "demonstrated so cogent an interest in obtaining and making public" the membership information sought to be obtained as to "justify the substantial abridgment of associational freedom which such disclosures will effect." *Bates v. Little Rock.* "Where there is a significant encroachment upon personal liberty, the State may prevail only upon showing a subordinating interest which is compelling."

Applying these principles to the facts of this case, the respondent Committee contends that the prior decisions of this Court compel a result here upholding the legislative right of inquiry. In *Barenblatt, Wilkinson,* and *Braden,* however, it was a refusal to answer a question or questions concerning the witness' own past or present membership in the Communist Party which supported his conviction. It is apparent that the necessary preponderating governmental interest and, in fact, the very result in those cases were founded on the holding that the Communist Party is not an ordinary or legitimate political party, as known in this country, and that, because of its particular nature, membership therein is itself a permissible subject of regulation and legislative scrutiny. Assuming the correctness of the premises on which those cases were decided, no further demonstration of compelling governmental interest was deemed necessary, since the direct object of the challenged questions there was discovery of membership in the Communist Party, a matter held pertinent to a proper subject then under inquiry.

Here, however, it is not alleged Communists who are the witnesses before the Committee and it is not discovery of their membership in that party which is the object of the challenged inquiries. Rather, it is the NAACP itself which is the subject of the investigation, and it is its local president, the petitioner, who was called before the Committee and held in contempt because he refused to divulge the contents of its membership records. There is no suggestion that the Miami branch of the NAACP or the national organization with which it is affiliated was, or is, itself a subversive organization. Nor is there any indication that the activities or policies of the NAACP were either Communist dominated or influenced. In fact, this very record indicates that the association was and is against communism and has voluntarily taken steps to keep Communists from being members. Each year since 1950, the NAACP has adopted resolutions barring Communists from membership in the organization. Moreover, the petitioner testified that all prospective officers of the local organization are thoroughly investigated for Communist or subversive connections and, though subversive activities constitute grounds for termination of association membership, no such expulsions from the branch occurred during the five years preceding the investigation.

Thus, unlike the situation in *Barenblatt, Wilkinson* and *Braden, supra,* the Committee was not here seeking from the petitioner or the records of which he was custodian any information as to whether he, himself, or even other persons were members of the Communist Party, Communist front or affiliated organizations, or other allegedly subversive groups; instead, the entire thrust of the demands on the petitioner was that he disclose whether other persons were members of the NAACP, itself a concededly legitimate and non-subversive organization. Compelling such an organization, engaged in the exercise of First and Fourteenth Amendment rights, to disclose its membership presents, under our cases, a question wholly different from compelling the Communist Party to disclose its own membership. Moreover, even to say, as in *Barenblatt,* that it is permissible to inquire into the subject of Communist infiltration of educational or other organizations does not mean that it is permissible to demand or require from such other groups disclosure of their membership by inquiry into their records when such disclosure will seriously inhibit or impair the exercise of constitutional rights and has not itself been demonstrated to bear a crucial relation to a proper governmental interest or to be essential to fulfillment of a proper governmental purpose. The prior holdings that governmental interest in controlling subversion and the particular character of the Communist Party and its objectives outweigh the right of individual Communists to conceal party membership or affiliations by no means require the wholly different conclusion that other groups—concededly legitimate—automatically forfeit their rights to privacy of association simply because the general subject matter of the legislative inquiry is Communist subversion or infiltration. The fact that governmental interest was deemed compelling in *Barenblatt, Wilkinson,* and *Braden* and held to support the inquiries there made into membership in the Communist Party does not resolve the issues here, where the challenged questions go to membership in an admittedly lawful organization.

III.

This summary of the evidence discloses the utter failure to demonstrate the existence of any substantial relationship between the NAACP and subversive or Communist activities. In essence, there is here merely indirect, less than unequivocal, and mostly hearsay testimony that in years past some 14 people who were asserted to be, or to have been, Communists or members of Communist front or "affiliated organizations" attended occasional meetings of the Miami branch of the NAACP "and/or" were members of that branch, which had a total membership of about 1,000.

On the other hand, there was no claim made at the hearings, or since, that the NAACP or its Miami branch was engaged in any subversive activities or that its legitimate activities have been dominated or influenced by Communists. Without any indication of present subversive infiltration in, or influence on, the Miami branch of the NAACP, and without any reasonable, demonstrated factual basis to believe that such infiltration or influence existed in the past, or was actively attempted or sought in the present—in short without any showing of a meaningful relationship between the NAACP, Miami branch, and subversives or subversive or other illegal activities—we are asked to find the compelling and subordinating state interest which must exist if essential freedoms are to be curtailed or inhibited. This we cannot do. The respondent Committee has laid no adequate foundation for its direct demands upon the officers and records of a wholly legitimate organization for disclosure of its membership; the Committee has neither demonstrated nor pointed out any threat to the State by virtue of the existence of the NAACP or the pursuit of its activities or the minimal associational ties of the 14 asserted Communists. The strong associational interest in maintaining the privacy of membership lists of groups engaged in the constitutionally protected free trade in ideas and beliefs may not be substantially infringed upon such a slender showing as here made by the respondent. While, of course, all legitimate organizations are the beneficiaries of these protections, they are all the more essential here, where the challenged privacy is that of persons espousing beliefs already unpopular with their neighbors and the deterrent and "chilling" effect on the free exercise of constitutionally enshrined rights of free speech, expression, and association is consequently the more immediate and substantial. What we recently said in *NAACP v. Button, supra,* with respect to the State of Virginia is, as appears from the record, equally applicable here: "We cannot close our eyes to the fact that the militant Negro civil rights movement has engendered the intense resentment and opposition of the politically dominant white community. . . ."

Nothing we say here impairs or denies the existence of the underlying legislative right to investigate or legislate with respect to subversive activities by Communists or anyone else; our decision today deals only with the manner in which such power may be exercised and we hold simply that groups which themselves are neither engaged in subversive or other illegal or improper activities nor demonstrated to have any substantial connections with such activities are to be protected in their rights of free and private association. . . .

To permit legislative inquiry to proceed on less than an adequate foundation would be to sanction unjustified and unwarranted intrusions into the very heart of the constitutional privilege to be secure in associations in legitimate organizations engaged in the exercise of First and Fourteenth Amendment rights; to impose a lesser standard than we here do would be inconsistent with the maintenance of those essential conditions basic to the preservation of our democracy.

The judgment below must be and is reversed.

Elfbrandt v. Russell (1966)

Arizona had passed a law requiring state employees to take an oath to support the federal and state constitutions and state laws. The legislature later passed a law providing that an employee is subject to prosecution for perjury and discharge from office if he "knowingly and willfully becomes or remains a member of the communist party of the United States or its successors or any of its subordinate organizations" or "any other organization" having for "one of its purposes" the overthrow of the state government if the employee knew of the unlawful purpose. The petitioner, a teacher, filed suit for declaratory relief, having decided that she could not in good conscience take the oath, uncertain of its meaning and unable to obtain a hearing to clarify the oath. The Court voted five to four to strike down the oath as enlarged by the legislature.

Decided April 18, 1966.

Mr. Justice DOUGLAS delivered the opinion of the Court.

This case . . . involves questions concerning the constitutionality of an Arizona Act requiring an oath from state employees. . . .

The oath reads in conventional fashion as follows:

"I, (type or print name) do solemnly swear (or affirm) that I will support the Constitution of the United States and the Constitution and laws of the State of Arizona; that I will bear true faith and allegiance to the same, and defend them against all enemies, foreign and domestic, and that I will faithfully and impartially discharge the duties of the office of (name of office) according to the best of my ability, so help me God (or so I do affirm)."

The Legislature put a gloss on the oath by subjecting to a prosecution for perjury and for discharge from public office anyone who took the oath and who "knowingly and willfully becomes or remains a member of the communist party of the United States or its successors or any of its subordinate organizations" or "any other organization" having for "one of its purposes" the overthrow of the government of Arizona or any of its political subdivisions where the employee had knowledge of the unlawful purpose. Petitioner, a teacher and a Quaker, decided she could not in good conscience take the oath, not knowing what it meant and not having any chance to get a hearing at which its precise scope and meaning could be determined.

We recognized in *Scales v. United States,* that "quasi-political parties or other groups . . . may embrace both legal and illegal aims." We noted that a "blanket prohibition of association with a group having both legal and illegal aims" would pose "a real danger that legitimate political expression or association would be impaired." The statute with which we dealt in *Scales,* the so-called "membership clause" of the Smith Act (18 U.S.C. 2385), was found not to suffer from this constitutional infirmity because, as the Court construed it, the statute reached only "active" membership with the "specific intent" of assisting in achieving the unlawful ends of the organization.

Any lingering doubt that proscription of mere knowing membership, without any showing of "specific intent," would run afoul of the Constitution was set at rest by our decision in *Aptheker v. Secretary of State.* We dealt there with a statute which provided that no member of a Communist organization ordered by the Subversive Activities Control Board to register shall apply for or use a passport. We concluded that the statute would not permit a narrow reading of the sort we gave in *Scales*. The statute, as we read it, covered membership which was not accompanied by a specific intent to further the unlawful aims of the organization, and we held it unconstitutional.

The oath and accompanying statutory gloss challenged here suffer from an identical constitutional infirmity. One who subscribes to this Arizona oath and who is, or thereafter becomes, a knowing member of an organization which has as "one of its purposes" the violent overthrow of the government, is subject to immediate discharge and criminal penalties. Nothing in the oath, the statutory gloss, or the construction of the oath and statutes given by the Arizona Supreme Court, purports to exclude association by one who does not subscribe to the organization's unlawful ends. Would it be legal to join a seminar group predominantly Communist and therefore subject to control by those who are said to believe in the overthrow of the Government by force and violence? Juries might convict though the teacher did not subscribe to the wrongful aims of the organization. And there is apparently no machinery provided for getting clearance in advance.

Those who join an organization but do not share its unlawful purposes and who do not participate in its unlawful activities surely pose no threat, either as citizens or as public employees. Laws such as this which are not restricted in scope to those who join with the "specific intent" to further illegal action impose, in effect, a conclusive presumption that the member shares the unlawful aims of the organization.

This Act threatens the cherished freedom of association protected by the First Amendment, made applicable to the States through the Fourteenth Amendment.

A statute touching those protected rights must be "narrowly drawn to define and punish specific conduct as constituting a clear and present danger to a substantial interest of the State." *Cantwell v. Connecticut.* Legitimate legislative goals "cannot be pursued by means that broadly stifle fundamental personal liberties when the end can be more narrowly achieved."

A law which applies to membership without the "specific intent" to further the illegal aims of the organization infringes unnecessarily on protected freedoms. It rests on the doctrine of "guilt by association" which has no place here.

Reversed.

Mr. Justice WHITE, with whom Mr. Justice CLARK, Mr. Justice HARLAN and Mr. Justice STEWART concur, dissenting.

According to unequivocal prior holdings of this Court, a State is entitled to condition public employment upon its employees abstaining from knowing membership in the Communist Party and other organizations advocating the violent overthrow of the government which employs them; the State is constitutionally authorized to inquire into such affiliations and it may discharge those who refuse to affirm or deny them. . . . The Court does not mention or purport to overrule these cases; nor does it expressly hold that a State must retain, even in its most sensitive positions, those who lend such support as knowing membership entails to those organizations, such as the Communist Party, whose purposes include the violent destruction of democratic government.

Under existing constitutional law, then, Arizona is free to require its teachers to refrain from knowing membership in the designated organizations and to bar from employment all knowing members as well as those who refuse to establish their qualifications to teach by executing the oath prescribed by the statute. Arizona need not retain those employees on the governor's staff, in the Phoenix police department or in its schools who insist on holding membership in and lending their name and influence to those organizations aiming at violent overthrow.

There is nothing in *Scales v. United States, Noto v. United States,* or *Aptheker v. Secretary of State,* dictating the result reached by the Court. *Scales* involved the construction of the Smith Act and a holding that the membership clause did not reach members who knew of the illegal aims of the Party but lacked an active membership and an intent to further the illegal ends. *Noto* also involved a construction of the Smith Act, the conviction there being reversed for insufficient evidence. *Aptheker* struck down a provision denying passports to members of the Communist Party which applied "whether or not one knows or believes that he is associated with an organization operating to further aims of the world Communist movement. . . . The provision therefore sweeps within its prohibition both knowing and unknowing members." In any event, *Scales, Noto* and *Aptheker* did not deal with the government employee who is a knowing member of the Communist Party. They did not suggest that the State or Federal Government should be prohibited from taking elementary precautions against its employees forming knowing and deliberate affiliations with those organizations who conspire to destroy the government by violent means. . . .

Even if Arizona may not take criminal action against its law enforcement officers or its teachers who become Communists knowing of the purposes of the Party, the Court's judgment overreaches itself in invalidating this Arizona statute. Whether or not Arizona may make knowing membership a crime, it need not retain the member as an employee and is entitled to insist that its employees disclaim, under oath, knowing membership in the designated organizations and to condition future employment upon future abstention from membership. It is, therefore, improper to invalidate the entire statute in this declaratory judgment action.

UNITED STATES V. ROBEL (1967)

This case involved a section of the Internal Security Act that denied employment in any defense facility to members of the Communist Party. Robel, who was a member of the party, was employed as a machinist in the Todd Shipyards in Seattle, which the secretary of defense had designated as a defense facility. Robel continued to work there and was indicted under that section of the Internal Security Act. The Federal District Court dismissed the indictment, and Robel went back to work. The government appealed to the Supreme Court, which by a vote of six to two affirmed the dismissal of the indictment.

Decided December 11, 1967.
Mr. Chief Justice WARREN delivered the opinion of the Court.
This appeal draws into question the constitutionality of 5 (a) (1) (D) of the Subversive Activities Control Act of 1950, which provides that, when a Communist-action organization is under a final order to register, it shall be unlawful for any member of the organization "to engage in any employment in any defense facility." . . .

We cannot agree with the District Court that [this law] can be saved from constitutional infirmity by limiting its application to active members of Communist-action organizations who have the specific intent of furthering the unlawful goals of such organizations. . . . In *Aptheker v.*

Secretary of State, (1964), we noted that the Smith Act's membership clause required a defendant to have knowledge of the organization's illegal advocacy, a requirement that "was intimately connected with the construction limiting membership to 'active' members." *Aptheker* involved a challenge to 6 of the Subversive Activities Control Act, 50 U.S.C. 785, which provides that, when a Communist organization is registered or under a final order to register, it shall be unlawful for any member thereof with knowledge or notice thereof to apply for a passport. We held that "[t]he clarity and preciseness of the provision in question make it impossible to narrow its indiscriminately cast and overly broad scope without substantial rewriting." We take the same view of 5 (a) (1) (D). It is precisely because that statute sweeps indiscriminately across all types of association with Communist-action groups, without regard to the quality and degree of membership, that it runs afoul of the First Amendment.

In *Aptheker,* we held 6 unconstitutional because it too broadly and indiscriminately infringed upon constitutionally protected rights. The Government has argued that, despite the overbreadth which is obvious on the face of 5 (a) (1) (D), *Aptheker* is not controlling in this case because the right to travel is a more basic freedom than the right to be employed in a defense facility. We agree that *Aptheker* is not controlling since it was decided under the Fifth Amendment. But we cannot agree with the Government's characterization of the essential issue in this case. It is true that the specific disability imposed by 5 (a) (1) (D) is to limit the employment opportunities of those who fall within its coverage, and such a limitation is not without serious constitutional implications. . . . But the operative fact upon which the job disability depends is the exercise of an individual's right of association, which is protected by the provisions of the First Amendment. Wherever one would place the right to travel on a scale of constitutional values, it is clear that those rights protected by the First Amendment are no less basic in our democratic scheme.

The Government seeks to defend the statute on the ground that it was passed pursuant to Congress' war power. The Government argues that this Court has given broad deference to the exercise of that constitutional power by the national legislature. That argument finds support in a number of decisions of this Court. However, the phrase "war power" cannot be invoked as a talismanic incantation to support any exercise of congressional power which can be brought within its ambit. More specifically in this case, the Government asserts that 5 (a) (1) (D) is an expression "of the growing concern shown by the executive and legislative branches of government over the risks of internal subversion in plants on which the national defense depend[s]." Yet, this concept of "national defense" cannot be deemed an end in itself, justifying any exercise of legislative power designed to promote such a goal. Implicit in the term "national defense" is the notion of defending those values and ideals which set this Nation apart. For almost two centuries, our country has taken singular pride in the democratic ideals enshrined in its Constitution, and the most cherished of those ideals have found expression in the First Amendment. It would indeed be ironic if, in the name of national defense, we would sanction the subversion of one of those liberties—the freedom of association—which makes the defense of the Nation worthwhile.

When Congress' exercise of one of its enumerated powers clashes with those individual liberties protected by the Bill of Rights, it is our "delicate and difficult task" to determine whether the resulting restriction on freedom can be tolerated. . . . The Government emphasizes that the purpose of 5 (a) (1) (D) is to reduce the threat of sabotage and espionage in the Nation's defense plants. The Government's interest in such a prophylactic measure is not insubstantial. But it cannot be doubted that the means chosen to implement that governmental purpose in this instance cut deeply into the right of association. Section 5 (a) (1) (D) put appellee to the choice of surrendering his organizational affiliation, regardless of whether his membership threatened the security of a defense facility, or giving up his job. When appellee refused to make that choice, he became subject to a possible criminal penalty of five years' imprisonment and a $10,000 fine. The statute quite literally establishes guilt by association alone, without any need to establish that an individual's association poses the threat feared by the Government in proscribing it. The inhibiting effect on the exercise of First Amendment rights is clear.

It has become axiomatic that "[p]recision of regulation must be the touchstone in an area so closely touching our most precious freedoms." *NAACP v. Button* (1963). . . . Such precision is notably lacking in 5 (a) (1) (D). That statute casts its net across a broad range of associational activities, indiscriminately trapping membership which can be constitutionally punished and membership which cannot be so proscribed. It is made irrelevant to the statute's operation that an individual may be a passive or inactive member of a designated organization, that he may be unaware of the organization's unlawful aims, or that he may disagree with those unlawful aims. It is also made irrelevant that an individual who is subject to the penalties of 5 (a) (1) (D) may occupy a nonsensitive position in a defense facility. Thus, 5 (a) (1) (D) contains the fatal defect of overbreadth because it seeks to bar employment both for association which may be proscribed and for association which may not be proscribed consistently with First Amendment rights. This the Constitution will not tolerate.

We are not unmindful of the congressional concern over the danger of sabotage and espionage in national defense industries, and nothing we hold today should be read to deny Congress the power under narrowly drawn legislation to keep from sensitive positions in defense facilities those who would use their positions to disrupt the Nation's production facilities. We have recognized that, while the Constitution protects against invasions of individual rights, it does not withdraw from the Government the power to safeguard its vital interests. . . . Spies and saboteurs do exist, and Congress can, of course, prescribe criminal penalties for those who engage in espionage and sabotage. The Government can deny access to its secrets to those who would use such information to harm the Nation. And Congress can declare sensitive positions in national defense industries off limits to those who would use such positions to disrupt the production of defense materials. The Government has told us that Congress, in passing 5 (a) (1) (D), made a considered judgment that one possible alternative to that statute—an industrial security screening program—would be inadequate and ineffective to protect against sabotage in defense facilities. It is not our function to examine the validity of that congressional judgment. Neither is it our function to determine whether an industrial security screening program exhausts the possible alternatives to the statute under review. We are concerned solely with determining whether the statute before us has exceeded the bounds imposed by the Constitution when First Amendment rights are at stake. The task of writing legislation which will stay within those bounds has been committed to Congress. Our decision today simply recognizes that, when legitimate legislative concerns are expressed in a statute which imposes a substantial burden on protected First Amendment activities, Congress must achieve its goal by means which have a "less drastic" impact on the continued vitality of First Amendment freedoms. The Constitution and the basic position of First Amendment rights in our democratic fabric demand nothing less.

Affirmed.

Mr. Justice WHITE, with whom Mr. Justice HARLAN joins, dissenting.

The Court holds that because of the First Amendment a member of the Communist Party who knows that the Party has been held to be a Communist-action organization may not be barred from employment in defense establishments important to the security of the Nation. It therefore refuses to enforce the contrary judgments of the Legislative and Executive Branches of the Government. Respectfully disagreeing with this view, I dissent.

The constitutional right found to override the public interest in national security defined by Congress is the right of association, here the right of appellee Robel to remain a member of the Communist Party after being notified of its adjudication as a Communist-action organization. Nothing in the Constitution requires this result. The right of association is not mentioned in the Constitution. It is a judicial construct appended to the First Amendment rights to speak freely, to assemble, and to petition for redress of grievances. While the right of association has deep roots in history and is supported by the inescapable necessity for group action in a republic as large and complex as ours, it has only recently blossomed as the controlling factor in constitutional litigation; its contours as yet lack delineation. Although official interference with First Amendment rights has drawn close scrutiny, it is now apparent that the right of association is not absolute and is subject to significant regulation by the State. The law of criminal conspiracy restricts the purposes for which men may associate and the means they may use to implement their plans. Labor unions, and membership in them, are intricately controlled by statutes, both federal and state, as are political parties and corporations. . . .

The national interest asserted by the Congress is real and substantial. After years of study, Congress prefaced the Subversive Activities Control Act of 1950, 64 Stat. 987, 50 U.S.C. 781–798, with its findings that there exists an international Communist movement which by treachery, deceit, espionage, and sabotage seeks to overthrow existing governments; that the movement operates in this country through Communist-action organizations which are under foreign domination and control and which seek to overthrow the Government by any necessary means, including force and violence; that the Communist movement in the United States is made up of thousands of adherents, rigidly disciplined, operating in secrecy, and employing espionage and sabotage tactics in form and manner evasive of existing laws. Congress therefore, among other things, defined the characteristics of Communist-action organizations, provided for their adjudication by the SACB, and decided that the security of the United States required the exclusion of Communist-action organization members from employment in certain defense facilities. After long and complex litigation, the SACB found the Communist Party to be a Communist-action organization within the meaning of the Act.

Against this background protective measures were clearly appropriate. One of them, contained in 50 U.S.C. 784 (a) (1) (D), which became activated with the affirmance of the Party's designation as a Communist-action organization, makes it unlawful "[f]or any member of such organization, with knowledge or notice ... that such order has become final ... to engage in any employment in any defense facility...." A defense facility is any of the specified types of establishment "with respect to the operation of which [the Secretary of Defense] finds and determines that the security of the United States requires" that members of such organizations not be employed. Given the characteristics of the Party, its foreign domination, its primary goal of government overthrow, the discipline which it exercises over its members, and its propensity for espionage and sabotage, the exclusion of members of the Party who know the Party is a Communist-action organization from certain defense plants is well within the powers of Congress.

Congress should be entitled to take suitable precautionary measures. Some Party members may be no threat at all, but many of them undoubtedly are, and it is exceedingly difficult to identify those in advance of the very events which Congress seeks to avoid. If Party members such as Robel may be barred from "sensitive positions," it is because they are potential threats to security. For the same reason they should be excludable from employment in defense plants which Congress and the Secretary of Defense consider of critical importance to the security of the country.

The statute does not prohibit membership in the Communist Party. Nor are appellee and other Communists excluded from all employment in the United States, or even from all defense plants. The touchstones for exclusion are the requirements of national security, and the facilities designated under this standard amount to only about one percent of all the industrial establishments in the United States.

It is this impact on associational rights, although specific and minimal, which the Court finds impermissible. But as the statute's dampening effect on associational rights is to be weighed against the asserted and obvious government interest in keeping members of Communist-action groups from defense facilities, it would seem important to identify what interest Robel has in joining and remaining a member of a group whose primary goals he may not share. We are unenlightened, however, by the opinion of the Court or by the record in this case, as to the purposes which Robel and others like him may have in associating with the Party. The legal aims and programs of the Party are not identified or appraised nor are Robel's activities as a member of the Party. The Court is left with a vague and formless concept of associational rights and its own notions of what constitutes an unreasonable risk to defense facilities.

The Court says that mere membership in an association with knowledge that the association pursues unlawful aims cannot be the basis for criminal prosecution. . . . But denying the opportunity to be employed in some defense plants is a much smaller deterrent to the exercise of associational rights than denial of a passport or a criminal penalty attached solely to membership, and the Government's interest in keeping potential spies and saboteurs from defense plants is much greater than its interest in keeping disloyal Americans from traveling abroad or in committing all Party members to prison. . . .

The Court's motives are worthy. It seeks the widest bounds for the exercise of individual liberty consistent with the security of the country. In so doing it arrogates to itself an independent judgment of the requirements of national security. These are matters about which judges should be wary.

ROBERTS V. UNITED STATES JAYCEES (1984)

The United States Jaycees, a nonprofit membership association, had as one of its stated objectives to "promote and foster the growth and devel-

opment of young men's civic organizations." Regular membership was available to men between the ages of eighteen and thirty-five; associate, nonvoting membership was available to women and older men. A Minnesota statute prohibiting gender discrimination in places of public accommodation was applied to the Jaycees and required them to admit women as regular members. The Jaycees argued that this restriction on their membership interfered with their members' freedom of association.

Decided July 3, 1984.

Mr. Justice BRENNAN delivered the opinion of the Court.

Our decisions have referred to constitutionally protected "freedom of association" in two distinct senses. In one line of decisions, the Court has concluded that choices to enter into and maintain certain intimate human relationships must be secured against undue intrusion by the State because of the role of such relationships in safeguarding the individual freedom that is central to our constitutional scheme. In this respect, freedom of association receives protection as a fundamental element of personal liberty. In another set of decisions, the Court has recognized a right to associate for the purpose of engaging in those activities protected by the First Amendment—speech, assembly, petition for the redress of grievances, and the exercise of religion. The Constitution guarantees freedom of association of this kind as an indispensable means of preserving other individual liberties.

The intrinsic and instrumental features of constitutionally protected association may, of course, coincide. In particular, when the State interferes with individuals' selection of those with whom they wish to join in a common endeavor, freedom of association in both of its forms may be implicated. The Jaycees contend that this is such a case. Still, the nature and degree of constitutional protection afforded freedom of association may vary depending on the extent to which one or the other aspect of the constitutionally protected liberty is at stake in a given case. We therefore find it useful to consider separately the effect of applying the Minnesota statute to the Jaycees on what could be called its members' freedom of intimate association and their freedom of expressive association.

A

The Court has long recognized that, because the Bill of Rights is designed to secure individual liberty, it must afford the formation and preservation of certain kinds of highly personal relationships a substantial measure of sanctuary from unjustified interference by the State. Without precisely identifying every consideration that may underlie this type of constitutional protection, we have noted that certain kinds of personal bonds have played a critical role in the culture and traditions of the Nation by cultivating and transmitting shared ideals and beliefs; they thereby foster diversity and act as critical buffers between the individual and the power of the State. Moreover, the constitutional shelter afforded such relationships reflects the realization that individuals draw much of their emotional enrichment from close ties with others. Protecting these relationships from unwarranted state interference therefore safeguards the ability independently to define one's identity that is central to any concept of liberty.

The personal affiliations that exemplify these considerations, and that therefore suggest some relevant limitations on the relationships that might be entitled to this sort of constitutional protection, are those that attend the creation and sustenance of a family—marriage, e.g., *Zablocki v. Redhail, supra;* childbirth, e.g., *Carey v. Population Services International, supra;* the raising and education of children, e.g., *Smith v. Organization of Foster Families, supra;* and cohabitation with one's relatives, e.g., *Moore v. East Cleveland, supra.* Family relationships, by their nature, involve deep attachments and commitments to the necessarily few other individuals with whom one shares not only a special community of thoughts, experiences, and beliefs but also distinctively personal aspects of one's life. Among other things, therefore, they are distinguished by such attributes as relative smallness, a high degree of selectivity in decisions to begin and maintain the affiliation, and seclusion from others in critical aspects of the relationship. As a general matter, only relationships with these sorts of qualities are likely to reflect the considerations that have led to an understanding of freedom of association as an intrinsic element of personal liberty. Conversely, an association lacking these qualities—such as a large business enterprise—seems remote from the concerns giving rise to this constitutional protection. Accordingly, the Constitution undoubtedly imposes constraints on the State's power to control the selection of one's spouse that would not apply to regulations affecting the choice of one's fellow employees.

Between these poles, of course, lies a broad range of human relationships that may make greater or lesser claims to constitutional protection from particular incursions by the State. Determining the limits of state authority over an individual's freedom to enter into a particular association therefore unavoidably entails a careful assessment of where that relationship's objective characteristics locate it on a spectrum from the most intimate to the most attenuated of personal attachments. We need not mark the potentially significant points on this terrain with any precision. We note only that factors that may be relevant include size, purpose, policies, selectivity, congeniality, and other characteristics that in a particular case may be pertinent. In this case, however, several features of the Jaycees clearly place the organization outside of the category of relationships worthy of this kind of constitutional protection.

In short, the local chapters of the Jaycees are neither small nor selective. Moreover, much of the activity central to the formation and maintenance of the association involves the participation of strangers to that relationship. Accordingly, we conclude that the Jaycees chapters lack the distinctive characteristics that might afford constitutional protection to the decision of its members to exclude women.

B

An individual's freedom to speak, to worship, and to petition the government for the redress of grievances could not be vigorously protected from interference by the State unless a correlative freedom to engage in group effort toward those ends were not also guaranteed. According protection to collective effort on behalf of shared goals is especially important in preserving political and cultural diversity and in shielding dissident expression from suppression by the majority. Consequently, we have long understood as implicit in the right to engage in activities protected by the First Amendment a corresponding right to associate with others in pursuit of a wide variety of political, social, economic, educational, religious, and cultural ends. In view of the various protected activities in which the Jaycees engages that right is plainly implicated in this case. . . .

There can be no clearer example of an intrusion into the internal structure or affairs of an association than a regulation that forces the group to accept members it does not desire. Such a regulation may impair the ability of the original members to express only those views that brought them together. Freedom of association therefore plainly presupposes a freedom not to associate.

The right to associate for expressive purposes is not, however, absolute. Infringements on that right may be justified by regulations adopted to serve compelling state interests, unrelated to the suppression of ideas, that cannot be achieved through means significantly less restrictive of associational freedoms. . . . We are persuaded that Minnesota's compelling interest in eradicating discrimination against its female citizens justifies the impact that application of the statute to the Jaycees may have on the male members' associational freedoms.

On its face, the Minnesota Act does not aim at the suppression of speech, does not distinguish between prohibited and permitted activity on the basis of viewpoint, and does not license enforcement authorities to administer the statute on the basis of such constitutionally impressible criteria. Nor does the Jaycees contend that the Act has been applied in this case for the purpose of hampering the organization's ability to express its views. Instead, as the Minnesota Supreme Court explained, the Act reflects the State's strong historical commitment to eliminating discrimination and assuring its citizens equal access to publicly available goods and services. That goal, which is unrelated to the suppression of expression, plainly serves compelling state interests of the highest order.

By prohibiting gender discrimination in places of public accommodation, the Minnesota Act protects the State's citizenry from a number of serious social and personal harms. In the context of reviewing state actions under the Equal Protection Clause, this Court has frequently noted that discrimination based on archaic and overbroad assumptions about the relative needs and capacities of the sexes forces individuals to labor under stereotypical notions that often bear no relationship to their actual abilities. It thereby both deprives persons of their individual dignity and denies society the benefits of wide participation in political, economic, and cultural life. . . .

The judgment of the Court of Appeals is reversed.

Justice O'CONNOR, concurring in part and concurring in the judgment.

. . . There is only minimal constitutional protection of the freedom of commercial association. There are, of course, some constitutional protections of commercial speech—speech intended and used to promote a commercial transaction with the speaker. But the State is free to impose any rational regulation on the commercial transaction itself. The Constitution does not guarantee a right to choose employees, customers, suppliers, or those with whom one engages in simple commercial transactions, without restraint from the State. A shopkeeper has no constitutional right to deal only with persons of one sex.

The dichotomy between rights of commercial association and rights of expressive association is also found in the more limited constitutional protections accorded an association's recruitment and solicitation activities and other dealings with its members and the public. Reasonable, content-neutral state regulation of the time, place, and manner of an organization's relations with its members or with the State can pass constitutional muster, but only if the regulation is "narrowly drawn" to serve a "sufficiently strong, subordinating interest" "without unnecessarily interfering with First Amendment freedoms."

By contrast, an organization engaged in commercial activity enjoys only minimal constitutional protection of its recruitment, training, and solicitation activities. While the Court has acknowledged a First Amendment right to engage in non-deceptive commercial advertising, governmental regulation of the commercial recruitment of new members, stockholders, customers, or employees is valid if rationally related to the government's ends.

Many associations cannot readily be described as purely expressive or purely commercial. No association is likely ever to be exclusively engaged in expressive activities, if only because it will collect dues from its members or purchase printing materials or rent lecture halls or serve coffee and cakes at its meetings. And innumerable commercial associations also engage in some incidental protected speech or advocacy. The standard for deciding just how much of an association's involvement in commercial activity is enough to suspend the association's First Amendment right to control its membership cannot, therefore, be articulated with simple precision. Clearly the standard must accept the reality that even the most expressive of associations is likely to touch, in some way or other, matters of commerce. The standard must nevertheless give substance to the ideal of complete protection for purely expressive association, even while it readily permits state regulation of commercial affairs.

In my view, an association should be characterized as commercial, and therefore subject to rationally related state regulation of its membership and other associational activities, when, and only when, the association's activities are not predominantly of the type protected by the First Amendment. It is only when the association is predominantly engaged in protected expression that state regulation of its membership will necessarily affect, change, dilute, or silence one collective voice that would otherwise be heard. An association must choose its market. Once it enters the marketplace of commerce in any substantial degree it loses the complete control over its membership that it would otherwise enjoy if it confined its affairs to the marketplace of ideas.

HURLEY V. IRISH-AMERICAN GAY, LESBIAN, AND BISEXUAL GROUP OF BOSTON (1995)

A Massachusetts state antidiscrimination law forbade discrimination on the basis of, inter alia, sexual orientation in the admission or treatment of any person in a place of public accommodation. The state courts found the annual Boston St. Patrick's Day parade to be a public accommodation and the exclusion of a gay rights group, Irish-American Gay, Lesbian, and Bisexual Group of Boston (GLIB), from the parade to be a violation of the law. The state courts ordered that GLIB be allowed to march in the parade. The organizers of the parade, John J. Hurley and the South Boston Allied War Veterans Council, appealed to the Supreme Court, arguing that this forced inclusion was a violation of their First Amendment rights. The Court unanimously sustained their claim.

Decided June 19, 1995.
Justice SOUTER delivered the opinion of the Court.
The issue in this case is whether Massachusetts may require private citizens who organize a parade to include among the marchers a group imparting a message the organizers do not wish to convey. We hold that such a mandate violates the First Amendment.

The protected expression that inheres in a parade is not limited to its banners and songs, however, for the Constitution looks beyond written or spoken words as mediums of expression. . . .

Not many marches, then, are beyond the realm of expressive parades, and the South Boston celebration is not one of them. Spectators line the streets; people march in costumes and uniforms, carrying flags and banners with all sorts of messages (e.g., "England get out of Ireland," "Say no to drugs"); marching bands and pipers play, floats are pulled along, and the whole show is broadcast over Boston. . . . But a private speaker does not forfeit constitutional protection simply by combining multifarious voices, or by failing to edit their themes to isolate an exact message as the exclusive subject matter of the speech. Nor, under our precedent, does First Amendment protection require a speaker to generate, as an original matter, each item featured in the communication.

C

In the case before us, however, the Massachusetts law has been applied in a peculiar way. Its enforcement does not address any dispute about the participation of openly gay, lesbian, or bisexual individuals in various units admitted to the parade. The petitioners disclaim any intent to exclude homosexuals as such, and no individual member of GLIB claims to have been excluded from parading as a member of any group that the Council has approved to march. Instead, the disagreement goes to the admission of GLIB as its own parade unit carrying its own banner. See App. to Pet. for Cert. B26-B27, and n. 28. Since every participating unit affects the message conveyed by the private organizers, the state courts' application of the statute produced an order essentially requiring petitioners to alter the expressive content of their parade. Although the state courts spoke of the parade as a place of public accommodation, see, e.g., 418 Mass., at 247–248, 636 N. E. 2d, at 1297–1298, once the expressive character of both the parade and the marching GLIB contingent is understood, it becomes apparent that the state courts' application of the statute had the effect of declaring the sponsors' speech itself to be the public accommodation. Under this approach any contingent of protected individuals with a message would have the right to participate in petitioners' speech, so that the communication produced by the private organizers would be shaped by all those protected by the law who wished to join in with some expressive demonstration of their own. But this use of the State's power violates the fundamental rule of protection under the First Amendment, that a speaker has the autonomy to choose the content of his own message.

Petitioners' claim to the benefit of this principle of autonomy to control one's own speech is as sound as the South Boston parade is expressive. Rather like a composer, the Council selects the expressive units of the parade from potential participants, and though the score may not produce a particularized message, each contingent's expression in the Council's eyes comports with what merits celebration on that day. Even if this view gives the Council credit for a more considered judgment than it actively made, the Council clearly decided to exclude a message it did not like from the communication it chose to make, and that is enough to invoke its right as a private speaker to shape its expression by speaking on one subject while remaining silent on another. The message it disfavored is not difficult to identify. Although GLIB's point (like the Council's) is not wholly articulate, a contingent marching behind the organization's banner would at least bear witness to the fact that some Irish are gay, lesbian, or bisexual, and the presence of the organized marchers would suggest their view that people of their sexual orientations have as much claim to unqualified social acceptance as heterosexuals and indeed as members of parade units organized around other identifying characteristics. The parade's organizers may not believe these facts about Irish sexuality to be so, or they may object to unqualified social acceptance of gays and lesbians or have some other reason for wishing to keep GLIB's message out of the parade. But whatever the reason, it boils down to the choice of a speaker not to propound a particular point of view, and that choice is presumed to lie beyond the government's power to control.

Unlike the programming offered on various channels by a cable network, the parade does not consist of individual, unrelated segments that happen to be transmitted together for individual selection by members of the audience. Although each parade unit generally identifies itself, each is understood to contribute something to a common theme, and accordingly there is no customary practice whereby private sponsors disavow "any identity of viewpoint" between themselves and the selected participants. Practice follows practicability here, for such disclaimers would be quite curious in a moving parade. . . . Without deciding on the precise significance of the likelihood of misattribution, it nonetheless becomes clear that in the context of an expressive parade, as with a protest march, the parade's overall message is distilled from the individual presentations along the way, and each unit's expression is perceived by spectators as part of the whole. . . .

New York State Club Association is also instructive by the contrast it provides. There, we turned back a facial challenge to a state antidiscrimination statute on the assumption that the expressive associational character of a dining club with over 400 members could be sufficiently attenuated to permit application of the law even to such a private organization, but we also recognized that the State did not prohibit exclusion of those whose views were at odds with positions espoused by the general club memberships. In other words, although the association provided public benefits to which a State could ensure equal access, it was also engaged in expressive activity; compelled access to the benefit, which was upheld, did not trespass on the organization's message itself. If we were to analyze this case strictly along those lines, GLIB would lose. Assuming the parade to be large enough and a source of benefits (apart from its expression) that would generally justify a mandated access provision, GLIB could nonetheless be refused admission as an expressive contingent with its own message just as readily as a private club could exclude an applicant whose manifest views were at odds with a position taken by the club's existing members.

IV

Our holding today rests not on any particular view about the Council's message but on the Nation's commitment to protect freedom of speech. Disapproval of a private speaker's statement does not legitimize use of the Commonwealth's power to compel the speaker to alter the message by including one more acceptable to others. Accordingly, the judgment of the Supreme Judicial Court is reversed and the case remanded for proceedings not inconsistent with this opinion.

It is so ordered.

ANTI-TERRORISM AND EFFECTIVE DEATH PENALTY ACT (1996)

After the 1993 bombing of the World Trade Center and the 1995 bombing of the Oklahoma City Federal Building, the Congress moved to give the Justice Department and the Federal Bureau of Investigation new tools to dig out terrorist cells. The following provision, which deals with material support for terrorist activities, engenders the most controversy. Opponents argued that it made even the most innocent contact with a group subject to criminal prosecution or deportation. Supporters claimed it was an essential weapon in cutting off funds for terrorist groups that hide behind the façade of a charitable organization.

Section 2339B. Providing material support or resources to designated foreign terrorist organizations

(a) Prohibited Activities.—

(1) Unlawful conduct.—Whoever, within the United States or subject to the jurisdiction of the United States, knowingly provides material

support or resources to a foreign terrorist organization, or attempts or conspires to do so, shall be fined under this title or imprisoned not more than 15 years, or both, and, if the death of any person results, shall be imprisoned for any term of years or for life.

(2) Financial institutions.—Except as authorized by the Secretary, any financial institution that becomes aware that it has possession of, or control over, any funds in which a foreign terrorist organization, or its agent, has an interest, shall—

(A) retain possession of, or maintain control over, such funds; and

(B) report to the Secretary the existence of such funds in accordance with regulations issued by the Secretary.

(b) Civil Penalty.—Any financial institution that knowingly fails to comply with subsection (a)(2) shall be subject to a civil penalty in an amount that is the greater of—

(A) $50,000 per violation; or

(B) twice the amount of which the financial institution was required under subsection (a)(2) to retain possession or control.

(c) Injunction.—Whenever it appears to the Secretary or the Attorney General that any person is engaged in, or is about to engage in, any act that constitutes, or would constitute, a violation of this section, the Attorney General may initiate civil action in a district court of the United States to enjoin such violation.

(d) Extraterritorial Jurisdiction.—There is extraterritorial Federal jurisdiction over an offense under this section.

(e) Investigations.—

(1) In general.—The Attorney General shall conduct any investigation of a possible violation of this section, or of any license, order, or regulation issued pursuant to this section.

(2) Coordination with the department of the treasury.—The Attorney General shall work in coordination with the Secretary in investigations relating to—

(A) the compliance or noncompliance by a financial institution with the requirements of subsection (a)(2); and

(B) civil penalty proceedings authorized under subsection (b).

(3) Referral.—Any evidence of a criminal violation of this section arising in the course of an investigation by the Secretary or any other Federal agency shall be referred immediately to the Attorney General for further investigation. The Attorney General shall timely notify the

Secretary of any action taken on referrals from the Secretary, and may refer investigations to the Secretary for remedial licensing or civil penalty action.

(f) Classified Information in Civil Proceedings Brought by the United States.—

(1) Discovery of classified information by defendants.—

(A) Request by United States.—In any civil proceeding under this section, upon request made ex parte and in writing by the United States, a court, upon a sufficient showing, may authorize the United States to—

(i) redact specified items of classified information from documents to be introduced into evidence or made available to the defendant through discovery under the Federal Rules of Civil Procedure;

(ii) substitute a summary of the information for such classified documents; or

(iii) substitute a statement admitting relevant facts that the classified information would tend to prove.

(B) Order granting request.—If the court enters an order granting a request under this paragraph, the entire text of the documents to which the request relates shall be sealed and preserved in the records of the court to be made available to the appellate court in the event of an appeal.

(C) Denial of request.—If the court enters an order denying a request of the United States under this paragraph, the United States may take an immediate, interlocutory appeal in accordance with paragraph (5). For purposes of such an appeal, the entire text of the documents to which the request relates, together with any transcripts of arguments made ex parte to the court in connection therewith, shall be maintained under seal and delivered to the appellate court.

(2) Introduction of classified information; precautions by court.—

(A) Exhibits.—To prevent unnecessary or inadvertent disclosure of classified information in a civil proceeding brought by the United States under this section, the United States may petition the court ex parte to admit, in lieu of classified writings, recordings, or photographs, one or more of the following:

(i) Copies of items from which classified information has been redacted.

(ii) Stipulations admitting relevant facts that specific classified information would tend to prove.

(iii) A declassified summary of the specific classified information.

(B) Determination by court.—The court shall grant a request under this paragraph if the court finds that the redacted item, stipulation, or summary is sufficient to allow the defendant to prepare a defense.

(3) Taking of trial testimony.—

(A) Objection.—During the examination of a witness in any civil proceeding brought by the United States under this subsection, the United States may object to any question or line of inquiry that may require the witness to disclose classified information not previously found to be admissible.

(B) Action by court.—In determining whether a response is admissible, the court shall take precautions to guard against the compromise of any classified information, including —

(i) permitting the United States to provide the court, ex parte, with a proffer of the witness's response to the question or line of inquiry; and

(ii) requiring the defendant to provide the court with a proffer of the nature of the information that the defendant seeks to elicit.

(C) Obligation of defendant.—In any civil proceeding under this section, it shall be the defendant's obligation to establish the relevance and materiality of any classified information sought to be introduced.

(4) Appeal.—If the court enters an order denying a request of the United States under this subsection, the United States may take an immediate interlocutory appeal in accordance with paragraph (5).

(5) Interlocutory appeal.—

(A) Subject of appeal.—An interlocutory appeal by the United States shall lie to a court of appeals from a decision or order of a district court—

(i) authorizing the disclosure of classified information;

(ii) imposing sanctions for nondisclosure of classified information; or

(iii) refusing a protective order sought by the United States to prevent the disclosure of classified information.

(B) Expedited consideration.—

(i) In general.—An appeal taken pursuant to this paragraph, either before or during trial, shall be expedited by the court of appeals.

(ii) Appeals prior to trial.—If an appeal is of an order made prior to trial, an appeal shall be taken not later than 10 days after the decision or order appealed from, and the trial shall not commence until the appeal is resolved.

(iii) Appeals during trial.—If an appeal is taken during trial, the trial court shall adjourn the trial until the appeal is resolved, and the court of appeals—

(I) shall hear argument on such appeal not later than 4 days after the adjournment of the trial;

(II) may dispense with written briefs other than the supporting materials previously submitted to the trial court;

(III) shall render its decision not later than 4 days after argument on appeal; and

(IV) may dispense with the issuance of a written opinion in rendering its decision.

(C) Effect of ruling.—An interlocutory appeal and decision shall not affect the right of the defendant, in a subsequent appeal from a final judgment, to claim as error reversal by the trial court on remand of a ruling appealed from during trial.

(6) Construction.—Nothing in this subsection shall prevent the United States from seeking protective orders or asserting privileges ordinarily available to the United States to protect against the disclosure of classified information, including the invocation of the military and State secrets privilege.

(g) Definitions.—As used in this section—

(1) the term "classified information" has the meaning given that term in section 1(a) of the Classified Information Procedures Act (18 U.S.C. App.);

(2) the term "financial institution" has the same meaning as in section 5312(a)(2) of title 31, United States Code;

(3) the term "funds" includes coin or currency of the United States or any other country, traveler's checks, personal checks, bank checks, money orders, stocks, bonds, debentures, drafts, letters of credit, any other negotiable instrument, and any electronic representation of any of the foregoing;

(4) the term "material support or resources" has the same meaning as in section 2339A;

(5) the term "Secretary" means the Secretary of the Treasury; and

(6) the term "terrorist organization" means an organization designated as a terrorist organization under section 219 of the Immigration and Nationality Act.

CALIFORNIA DEMOCRATIC PARTY V. JONES (2000)

In 1996 the voters of California passed Proposition 198, which changed the state's partisan primary from a closed primary, in which only a political party's members can vote on its nominees, to a blanket primary, in which each voter's ballot lists every candidate regardless of party affiliation, allowing the voter to choose freely among them. The candidate of each party who wins the most votes then becomes that party's nominee for the general election. The political parties filed suit alleging, inter alia, that the blanket primary violated their First Amendment rights of association. The district court held that the primary's burden on petitioners' associational rights was not severe and was justified by substantial state interests. The Ninth Circuit affirmed. The decision was appealed to the Supreme Court, which reversed the lower courts.

Decided June 26, 2000.

Mr. Justice SCALIA delivered the opinion of the Court.

This case presents the question whether the State of California may, consistent with the First Amendment to the United States Constitution, use a so-called "blanket" primary to determine a political party's nominee for the general election.

Respondents rest their defense of the blanket primary upon the proposition that primaries play an integral role in citizens' selection of public officials. As a consequence, they contend, primaries are public rather than private proceedings, and the States may and must play a role in ensuring that they serve the public interest. Proposition 198, respondents conclude, is simply a rather pedestrian example of a State's regulating its system of elections.

We have recognized, of course, that States have a major role to play in structuring and monitoring the election process, including primaries. . . . What we have not held, however, is that the processes by which political parties select their nominees are, as respondents would have it, wholly public affairs that States may regulate freely. To the contrary, we have continually stressed that when States regulate parties' internal processes they must act within limits imposed by the Constitution. In this regard, respondents' reliance on *Smith v. Allwright* (1944), and *Terry v. Adams* (1953), is misplaced. In *Allwright,* we invalidated the Texas Democratic

Party's rule limiting participation in its primary to whites; in *Terry,* we invalidated the same rule promulgated by the Jaybird Democratic Association, a "self-governing voluntary club." These cases held only that, when a State prescribes an election process that gives a special role to political parties, it "endorses, adopts and enforces the discrimination against Negroes," that the parties . . . bring into the process—so that the parties' discriminatory action becomes state action under the Fifteenth Amendment. They do not stand for the proposition that party affairs are public affairs, free of First Amendment protections—and our later holdings make that entirely clear.

In no area is the political association's right to exclude more important than in the process of selecting its nominee. That process often determines the party's positions on the most significant public policy issues of the day, and even when those positions are predetermined it is the nominee who becomes the party's ambassador to the general electorate in winning it over to the party's views. . . .

Unsurprisingly, our cases vigorously affirm the special place the First Amendment reserves for, and the special protection it accords, the process by which a political party "select[s] a standard bearer who best represents the party's ideologies and preferences." The moment of choosing the party's nominee, we have said, is "the crucial juncture at which the appeal to common principles may be translated into concerted action, and hence to political power in the community." *Tashjian.* . . .

Proposition 198 forces political parties to associate with—to have their nominees, and hence their positions, determined by—those who, at best, have refused to affiliate with the party, and, at worst, have expressly affiliated with a rival. In this respect, it is qualitatively different from a closed primary. Under that system, even when it is made quite easy for a voter to change his party affiliation the day of the primary, and thus, in some sense, to "cross over," at least he must formally *become a member of the party;* and once he does so, he is limited to voting for candidates of that party.

In any event, the deleterious effects of Proposition 198 are not limited to altering the identity of the nominee. Even when the person favored by a majority of the party members prevails, he will have prevailed by taking somewhat different positions—and, should he be elected, will continue to take somewhat different positions in order to be renominated. . . . In effect, Proposition 198 has simply moved the general election one step earlier in the process, at the expense of the parties' ability to perform the "basic function" of choosing their own leaders.

Nor can we accept the Court of Appeals' contention that the burden imposed by Proposition 198 is minor because petitioners are free to endorse and financially support the candidate of their choice in the primary. The ability of the party leadership to endorse a candidate is simply no substitute for the party members' ability to choose their own nominee. . . .

We are similarly unconvinced by respondents' claim that the burden is not severe because Proposition 198 does not limit the parties from engaging fully in *other* traditional party behavior, such as ensuring orderly internal party governance, maintaining party discipline in the legislature, and conducting campaigns. The accuracy of this assertion is highly questionable, at least as to the first two activities. That party nominees will be equally observant of internal party procedures and equally respectful of party discipline when their nomination depends on the general electorate rather than on the party faithful seems to us improbable. . . . There is simply no substitute for a party's selecting its own candidates.

In sum, Proposition 198 forces petitioners to adulterate their candidate-selection process—the "basic function of a political party"—by opening it up to persons wholly unaffiliated with the party. Such forced association has the likely outcome—indeed, in this case the *intended* outcome—of changing the parties' message. We can think of no heavier burden on a political party's associational freedom. Proposition 198 is therefore unconstitutional unless it is narrowly tailored to serve a compelling state interest. ("Regulations imposing severe burdens on [parties'] rights must be narrowly tailored and advance a compelling state interest"). . . .

Respondents' legitimate state interests and petitioners' First Amendment rights are not inherently incompatible. To the extent they are in this case, the State of California has made them so by forcing political parties to associate with those who do not share their beliefs. And it has done this at the "crucial juncture" at which party members traditionally find their collective voice and select their spokesman. *Tashjian*, 479 U.S., at 216. The burden Proposition 198 places on petitioners' rights of political association is both severe and unnecessary. The judgment for the Court of Appeals for the Ninth Circuit is reversed.

It is so ordered.

Justice STEVENS, with whom Justice GINSBURG joins as to Part I, dissenting.

Today the Court construes the First Amendment as a limitation on a State's power to broaden voter participation in elections conducted by the State. The Court's holding is novel and, in my judgment, plainly wrong. I am convinced that California's adoption of a blanket primary pursuant to Proposition 198 does not violate the First Amendment, and that its use in primary elections for state offices is therefore valid.

I

The so-called "right not to associate" that the Court relies upon, then, is simply inapplicable to participation in a state election. A political party, like any other association, may refuse to allow non-members to participate in the party's decisions when it is conducting its own affairs; California's blanket primary system does not infringe this principle. But an election, unlike a convention or caucus, is a public affair. Although it is true that we have extended First Amendment protection to a party's right to invite independents to participate in its primaries, *Tashjian v. Republican Party of Conn.*, 479 U.S. 208 (1986), neither that case nor any other has held or suggested that the "right not to associate" imposes a limit on the State's power to open up its primary elections to all voters eligible to vote in a general election. In my view, while state rules abridging participation in its elections should be closely scrutinized, the First Amendment does not inhibit the State from acting to broaden voter access to state-run, state-financed elections. When a State acts not to limit democratic participation but to expand the ability of individuals to participate in the democratic process, it is acting not as a foe of the First Amendment but as a friend and ally.

A meaningful "right not to associate," if there is such a right in the context of limiting an electorate, ought to enable a party to insist on choosing its nominees at a convention or caucus where non-members could be excluded. In the real world, however, anyone can "join" a political party merely by asking for the appropriate ballot at the appropriate time or (at most) by registering within a state-defined reasonable period of time before an election; neither past voting history nor the voter's race, religion, or gender can provide a basis for the party's refusal to "associate" with an unwelcome new member. . . .

The Court's reliance on a political party's "right not to associate" as a basis for limiting a State's power to conduct primary elections will inevitably require it either to draw unprincipled distinctions among various primary configurations or to alter voting practices throughout the Nation in fundamental ways. Assuming that a registered Democrat or independent who wants to vote in the Republican gubernatorial primary can do so merely by asking for a Republican ballot, the Republican Party's constitutional right "not to associate" is pretty feeble if the only cost it imposes on that Democrat or independent is a loss of his right to vote for non-Republican candidates for other offices. Subtle distinctions of this minor import are grist for state legislatures, but they demean the process of constitutional adjudication.

In my view, the First Amendment does not mandate that a putatively private association be granted the power to dictate the organizational structure of state-run, state-financed primary elections. It is not this Court's constitutional function to choose between the competing visions of what makes democracy work—party autonomy and discipline versus progressive inclusion of the entire electorate in the process of selecting their public officials—that are held by the litigants in this case. That choice belongs to the people.

BOY SCOUTS OF AMERICA V. DALE (2000)

James Dale was dismissed from his post as scoutmaster and his adult membership in the Boy Scouts revoked when the organization found out that he was a homosexual and a gay rights activist. He filed suit in the New Jersey Superior Court, alleging that the Boy Scouts had violated a state statute prohibiting discrimination on the basis of sexual orientation in places of public accommodation. That court's chancery division granted summary judgment for the Boy Scouts, but its appellate division reversed in pertinent part and remanded. The state supreme court affirmed. The Boys Scouts appealed to the Supreme Court and won the case on a 5–4 vote.

Decided June 28, 2000.
Chief Justice REHNQUIST delivered the opinion of the Court.
Petitioners are the Boy Scouts of America and the Monmouth Council, a division of the Boy Scouts of America (collectively, Boy Scouts). The Boy Scouts is a private, not-for-profit organization engaged in instilling its system of values in young people. The Boy Scouts asserts that homosex-

ual conduct is inconsistent with the values it seeks to instill. Respondent is James Dale, a former Eagle Scout whose adult membership in the Boy Scouts was revoked when the Boy Scouts learned that he is an avowed homosexual and gay rights activist. The New Jersey Supreme Court held that New Jersey's public accommodations law requires that the Boy Scouts admit Dale. This case presents the question whether applying New Jersey's public accommodations law in this way violates the Boy Scouts' First Amendment right of expressive association. We hold that it does.

II

In *Roberts v. United States Jaycees*, 468 U. S. 609, 622 (1984), we observed that "implicit in the right to engage in activities protected by the First Amendment" is "a corresponding right to associate with others in pursuit of a wide variety of political, social, economic, educational, religious, and cultural ends." This right is crucial in preventing the majority from imposing its views on groups that would rather express other, perhaps unpopular, ideas. . . .Government actions that may unconstitutionally burden this freedom may take many forms, one of which is "intrusion into the internal structure or affairs of an association" like a "regulation that forces the group to accept members it does not desire." Forcing a group to accept certain members may impair the ability of the group to express those views, and only those views, that it intends to express. Thus, "[f]reedom of association . . . plainly presupposes a freedom not to associate."

The forced inclusion of an unwanted person in a group infringes the group's freedom of expressive association if the presence of that person affects in a significant way the group's ability to advocate public or private viewpoints. *New York State Club Assn., Inc. v. City of New York* (1988). But the freedom of expressive association, like many freedoms, is not absolute. We have held that the freedom could be overridden "by regulations adopted to serve compelling state interests, unrelated to the suppression of ideas, that cannot be achieved through means significantly less restrictive of associational freedoms." *Roberts, supra,* at 623.

To determine whether a group is protected by the First Amendment's expressive associational right, we must determine whether the group engages in "expressive association." The First Amendment's protection of expressive association is not reserved for advocacy groups. But to come within its ambit, a group must engage in some form of expression, whether it be public or private.

Because this is a First Amendment case where the ultimate conclusions of law are virtually inseparable from findings of fact, we are obligated to independently review the factual record to ensure that the state court's judgment does not unlawfully intrude on free expression. The record reveals the following. The Boy Scouts is a private, nonprofit organization. According to its mission statement:

"It is the mission of the Boy Scouts of America to serve others by helping to instill values in young people and, in other ways, to prepare them to make ethical choices over their lifetime in achieving their full potential.

"The values we strive to instill are based on those found in the Scout Oath and Law:

"Scout Oath

"On my honor I will do my best

To do my duty to God and my country and to obey the Scout Law;

To help other people at all times;

To keep myself physically strong, mentally awake, and morally straight.

"Scout Law

"A Scout is:

"Trustworthy

Obedient

Loyal

Cheerful

Helpful

Thrifty

Friendly

Brave

Courteous

Clean

Kind

Reverent." App. 184.

It seems indisputable that an association that seeks to transmit such a system of values engages in expressive activity. . . .

Given that the Boy Scouts engages in expressive activity, we must determine whether the forced inclusion of Dale as an assistant scoutmaster would significantly affect the Boy Scouts' ability to advocate public or private viewpoints. This inquiry necessarily requires us first to explore, to a limited extent, the nature of the Boy Scouts' view of homosexuality. . . .

Obviously, the Scout Oath and Law do not expressly mention sexuality or sexual orientation. And the terms "morally straight" and "clean" are by no means self-defining. Different people would attribute to those terms very different meanings. For example, some people may believe that engaging in homosexual conduct is not at odds with being "morally straight" and "clean." And others may believe that engaging in homosexual conduct is contrary to being "morally straight" and "clean." The Boy Scouts says it falls within the latter category.

The New Jersey Supreme Court analyzed the Boy Scouts' beliefs and found that the "exclusion of members solely on the basis of their sexual orientation is inconsistent with Boy Scouts' commitment to a diverse and 'representative' membership . . . [and] contradicts Boy Scouts' overarching objective to reach 'all eligible youth.'" 160 N. J., at 618, 734 A. 2d, at 1226. The court concluded that the exclusion of members like Dale "appears antithetical to the organization's goals and philosophy." But our cases reject this sort of inquiry; it is not the role of the courts to reject a group's expressed values because they disagree with those values or find them internally inconsistent.

The Boy Scouts asserts that it "teach[es] that homosexual conduct is not morally straight," and that it does "not want to promote homosexual conduct as a legitimate form of behavior." We accept the Boy Scouts' assertion. We need not inquire further to determine the nature of the Boy Scouts' expression with respect to homosexuality.

We must then determine whether Dale's presence as an assistant scoutmaster would significantly burden the Boy Scouts' desire to not "promote homosexual conduct as a legitimate form of behavior." As we give deference to an association's assertions regarding the nature of its expression, we must also give deference to an association's view of what would impair its expression. . . . That is not to say that an expressive association can erect a shield against anti-discrimination laws simply by asserting that mere acceptance of a member from a particular group would impair its message. But here Dale, by his own admission, is one of a group of gay Scouts who have "become leaders in their community and are open and honest about their sexual orientation." Dale was the co-president of a gay and lesbian organization at college and remains a gay rights activist. Dale's presence in the Boy Scouts would, at the very least, force the organization to send a message, both to the youth members and the world, that the Boy Scouts accepts homosexual conduct as a legitimate form of behavior.

Hurley is illustrative on this point. There we considered whether the application of Massachusetts' public accommodations law to require the organizers of a private St. Patrick's Day parade to include among the marchers an Irish-American gay, lesbian, and bisexual group, GLIB, violated the parade organizers' First Amendment rights. We noted that the parade organizers did not wish to exclude the GLIB members because of their sexual orientations, but because they wanted to march behind a GLIB banner.

Here, we have found that the Boy Scouts believes that homosexual conduct is inconsistent with the values it seeks to instill in its youth members; it will not "promote homosexual conduct as a legitimate form of behavior." As the presence of GLIB in Boston's St. Patrick's Day parade would have interfered with the parade organizers' choice not to propound a particular point of view, the presence of Dale as an assistant scoutmaster would just as surely interfere with the Boy Scout's choice not to propound a point of view contrary to its beliefs.

First, associations do not have to associate for the "purpose" of disseminating a certain message in order to be entitled to the protections of the First Amendment. An association must merely engage in expressive activity that could be impaired in order to be entitled to protection. For example, the purpose of the St. Patrick's Day parade in *Hurley* was not to espouse any views about sexual orientation, but we held that the parade organizers had a right to exclude certain participants nonetheless.

Second, even if the Boy Scouts discourages Scout leaders from disseminating views on sexual issues—a fact that the Boy Scouts disputes with contrary evidence—the First Amendment protects the Boy Scouts' method of expression. If the Boy Scouts wishes Scout leaders to avoid questions of sexuality and teach only by example, this fact does not negate the sincerity of its belief discussed above.

Third, the First Amendment simply does not require that every member of a group agree on every issue in order for the group's policy to be "expressive association." The Boy Scouts takes an official position with respect to homosexual conduct, and that is sufficient for First Amendment purposes. In this same vein, Dale makes much of the claim that the Boy Scouts does not revoke the membership of heterosexual Scout leaders that openly disagree with the Boy Scouts' policy on sexual orientation. But if this is true, it is irrelevant. The presence of an avowed homosexual and gay rights activist in an assistant scoutmaster's uniform sends a distinctly different message from the presence of a heterosexual assistant scoutmaster who is on record as disagreeing with Boy Scouts policy. The Boy Scouts has a First Amendment right to choose to send one message but not the other. The fact that the organization does not trumpet its views from the housetops, or that it tolerates dissent within its ranks, does not mean that its views receive no First Amendment protection.

Having determined that the Boy Scouts is an expressive association and that the forced inclusion of Dale would significantly affect its expression, we inquire whether the application of New Jersey's public accommodations law to require that the Boy Scouts accept Dale as an assistant scoutmaster runs afoul of the Scouts' freedom of expressive association. We conclude that it does.

State public accommodations laws were originally enacted to prevent discrimination in traditional places of public accommodation—like inns and trains. Over time, the public accommodations laws have expanded to cover more places. New Jersey's statutory definition of "[a] place of public accommodation" is extremely broad. The term is said to "include, but not be limited to," a list of over 50 types of places. Many on the list are what one would expect to be places where the public is invited. For example, the statute includes as places of public accommodation taverns, restaurants, retail shops, and public libraries. But the statute also includes places that often may not carry with them open invitations to the public, like summer camps and roof gardens. In this case, the New Jersey Supreme Court went a step further and applied its public accommodations law to a private entity without even attempting to tie the term "place" to a physical location. As the definition of "public accommodation" has expanded from clearly commercial entities, such as restaurants, bars, and hotels, to membership organizations such as the Boy Scouts, the potential for conflict between state public accommodations laws and the First Amendment rights of organizations has increased.

Justice Stevens' dissent makes much of its observation that the public perception of homosexuality in this country has changed. Indeed, it appears that homosexuality has gained greater societal acceptance. But this is scarcely an argument for denying First Amendment protection to those who refuse to accept these views. The First Amendment protects expression, be it of the popular variety or not. And the fact that an idea may be embraced and advocated by increasing numbers of people is all the more reason to protect the First Amendment rights of those who wish to voice a different view. . . .

We are not, as we must not be, guided by our views of whether the Boy Scouts' teachings with respect to homosexual conduct are right or wrong; public or judicial disapproval of a tenet of an organization's expression does not justify the State's effort to compel the organization to accept members where such acceptance would derogate from the organization's expressive message.

The judgment of the New Jersey Supreme Court is reversed, and the cause remanded for further proceedings not inconsistent with this opinion.

It is so ordered.

Justice STEVENS, with whom Justice SOUTER, Justice GINSBURG and Justice BREYER join, dissenting.

BSA's claim finds no support in our cases. We have recognized "a right to associate for the purpose of engaging in those activities protected by the First Amendment—speech, assembly, petition for the redress of grievances, and the exercise of religion." *Roberts.* And we have acknowledged that "when the State interferes with individuals' selection of those with whom they wish to join in a common endeavor, freedom of association . . . may be implicated." But "[t]he right to associate for expressive purposes is not . . . absolute"; rather, "the nature and degree of constitutional protection afforded freedom of association may vary depending on the extent to which . . . the constitutionally protected liberty is at stake in a given case." Indeed, the right to associate does not mean "that in every setting in which individuals exercise some discrimination in choosing associates, their selective process of inclusion and exclusion is protected by the Constitution." For example, we have routinely and easily rejected assertions of this right by expressive organizations with discriminatory membership policies, such as private schools, law firms, and labor organizations. In fact, until today, we have never once found a claimed right to associate in the selection of members to prevail in the face of a State's antidiscrimination law. To the contrary, we have squarely held that a State's antidiscrimination law does not vio-

late a group's right to associate simply because the law conflicts with
that group's exclusionary membership policy.

In *Roberts v. United States Jaycees* (1984), we addressed just such a
conflict. The Jaycees was a nonprofit membership organization "designed to inculcate in the individual membership . . . a spirit of genuine
Americanism and civic interest, and . . . to provide . . . an avenue for in-
telligent participation by young men in the affairs of their community."
The organization was divided into local chapters, described as "young
men's organization[s]," in which regular membership was restricted to
males between the ages of 18 and 35. But Minnesota's Human Rights
Act, which applied to the Jaycees, made it unlawful to "deny any person
the full and equal enjoyment of . . . a place of public accommodation because of . . . sex." The Jaycees, however, claimed that applying the law to
it violated its right to associate—in particular its right to maintain its selective membership policy.

We rejected that claim. Cautioning that the right to associate is not
"absolute," we held that "[i]nfringements on that right may be justified
by regulations adopted to serve compelling state interests, unrelated to
the suppression of ideas, that cannot be achieved through means significantly less restrictive of associational freedoms." We found the State's
purpose of eliminating discrimination is a compelling state interest that
is unrelated to the suppression of ideas. We also held that Minnesota's
law is the least restrictive means of achieving that interest. The Jaycees
had "failed to demonstrate that the Act imposes any serious burdens on
the male members' freedom of expressive association." Though the
Jaycees had "taken public positions on a number of diverse issues,
[and] . . . regularly engage in a variety of . . . activities worthy of constitutional protection under the First Amendment," there was "no basis in
the record for concluding that admission of women as full voting members will impede the organization's ability to engage in these protected
activities or to disseminate its preferred views." "The Act," we held, "requires no change in the Jaycees' creed of promoting the interest of
young men, and it imposes no restrictions on the organization's ability
to exclude individuals with ideologies or philosophies different from
those of its existing members."

Several principles are made perfectly clear by *Jaycees* and *Rotary
Club*. First, to prevail on a claim of expressive association in the face of
a State's antidiscrimination law, it is not enough simply to engage in

some kind of expressive activity. Both the Jaycees and the Rotary Club engaged in expressive activity protected by the First Amendment, yet that fact was not dispositive. Second, it is not enough to adopt an openly avowed exclusionary membership policy. Both the Jaycees and the Rotary Club did that as well. Third, it is not sufficient merely to articulate *some* connection between the group's expressive activities and its exclusionary policy.

The evidence before this Court makes it exceptionally clear that BSA has, at most, simply adopted an exclusionary membership policy and has no shared goal of disapproving of homosexuality. BSA's mission statement and federal charter say nothing on the matter; its official membership policy is silent; its Scout Oath and Law—and accompanying definitions—are devoid of any view on the topic; its guidance for Scouts and Scoutmasters on sexuality declare that such matters are "not construed to be Scouting's proper area," but are the province of a Scout's parents and pastor; and BSA's posture respecting religion tolerates a wide variety of views on the issue of homosexuality. Moreover, there is simply no evidence that BSA otherwise teaches anything in this area, or that it instructs Scouts on matters involving homosexuality in ways not conveyed in the Boy Scout or Scoutmaster Handbooks. In short, Boy Scouts of America is simply silent on homosexuality. There is no shared goal or collective effort to foster a belief about homosexuality at all—let alone one that is significantly burdened by admitting homosexuals.

Equally important is BSA's failure to adopt any clear position on homosexuality. BSA's temporary, though ultimately abandoned, view that homosexuality is incompatible with being "morally straight" and "clean" is a far cry from the clear, unequivocal statement necessary to prevail on its claim. Despite the solitary sentences in the 1991 and 1992 policies, the group continued to disclaim any single religious or moral position as a general matter and actively eschewed teaching any lesson on sexuality. It also continued to define "morally straight" and "clean" in the Boy Scout and Scoutmaster Handbooks without any reference to homosexuality. As noted earlier, nothing in our cases suggests that a group can prevail on a right to expressive association if it, effectively, speaks out of both sides of its mouth. A State's antidiscrimination law does not impose a "serious burden" or a "substantial restraint" upon the group's "shared goals" if the group itself is unable to identify its own stance with any clarity.

IV

I am unaware of any previous instance in which our analysis of the scope of a constitutional right was determined by looking at what a litigant asserts in his or her brief and inquiring no further. . . . An organization can adopt the message of its choice, and it is not this Court's place to disagree with it. But we must inquire whether the group is, in fact, expressing a message (whatever it may be) and whether that message (if one is expressed) is significantly affected by a State's antidiscrimination law. More critically, that inquiry requires our *independent* analysis, rather than deference to a group's litigating posture. Reflection on the subject dictates that such an inquiry is required.

Surely there are instances in which an organization that truly aims to foster a belief at odds with the purposes of a State's antidiscrimination laws will have a First Amendment right to association that precludes forced compliance with those laws. But that right is not a freedom to discriminate at will, nor is it a right to maintain an exclusionary membership policy simply out of fear of what the public reaction would be if the group's membership were opened up. It is an implicit right designed to protect the enumerated rights of the First Amendment, not a license to act on any discriminatory impulse. To prevail in asserting a right of expressive association as a defense to a charge of violating an antidiscrimination law, the organization must at least show it has adopted and advocated an unequivocal position inconsistent with a position advocated or epitomized by the person whom the organization seeks to exclude. If this Court were to defer to whatever position an organization is prepared to assert in its briefs, there would be no way to mark the proper boundary between genuine exercises of the right to associate, on the one hand, and sham claims that are simply attempts to insulate nonexpressive private discrimination, on the other hand. Shielding a litigant's claim from judicial scrutiny would, in turn, render civil rights legislation a nullity, and turn this important constitutional right into a farce. . . .

The only apparent explanation for the majority's holding, then, is that homosexuals are simply so different from the rest of society that their presence alone—unlike any other individual's—should be singled out for special First Amendment treatment. Under the majority's reasoning, an openly gay male is irreversibly affixed with the label "homosexual." That label, even though unseen, communicates a message that permits his exclusion wherever he goes. His openness is the sole and sufficient justification for his ostracism. Though unintended, reliance on such a justification is tantamount to a constitutionally prescribed symbol of inferiority. . . .

That such prejudices are still prevalent and that they have caused serious and tangible harm to countless members of the class New Jersey seeks to protect are established matters of fact that neither the Boy Scouts nor the Court disputes. That harm can only be aggravated by the creation of a constitutional shield for a policy that is itself the product of a habitual way of thinking about strangers. As Justice Brandeis so wisely advised, "we must be ever on our guard, lest we erect our prejudices into legal principles."

If we would guide by the light of reason, we must let our minds be bold. I respectfully dissent.

CHRONOLOGY

1791	The states ratify the Bill of Rights, including the First Amendment, with its guarantee of freedom of speech and assembly. It is this amendment that is most frequently cited as providing the basis for freedom of association.
1798	President John Adams signs the Sedition Act of 1798, which codifies the English common law of seditious libel by making it a crime to speak disparagingly of the national government. It liberalizes the common law by allowing truth to be a defense. The act is passed as a consequence of the fear that societies supporting the French Revolution might take root in America. Its passage is also a reflection of an early fear concerning the role of political associations. Thomas Jefferson and James Madison oppose the law, and its growing unpopularity contributes to Jefferson's victory over Adams in the 1800 election.
1835	Alexis de Tocqueville publishes his first volume of *Democracy in America*, which many consider the best book ever written about America. It is also one of the first studies of democracy to appreciate the value of associational life in establishing a stable and prosperous society.

1868   The states ratify the Fourteenth Amendment with its important due process clause, which later becomes the basis for the Court's incorporating the provisions of most of the Bill of Rights, including the First Amendment, into state law. This will eventually give the Court broad authority over state and local laws that infringe upon freedom of association.

1875   *United States v. Cruikshank* becomes the first Supreme Court decision to recognize a broad constitutional right of people to assemble for the purposes of free speech.

1937   With *De Jonge v. State of Oregon* the Supreme Court incorporates the right of peaceable assembly into the Fourteenth Amendment and overturns the conviction of a political organizer who had simply attended a Communist Party rally.

1940   Congress passes the Smith Act, a peacetime sedition law designed to curb Communist Party activities.

1944   The Supreme Court declares in *Smith v. Allwright* that white primaries are a violation of the Constitution and in doing so considers primary elections are subject to constitutional scrutiny.

1947   The Hollywood Ten refuse to disclose to the House Un-American Activities Committee their membership in the Communist Party. They are later cited for contempt of Congress and given prison terms.

1947   Heads of the major film studios issue the Waldorf Statement committing them not to hire known members of the Communist Party.

1948	The Truman administration uses the Smith Act to indict the top eleven members of the Communist Party. They are all convicted in federal court.
1950	Congress passes the Internal Security Act over the veto of President Truman.
1951	The Supreme Court upholds the convictions of the leadership of the Communist Party of America in *Dennis v. United States.*
1952	The Supreme Court upholds the constitutionality of anticommunist loyalty oaths in *Adler v. Board of Education.*
1952	Congress passes the McCarran-Walter Immigration Act, which places restrictions on immigrants with connections to subversive organizations.
1956	The Supreme Court lectures the House Un-American Activities Committee on the dangers of forcing people to disclose their political views and associations but falls short of declaring the committee's charter unconstitutional.
1958	An historic moment in the history of freedom of association when the Supreme Court in *NAACP v. Alabama ex rel. Patterson* gives the right constitutional standing as implicit in the First and Fourteenth Amendments.
1959	In *Barenblatt v. United States* the Supreme Court backs away from its position in *Watkins* and upholds the rights of Congress to investigate into the political associations of suspected Communists.
1959	The hiring of Hollywood Ten writer Dalton Trumbo by Kirk Douglas, producer of the film *Spartacus,* and Otto Preminger, producer of the film *Exodus,* signals an end to the blacklist.

1961   The Supreme Court limits the scope of the government's ability to prosecute members of the Communist Party in two decisions, *Scales v. United States* and *Noto v. United States.*

1965   In *Albertson v. SACB,* the Supreme Court strikes the registration provisions of the Internal Security Act as a violation of the Fifth Amendment right against self-incrimination.

1967   In *United States v. Robel,* the Supreme Court invalidates another provision of the Internal Security Act denying employment in a defense facility to members of the Communist Party.

1973   The Congress abolishes the Subversive Activities Control Board.

1975   The House of Representatives eliminates the House Un-American Activities Committee.

1976   In *Runyon v. McCrary,* the Supreme Court denies that whites-only private schools are not protected by freedom of association in barring admission to African American students.

1981   In *Democratic Party of the United States v. Wisconsin ex rel. La Follette et al.,* the Supreme Court rules that states cannot require a national party convention to accept delegates chosen in an open primary if that violates party convention rules. This ruling thus grants some freedom of association protection to political parties.

1984   In *Roberts v. United States Jaycees,* the Supreme Court upholds the authority of Minnesota, under its antidiscrimination code, to require that an all-male civic association, the Jaycees, accept women as full members.

1995   In *Hurley v. Irish-American Gay, Lesbian, and Bisexual Group of Boston,* the Supreme Court upholds the right of parade organizers to exclude participation of those who impose their own message on a parade. This is a major First Amendment case with freedom of association implications.

1996   President Bill Clinton signs the Antiterrorism and Effective Death Penalty Act, which states in part, "Whoever within the United States or subject to the jurisdiction of the United States, knowingly provides material support or resources to a foreign terrorist organization, or attempts or conspires to do so, shall be fined under this title or imprisoned not more than 10 years, or both."

2000   The Supreme Court decides *Boy Scouts of America v. Dale* and *California Democratic Party v. Jones,* providing a clearer delineation of the contours of freedom of association.

2001   President George W. Bush signs the Patriot Act, granting greater powers to the federal government to punish those who give material support to terrorist groups.

TABLE OF CASES

ANNOTATED
BIBLIOGRAPHY

HISTORICAL ORIGINS AND
GENERAL CONCEPTS

The early notion that freedom of association was a fundamental right re-
quiring constitutional protection can be found in the writings of Jeremy
Bentham, brought together in J. H. Burns and H. L. A. Hart, *The Collected
Works of Jeremy Bentham* (London: Athlone Press, 1977), and in the works
of the great pamphleteer of the American Revolution Thomas Paine, whose
writings are collected in *Rights of Man, Common Sense, and Other Political
Writings*, edited by Mark Philp (Oxford: Oxford University Press, 1995).
One should also consult *The Federalist*, the historical defense of the Constitution by Alexander Hamilton, John Jay, and James Madison. Madison's
Federalist Nos. 10 and 51 remain classic essays that express a suspicion of
political associations. A new edition edited by George W. Carey and James
McClellan, *The Federalist: The Gideon Edition* (Indianapolis: Liberty Fund,
2001), contains both an editors' introduction and a readers' guide. By far the
most important volume on early American democracy and the concept of
associational rights is Alexis de Tocqueville's *Democracy in America*. A recent translation by Harvey C. Mansfield and Delba Winthrop (Chicago:
University of Chicago Press, 2000) includes a valuable introductory essay
and helpful annotations.

Two of the most comprehensive treatises on constitutional law, both of
which have insightful sections on freedom of association, are Laurence H.
Tribe, *American Constitutional Law*, second edition (Mineola, NY: Founda-

tion Press, 1998), and Gerald Gunther and Kathleen M. Sullivan, *Constitutional Law*, fourteenth edition (Westbury, NY: Foundation Press, 2003). Thomas I. Emerson's discussion of freedom of association in *The System of Freedom of Expression* (New York: Random House, 1970) is still unique and provocative. Alexander Meiklejohn, *Free Speech and Its Relation to Self Government* (New York: Harper Brothers, 1948), remains a classic.

A most valuable collection of essays on the general topic of voluntary associations and democracy is found in *Freedom of Association*, edited by Amy Guttman (Princeton, NJ: Princeton University Press, 1998). Amy Guttman, George Kateb, Nancy L. Rosenblum, Kent Greenawalt, and Peter de Marneff have essays in this collection of particular interest to constitutional scholars. Nancy L. Rosenblum's *Membership and Morals: The Personal Uses of Pluralism in America* (Princeton, NJ: Princeton University Press, 1998) is a discussion of the state of civil society, with an excellent chapter on membership and voice. Robert D. Putnam's *Bowling Alone: The Collapse and Revival of American Community* (New York: Simon and Schuster, 2000) is an exhaustive and somewhat pessimistic study of the state of civic engagement. Mark E. Warren, *Democracy and Association* (Princeton, NJ: Princeton University Press, 2001), is an assessment of various types of associations and their impact on democracy, as is Sidney Verba, Kay Lehman Schlozman, and Henry E. Brady, *Voice and Equality: Civic Voluntarism in American Politics* (Cambridge: Harvard University Press, 1995). William A. Galston, *Liberal Pluralism: The Implications of Value Pluralism for Political Theory and Practice* (Cambridge: Cambridge University Press, 2002), places voluntary associations in the context of American pluralism. Students of the problems of democracy and civic society may also want to consult Stephen Macedo, *Diversity and Distrust: Civic Education in a Multicultural Democracy* (Cambridge: Harvard University Press, 2000), and Aviam Soifer, *Law and the Company We Keep* (Cambridge: Harvard University Press, 1995).

Some very thoughtful articles looking at the legal and philosophical dimension of freedom of association are Richard W. Garnett, "The Freedom of Expressive Association: The Story of Henry Adams' Soul: Education and the Expression of Associations," *Minnesota Law Review* 85 (June 2001): 1841–1883; Jason Mazzone, "Freedom's Associations," *Washington Law Review* 77 (July 2002): 639–767; Laurence H. Tribe, "Disentangling Symmetries: Speech, Association, Parenthood," *Pepperdine Law Review* 28 (2001): 641–665; and Evelyn Brody, "Entrance, Voice, and Exit: The Constitutional Bounds of the Right of Association," *University of California–Davis Law Review* 35 (April 2002): 821–901.

GUILT BY ASSOCIATION DURING
THE COLD WAR ERA

The literature on the constitutional issues associated with domestic communism and the Cold War is considerable. Two works on the history of the House Un-American Activities Committee that have different perspectives are William F. Buckley Jr., *The Committee and Its Critics: A Calm Review of the House Committee on Un-American Activities* (New York: G. P. Putnam's Sons, 1962), and Walter Goodman, *The Committee: The Extraordinary Career of the House Committee on Un-American Activities* (London: History Book Club, 1964). Sidney Hook, *Heresy, Yes, Conspiracy, No* (New York: John Day and Company, 1953), provides a philosophic justification for some restrictions on associational freedom concerning the Communist Party. Victor S. Navasky, *Naming Names* (New York: Viking Press, 1980), and David Caute, *The Great Fear: The Anti-Communist Purge under Truman and Eisenhower* (New York: Simon and Schuster, 1978), are highly critical of the entire anticommunist enterprise during the 1940s and 1950s. Recent scholarship on the implications for associational freedom of the so-called McCarthy era includes Ellen Schrecker, *Many Are the Crimes: McCarthyism in America* (Princeton, NJ: Princeton University Press, 1998), whose viewpoint is close to that of Navasky and Caute. A more sympathetic view of the government's effort to curb Communist activity can be found in John Earl Haynes and Harvey Klehr, *Venona: Decoding Soviet Espionage in America* (New Haven, CT: Yale University Press, 2000); Harvey Klehr, John Earl Haynes, and Fridrikh Igorevich Firsov, *The Secret World of American Communism* (New Haven, CT: Yale University Press, 1995); and Hilton Kramer, *The Twilight of the Intellectuals: Culture and Politics in the Era of the Cold War* (Chicago: Ivan Dee, 1999). Albert Fried, ed., *McCarthyism: The Great American Red Scare* (New York: Oxford University Press, 1997), includes many documents not found elsewhere.

The Hollywood blacklist literature is voluminous, and most of it is critical. Robert Vaughn, *Only Victims: A Study of Show Business Blacklisting* (New York: Limelight Editions, 1996), first published in 1972, provides a valuable history, as do John Cogley's *Report on Blacklisting I: Movies* (New York: Fund for the Republic, 1956) and *Blacklisting: Two Key Documents* (New York: Arno Press and the New York Times, 1971). A critical view of the role of the Communist Party in Hollywood is Kenneth Lloyd Billingsley, *Hollywood Party: How Communism Seduced the American Film Industry in the 1930s and 1940s* (Rocklin, CA: Prima Publishing, 1998). A new volume in an outstanding historical film reference series is Peter Lev, *His-*

tory of the American Cinema, vol. 7: *Transforming the Screen, 1950–59* (New York: Charles Scribner's Sons, 2003). It includes a thoroughly researched chapter on the blacklist. An unusual perspective on the associational rights of film studios and television networks in regard to the blacklist can be found in Martin H. Redish and Christopher R. McFadden, "HUAC, the Hollywood Ten and the First Amendment Right of Non-Association," *Minnesota Law Review* 85 (June 2001): 1669–1728.

The efforts of the NAACP's fight for survival in the South during the 1950s is chronicled in Taylor Branch, *Parting the Waters* (New York: Simon and Shuster, 1988). A thoughtful article on Justice Harlan's landmark decision in *NAACP v. Alabama* is Robert M. O'Neill, "Tribute: The Neglected First Amendment Jurisprudence of the Second Justice Harlan," *New York University Annual Survey of American Law* 58 (2001): 57–66. Tinsley E. Yarbrough, *John Marshall Harlan: Great Dissenter of the Warren Court* (New York: Oxford University Press, 1992), includes important material on the freedom of association cases decided during the Warren Court. An insider's look at the Supreme Court's deliberations in that period is found in Bernard Schwartz, *Super Chief: Earl Warren and His Supreme Court—A Judicial Biography* (New York: New York University Press, 1983).

Freedom of Association and Antidiscrimination Laws

Douglas O. Linder, "Freedom of Association after *Roberts v. United States Jaycees,*" *Michigan Law Review* 82 (August 1984): 1878–1903; and William P. Marshall, "Discrimination and the Right of Association," *Northwestern University Law Review* 81 (Fall 1986): 68–105, are comprehensive analyses of the state of associational rights after *Roberts.* Another reflection on that landmark decision from the perspective of intimate association is Colin O'-Connor Udell, "Intimate Association: Resurrecting a Hybrid Right," *Texas Journal of Women and the Law* 7 (Spring 1998): 231–285.

The *Dale* decision triggered a host of law review articles on freedom of association. A symposium on the subject published in the *Minnesota Law Review* 85 (June 2001) includes several articles of special note: Dale Carpenter, "Expressive Association and Anti-Discrimination Law After *Dale:* A Tripartite Approach," pp. 1515–1589; Michael Stokes Paulsen, "Scouts, Families, and Schools," pp. 1917–1955; and Daniel A. Faber, "Speaking in the First Person Plural: Expressive Associations and the First Amendment," pp. 1483–1513. Looking at the issue from the angle of "anti-coercion" the-

ory is Roderick H. Hills, "The Constitutional Rights of Private Governments," *New York University Law Review* 78 (April 2003): 144–238.
Richard A. Epstein, "The Constitutional Perils of Moderation: The Case of
the Boy Scouts," *University of Southern California Law Review* 74
(November 2000): 119–143, examines the dangers of requiring associations
to have clear messages in order to secure associational rights. Three particularly critical accounts of the Court's decision in *Dale* are Erwin Chemerinsky and Catherine Fisk, "*Boy Scouts of America v. Dale:* The Expressive Interest of Associations," *William and Mary Bill of Rights Journal* 9 (April
2001): 595–617; James P. Madigan, "Questioning the Coercive Effect of Self-
Identifying Speech," *Iowa Law Review* 87 (October 2001): 75–144; and
David McGowan, "Making Sense of *Dale*," *Constitutional Commentary* 18
(Spring 2001): 121–175. A more sympathetic view of both the Boy Scouts'
position and the Court's decision in *Dale* is found in John C. O'Quinn,
"How Solemn Is the Duty of the Mighty Chief: Mediating the Conflict of
Rights in *Boy Scouts of America v. Dale*," *Harvard Journal of Law and
Public Policy* 34 (Fall 2001): 319–367; and David E. Bernstein, "Antidis-
crimination Laws and the First Amendment," *Missouri Law Review* 66
(Winter 2001): 83–138. A valuable discussion of the dilemma between lib-
erty and equality in *Dale* appears in Christopher S. Hargis, "*Romer, Hurley,
and Dale:* How the Supreme Court Languishes with 'Special Rights,'" *Kentucky Law Journal* 89 (Summer 2000): 1189–1225. A unique perspective on
Dale's impact on higher education is found in David E. Bernstein, "*Boy
Scouts of America v. Dale:* The Right of Expressive Association and Private
Universities' Racial Preferences and Speech Codes," *William and Mary Bill
of Rights Journal* 9 (April 2001): 619–643. Also see John O. McGinnis, "Reviving Tocqueville's America: The Rehnquist Court's Jurisprudence of Social Discovery," *California Law Review* 90 (March 2002): 530–571.

THE ASSOCIATIONAL RIGHTS OF
POLITICAL PARTIES

Kathleen M. Sullivan, "Sex, Money, and Groups: Free Speech and Association Decisions in the October 1999 Term," *Pepperdine Law Review* 28
(2001): 723–746, is an excellent review of both *Dale* and *California Democratic Party v. Jones* in the context of recent free speech cases. A critical discussion of the Court's decision in *Jones* with a view of its impact on the political process is Samuel Issacharoff, "Private Parties with Public Purposes:
Political Parties, Associational Freedoms, and Partisan Competition,"

Columbia Law Review 101 (March 2001): 274–313. Other critical discussions of Jones are in Seamus K. Barry, "Stealing the Covers: The Supreme Court's Ban on Blanket Primary Elections and Its Effect on a Citizen's First Amendment Right 'to Petition the Government for a Redress of Grievances,'" *Common Law Conspectus* 9 (2001): 71–85 and Teresa Mac-Donald, "*California Democratic Party v. Jones:* Invalidation of the Blanket Primary," *Pepperdine Law Review* 29 (2002): 319–341. A fine election law casebook is Samuel Issacharoff, Pamela S. Kaplan, and Richard H. Pildes, *The Law of Democracy: The Legal Structure of the Political Process,* revised second edition (New York: Foundation Press, 2002).

TERRORISM AND ASSOCIATIONAL RIGHTS

A critical view of the impact that recent laws to curb terrorism have had on freedom of association can be found in the writings of David Cole: "Hanging with the Wrong Crowd: Of Gangs, Terrorists, and the Right of Association," *Supreme Court Review* 199: 203–252; "The New McCarthyism: Repeating History in the War on Terrorism," *Harvard Civil Rights–Civil Liberties Law Review* 38 (Winter 2003): 1–29; and (with James X. Dempsey), *Terrorism and the Constitution: Sacrificing Civil Liberties in the Name of National Security,* second edition (New York: New Press, 2002). For a critique of Cole, see Stuart Taylor Jr., "Making Plans with al Qaeda: The War on Terrorism Justifies Some Limits on American Freedom to Associate," *Legal Times,* October 28, 2002, p. 86.

INTERNET SITES

For Internet access to federal court decisions, congressional laws, and a vast amount of other legal information, go to: *www.findlaw.com.* A libertarian perspective on freedom of association can be found at the Web site of the Cato Institute: *http://www.cato.org.* The American Civil Liberties Union, at *http://www.aclu.org/,* offers a more egalitarian approach. The site of the American Library Association, at *http://www.ala.org,* includes valuable material on the First Amendment. The University of Chicago Library has an extensive site on researching the Constitution: *http://www.lib.uchicago.edu/~llou/conlaw.html.*

INDEX

ABOUT THE AUTHOR

Robert J. Bresler is professor emeritus of public policy at Pennsylvania State University, where he taught for thirty-two years. From 2001 to 2004 he was visiting professor of government at Franklin and Marshall College. Before arriving at Penn State in 1969, he taught at the University of Wisconsin–Green Bay and the University of Delaware. He has also been a visiting professor at the U.S. Army War College and a senior Fulbright scholar at the National University of Singapore.

A native of Washington, D.C., he received his undergraduate degree from Earlham College and his Ph.D. from Princeton University. His books include *Us versus Them: American Political and Cultural Conflict from World War II to Watergate* (2000), *Contemporary Controversies* (1993), and *American Government* (coauthored, 1988, 1992, 1994). He has published articles in *Political Science Quarterly, Telos, Politics and Society, Inquiry, Bulletin of Atomic Scientists, The Nation,* and *Commonweal.* He is the national affairs editor at *USA Today: The Magazine of the American Scene,* where he writes a bimonthly column on U.S. politics.